GOOD FRIDAY
The Death of Irish Republicanism

GOOD FRIDAY
The Death of Irish Republicanism

Anthony McIntyre

Foreword by Ed Moloney

Ausubo Press
New York, New York

For information, address
Ausubo Press
130 Seventh Avenue
New York, New York 10011-1803
www.ausubopress.com

Front Cover Photo: AP IMAGES/PA PHOTOS

Library of Congress Cataloging-in-Publication Data

McIntyre, Anthony, 1954-
  Good Friday : the death of Irish republicanism / Anthony McIntyre ; foreword Ed
Moloney.
     p. cm.
  ISBN 978-1-932982-74-9
  1. Northern Ireland--Politics and government--1994- 2. Peace movements--
Northern Ireland--History--20th century. 3. Great Britain. Treaties,
etc. Ireland, 1998 Apr. 10. 4. Republicanism--Northern Ireland. 5. Irish unifica-
tion question. I. Title.

  DA990.U46M1435 2008
  941.60824--dc22
                              2008026847

CONTENTS

CONTENTS

FOREWORD

As I write these words, the final touches are being made in Belfast to the construction of a power-sharing government whose principal participants will be drawn from two political parties that for more than thirty years were the ideological equivalent in Ireland of oil and water.

If all goes according to plan the first or prime minister of the new Northern Ireland government will be the octogenarian Protestant fundamentalist leader, Reverend Ian Paisley who, since the 1950s, has played a political and social role in Ireland not unlike that performed in American political life by someone who combined the worldviews of Strom Thurmond and Jerry Falwell.

His deputy first minister will be Martin McGuinness, the Derry-born Republican leader who is the chief negotiator for Sinn Fein, the party that has always been recognised as the political arm of the Provisional Irish Republican Army. Alongside Gerry Adams, the Sinn Fein president, he has charted and guided IRA strategy for over two decades.

Paisley's role in Northern Irish politics has been every bit as reactionary as that played by Thurmond and Falwell in the United States. He made his name and won his political support by opposing, invariably successfully, every attempt to reform Northern Ireland to make it a warmer place for the large Catholic minority who found themselves unwelcome citizens of the partitioned state created by the Anglo-Irish treaty of 1921.

In the cause of preserving the union between Northern Ireland and Britain, he was like the Dixie Democrat of 1960 roaring to a cheering crowd of poor whites in Mississippi: 'Segregation today! Segregation tomorrow! Segregation forever'! Honoured by Bob Jones University in South Carolina with an honorary degree, not for nothing was Paisley known as Doctor No.

It would be hard to find someone as polar opposite to Paisley as Martin McGuinness. The offspring of poor Derry Catholics, McGuinness' people were the equivalent of the blacks of Mississippi, kept in place for decades by fear and repression by those who saw people like Paisley as their champion.

Like the Deep South in the 1960s, the Catholics of Northern Ireland stirred from their slumber and by 1968 the place was shaken to its core by a civil rights movement consciously modelled on that led by Martin Luther King and others. But while the black civil rights movement by and large saw their future in a reformed America, many of Martin McGuinness' contemporaries believed that Northern Ireland was irreformable, that the state had to be destroyed and that the unfinished business of 1921—the reunification of Ireland and final separation from Britain—had to be addressed before Catholics could enjoy equality and justice.

Many of them were drawn to the ranks of the Provisional IRA, which was committed to a military campaign to force the withdrawal of Britain from the last piece of Ireland through which her writ still ran. Martin McGuinness was one of them and, to judge by his meteoric rise through the ranks, he was a very efficient IRA member. He soon became commander of the IRA in Derry and in later years was chief of staff, the IRA's overall military chief. For many years he also ran the IRA's day-to-day war against the British in the 'war zone' of Northern Ireland. The war he and others in the IRA leadership waged lasted for the best part of three decades and the overall conflict produced a death toll of some 3,500, whose proportionate equivalent in America would be around the 600,000 mark, as large as the military fatalities of the Civil War.

Little wonder, then, when in March 2007 an agreement by Paisley and Sinn Fein to share power was announced, the reaction ranged from astonishment to bewilderment. The bulk of comment, especially from the media, concentrated on what appeared to be Paisley's remarkable volte-face, accompanied by all-too-predictable headlines such as:

'Dr. No finally says Yes'! But not for the first time, the Irish media had viewed and interpreted an important event in the Irish peace process in a superficial and noncontextual fashion.

The deal between Paisley and the Provos did not come out of nowhere. It was the culmination of a twenty-year peace process whose defining characteristic was the gradual but inexorable jettisoning of Republican ideology by the IRA under the guiding hands of the Adams/McGuinness leadership. By the time Paisley appeared in public with Adams to announce their partnership, the IRA was utterly unrecognisable from the guerrilla army that had declared war against Britain in 1970.

The list of concessions is long and significant and included:

- the total decommissioning and destruction of all IRA weaponry, the first time in Irish history any revolutionary group had done so.

- the formal ending of the IRA's war against Britain along with acceptance of the constitutional status of Northern Ireland as part of Britain.

- the agreement by IRA and Sinn Fein leaders to become ministers, legally ministers of the (British) Crown, in order to administer a state they had previously been pledged to destroy.

- and finally, and most crucially, acceptance of the mechanisms that had previously been used in an effort to crush the IRA: the police service, the criminal justice system, and the prison system.

Seen from this angle, what Paisley had done by going into government with Adams and McGuinness was much less a volte-face on his part and more an effective acceptance of the final act in the IRA's surrender and transformation into political respectability. The media's astonishment should have been reserved for Sinn Fein's remarkable U-turn rather than Paisley's, but not for the first time it wasn't.

The timidity of the Irish media while covering the metamorphosis of Sinn Fein and the IRA is by now well known, as depressing an episode for Irish journalism as was the media's paralysis in America during George Bush's drumbeat for the war in Iraq. For fear of being accused of being 'unhelpful' to the peace process, the Provos' flip-flops were always applauded but rarely closely scrutinised by the Irish media (invariably, one suspects, for fear of what they might have discovered).

Silence and hesitancy on the part of the media after a thirty-year war of counterinsurgency that included both state-imposed and self-censorship is perhaps to be expected. But what about the IRA's foot soldiers, those who had killed and seen comrades killed, who had bombed and shot and in turn had been bombed and shot, men and women who had spent decades behind bars in the IRA's cause? How did they feel about what their leaders were doing? How many of them spoke up or questioned what was happening?

Some rebelled by joining or founding dissident Republican groups; others attempted to subvert the Adams/McGuinness leadership from within. Both efforts failed for the same reason. The vast bulk of the IRA and Sinn Fein rank and file in the north, in the war zone where it mattered, stayed loyal to the Adams/McGuinness leadership.

They did so for a number of reasons. Some were motivated by fear, not so much that the IRA would physically punish them but that they would be shunned and made jobless and friendless in communities controlled and dominated by the IRA. Others were bought off, either by the scores of well-paid, community-style jobs funded by the British, Irish, or European authorities that flowed in the wake of the IRA's first moves into peace, or by the prospect of political office that would come with a settlement. Others genuinely believed in the new strategy while many—one suspects the bulk of the grassroots—just had no political understanding of what was happening or if they had, they just didn't care.

There was another reason. The Adams/McGuinness leadership spent nearly two decades constructing and implementing the strategy to move from revolution to reform. They moved slowly and carefully. One activist compared the process to a parked car being moved an inch a day down the driveway outside your house. After a while the car has shifted from the house to the road but no-one ever saw it move or can understand how it got there.

They also disguised their true intentions by employing ambiguity, secrecy, deception, dishonesty, betrayal, duplicity, ruthlessness, dissemblance, and outright lies with a skill and determination that was sometimes breathtaking. There is no room here to tell the full story of how Adams and McGuinness delivered the IRA into reformist politics but it is without doubt one of the most extraordinary tales of political counterfeiting in Irish history.

Many in the IRA either guessed or suspected what was going on but only a handful or so went public with their thoughts. The most persistent, thoughtful, incisive and, from the IRA leadership's point of view, troublesome and penetrating of these critics was Anthony McIntyre, whose articles and thoughts about the Adams/McGuinness leadership's handling of the peace process constitute this valuable book.

McIntyre was an IRA volunteer from his teenage years and spent some eighteen years in jail for the IRA, many of those years on the blanket and dirty protests staged by Republican prisoners in a bid to win back their political status. Ten of his friends died on a hunger strike in the same cause.

In jail he studied for a university degree and on release completed a Ph.D. thesis on the early years of the IRA's development. That coincided with the first public signs of the hitherto secret peace process and these were the signal for McIntyre to first question where the leadership was taking the Republican movement and then to criticise them. He was not motivated, as were other dissidents, by a wish to resuscitate the armed struggle being abandoned by Adams and McGuinness. Like all the more thoughtful critics of the process, he had long since concluded that violence was a hopeless cul de sac leading only to jail, death, and needless suffering.

What did motivate him was anger at the secrecy, lies, and duplicity of the Adams leadership and anger also, perhaps, at the bovine complacence of the IRA rank and file for staying silent in the face of such outrageous and obvious deception.

This was not an easy path to take. He was shunned by many in his community, by former friends and neighbors, and faced threats and intimidation. At one point his home was picketed by a mob of Adams' supporters. By doing so, the IRA leadership ironically confirmed one of McIntyre's central assertions about them, which was that they were a bunch of authoritarian, Stalinist control freaks whose instinctive and only response to criticism or dissent was to crush it.

Having analysed what the IRA's leadership was doing, it was clear to McIntyre that the only possible terminus of the journey would be its absorption into constitutional politics, the winding up of the IRA, and the acceptance of a settlement almost entirely constructed on British terms. That this would be dressed up as victory or as a transitional stage to victory by the Adams/McGuinness leadership served only as confirmation of their deceit.

In return, Adams, McGuinness, and their allies would escape, Houdini-like, from the straitjacket of IRA violence and by so doing would ensure they would never meet the violent end that was the fate of so many of their comrades. They would become respectable (and affluent) politicians instead, feted abroad as statesmen and welcome guests even in George W. Bush's Oval Office. A rich electoral harvest from grateful voters would follow and then the prospect of political power.

When McIntyre wrote about all this, either in the e-zine *The Blanket*, or in media articles and predicted, for instance, that the IRA would decommission its weapons despite the public pledges to the contrary by its leaders, he was scorned and ridiculed. The passage of time has brought vindication and the knowledge that while the Adams/McGuinness leadership has prevailed, it was not entirely cost-free for them. It has also brought this collection of articles to a wider audience. Read and enjoy.

ED MOLONEY
New York
April 2007

CHAPTER 1

The Good Friday Agreement

Why Stormont Reminded Me of Animal Farm

Sunday Tribune, 12 April 1998

'Good Friday—Republicanism crucified—Sunday's resurrection postponed' is the type of comment a cynical graffiti artist might be prompted to write on the walls of poorer nationalist areas in the aftermath of this week's Stormont Agreement. And if, as Michael Ignatieff once claimed, a cynic is someone with a healthy awareness of the gulf between what people practice and what they preach, then such graffiti would certainly be more accurate than the leader headlines we have been exposed to in today's papers. It seems to be that the hype machine has been given full throttle and a 'regime of truth' has been feverishly constructed in which certain concepts, perspectives, and even words will be prohibited regardless of—and maybe because of—their explanatory power. So much for tolerance and a plurality of ideas.

We are often told that at some point in the 1990s London and Dublin agreed that the old policy of excluding Republicans was futile and that the only strategic alternative was one of inclusion. What goes unmentioned is that the strategic objective was to include Republicans while excluding republicanism. And Saturday's *Irish Times* illustrated the success of such a strategy when it commented that the logic of the latest agreement was that 'Nationalists have had to swallow the bitter truth that there will be no united Ireland in the foreseeable future and that if it comes, it will only do so with the consent of Northern Ireland's majority'.

For those Republicans unconcerned with Orwellian doublethink, the Stormont Agreement amounts to the following: The British state has repeated its Sunningdale declaration of intent to remain in the north until a majority here asks it to do otherwise; the British state has made it clear that the Unionist veto shall remain in place and has strengthened the partitionist ethos underlying that veto by having it enshrined in the revised southern constitution; the British state has ruled out any transition to a united Ireland by refusing to state that by a certain date—no matter how far in the distant future—it will no longer have a presence in Ireland.

In such a context, only those Republicans who had forsaken the ballot box and ArmaLite strategy in favour of a ballot box in one hand and a white stick in the other alone might argue that the Stormont Agreement constitutes a stepping-stone to a united Ireland. On the contrary, it is a stumbling block to the unification of the country.

Republicans have not yet signed up for the deal. It is difficult to see how they can in the foreseeable future given the clearly partitionist shape of the outcome. One Republican activist—admittedly opposed to the leadership strategy from the outset—observed yesterday that what had started out as a victory cavalcade on the Falls Road had ended up as a funeral cortege. But of more significance than the absence of any signature on the dotted line is the fact that Republicans, by their involvement in the process, have helped to usher in the new partitionist outcome. Consequently, over time—and dependent to a large extent on how unionism performs—the situational logic may be such that the pressure to 'accept by instalment' could prove irresistible.

Some are inclined to heap praise on the efforts of Ahern and Blair whose frantic efforts and negotiating skills in the final days of the talks allegedly were decisive in securing an outcome. A more measured view would be that their input was vital only to the sprint finish. The marathon itself and the predetermined course that it took was made possible only by all the participants, including Republicans, consenting to an agreed Ireland. But any agreed Ireland, by implication subject to the agreement of the Unionists, could *never* have been a united Ireland.

Ultimately, the Stormont Agreement most suits partitionist nationalism and the British state. The former emerges feeling it has snatched back what was originally snatched from it in 1974. The British have secured agreement that they will leave the country only on the terms they have always insisted upon—by consent of a majority in the north.

Unionism had to give, but no more than the normal asking price in return for the copperfastening of partition.

As one of 'the creatures outside', peering in at the Stormont talks, where they had all agreed secrecy and confidentiality, concealing in the process from their respective democratic bases the haggling of our collective future, I was reminded of the final words in George Orwell's *Animal Farm*:

> Twelve voices were shouting in anger, and they were all alike. No question now, what had happened to the faces of the pigs. The creatures outside looked from pig to man, and from man to pig, and from pig to man again; but already it was impossible to say which was which.

We, the IRA, Have Failed

Guardian, 22 May 1998, and *Guardian Yearbook,* 1998

Once upon a time in the H-Blocks of Long Kesh prison camp when victory for the IRA seemed a foregone conclusion, 'doing time', despite the harshness of prison life, was relatively easy. Conviction rather than conditions sustained most of us. Our view of the world was simple, perhaps simplistic. Britain had no right to be in our country. It seemed as daft to us for British soldiers to die—as John Cleese once said—to keep China British as it was to keep Ireland so.

Part of the time spent in prison was under the leadership of the late Bobby Sands. He led us in an era when the British state had yet to get the measure of the IRA. And like many others who joined him in prison protest, he was arrested at a very difficult time for republicanism. The Republican movement was in a state of strategic turbulence, desperately trying to anchor itself in the wake of a truce later described as 'disastrous' and a 'virtual surrender' by Republican leaders such as Danny Morrison and Martin McGuinness. The strategic alternative to all of this was to wage a 'Long War'.

As an eighteen-year-old IRA volunteer in prison for the second time, I was blissfully unaware of much of this. It seemed there was a war to be fought and enemies to be killed. I and others succeeded on both counts. On a cold January morning in 1977 in Belfast's Crown Court with my mother gazing on in stunned disbelief, Lord Chief Justice Lowry informed me that I would serve at least twenty-five years in prison for ending the life of a member of the UVF. I merely laughed at him, prompting tabloid headlines of 'laughing killer jailed for life'. Nothing to worry about there. It had been sectarian attacks carried out by young Protestant kids that initially led me to develop an interest in the IRA. They had their orange parades—and we had our IRA. Although where it was no one seemed to know. But it was comforting to 'feel' that it was there and would 'settle up' on our behalf at some time.

And now I was part of it. Membership of it armed me with the arrogance of the damned—I simply did not care what the Lord Chief Justice had to say. In the IRA I was immune from his concerns. As readily as I had 'settled up' I prepared to settle down for the long haul.

And a long haul it proved to be—seventeen years of it. But the British had cause to fear Republicans and went to incredible ends to defeat us. They could never hope to buy us off. So they put our leader in a coffin after sixty-six days of hunger strike and sent him to his grave at the age of twenty-seven. And it was upon this that I was forced to reflect when I witnessed the present Republican jail leader being allowed to attend the Sinn Fein Ard Fheis. Padraig Wilson, like Bobby Sands, was and remains a selfless volunteer; his integrity is beyond dispute. But I did not share the euphoria of the Sinn Fein delegates at his presence. He was not there as a result of a deserved amnesty reluctantly and grudgingly conceded, but was allowed to attend because the British wanted to bolster up their long-term strategy in Ireland by securing a 'yes' vote for the Stormont Agreement at the Ard Fheis.

And in that context the conference was less a case of chickens coming home to roost and more one of turkeys celebrating Christmas. In trade union terms, the Republican leadership informed those it represents that it had secured for them a six day week and lower wages. That the body of the hall did not storm the podium in anger at the Ard Comhairle is an indication of just how defeated the original Provisional Republican project actually is.

Danny Morrison's commentary piece in the *Guardian* (11 May) was an exercise in putting a smile on the face of the corpse. To claim as he does that the IRA did not win but had not lost either is demonstrably wrong. The political objective of the Provisional IRA was to secure a British declaration of intent to withdraw. It failed. The objective of the British state was to force the Provisional IRA to accept—and subsequently respond with a new strategic logic—that it would not leave Ireland until a majority in the north consented to such a move. It succeeded.

GOOD FRIDAY

I concur with Danny Morrison's hope that the war is over. But it would have been over twenty-plus years ago, and in less ignominious fashion, had the post-truce leadership not insisted on fighting it to an inglorious conclusion. And then we would have been spared the twin sorrows of one jail OC dying to resist British state strategy and a second, through no fault of his own, appearing to legitimise it.

Another Victory for Unionism

Sunday Tribune, 4 July 1999

*T*he joke doing the rounds among Republican cynics while the Sinn Fein leadership were involved in the latest bout of negotiating up at Stormont was 'what time do you think they will sell us out at'? It was nothing more than a witticism as the vast majority of Republicans firmly support the Republican leadership. But such facetious barbs have emerged against an atmosphere of unease and hesitancy. And the feeling on the ground in West Belfast on Friday was no longer one of outright confidence that leadership integrity would not disappear in the vortex of decommissioning.

If the proposals announced by Blair and Ahern are carried unionism will have secured a major victory. Not only will Republicans be consigned to administer British rule for the foreseeable future, the acceptance by them of the principle of decommissioning has served to delegitimise and criminalise the previous Republican resistance to that rule. It also elevates to a higher moral plateau British state weaponry. Basically Republicans are being told that the weapons used by Francis Hughes, the deceased hunger striker, to kill a member of the British SAS death squad are contaminated in a manner which the weapons used to slaughter the innocent of Bloody Sunday and the victims of shoot to kill are not.

Sinn Fein played it poorly. The strategy of 'never but will' merely encouraged unionism to hold out for a better deal. Many positions previously held had been abandoned in spite of 'never never never' ad infinitum. Unionism learned the only never is never listen to what the Sinn Fein leadership say they will never do. And this helped sustain it throughout the recent months of Ping-Pong pressure as each side in the dispute was probed for some sign of weakness. Why blink first when experience showed that Sinn Fein always did?

Now we are beginning to see what the Good Friday Agreement

really meant. Despite repeated promises of no decommissioning, Sinn Fein now accept that decommissioning as part of the agreement is valid. Republican activists were not told that at the time when they were asked to support the Sinn Fein's leadership endorsement of that agreement. People who ventured the opinion that the process might lead to decommissioning were angrily dismissed and ridiculed.

In a bid to shield the reality from the grassroots the silly statement of the year for 1998 was manufactured by a leading member of Sinn Fein who informed his audience that while not transitional it remained possible to view the Good Friday Agreement as a transition to a transition. Which by logical extension meant that the week before Good Friday constituted a transition to a transition to a transition. Perhaps now the audience will be told that this week's outcome while a transition away from a transition to a transition is still endowed with transitory potential none the less.

One would imagine that this sort of nonsense could only have a limited shelf life. But it has carried the day. Like the pickpocket who tells his victim while he robs him 'your personal security is brilliant', Sinn Fein told the Republican base they were the most politicised people in Western Europe while republicanism was stripped away in front of their very eyes. In this sense the decommissioning issue actually assisted Sinn Fein. The base were told if they could not follow the complexities and intricacies nor penetrate the undemocratic secrecy surrounding the negotiations, then watch the ball of decommissioning. Trust in the process became reduced to that one issue.

Therein now lies the problem for Sinn Fein. Having thrown the baby out they now need to get rid of the bathwater. But in the process of deceiving their base they have depicted the bathwater as the baby. And the base are reluctant to let it go. The Unionists may yet snatch defeat from the jaws of victory. It would be nice if they did. But ultimately a partitionist administration is their baby. And the likelihood remains that this paper will be reviewing the book by a Sinn Fein cabinet minister *My Fight for a Reformed Stormont*.

Republicans Acknowledging a Democratic Basis to Partition

The Blanket, 10 February 2002

The notion of Republicans accepting the necessity of winning Unionist consent for a united Ireland, despite stirring considerable media interest throughout the week, is not a new element devoid of all previous trace and suddenly inserted into Sinn Fein discourse. Although one historian of the IRA, J. Bowyer Bell, claimed some time ago that all Republicans would regard as heresy any endorsement of the Unionist claim to a right to veto the unity of Ireland, Sinn Fein on their journey to becoming what some critics term 'Provisional Fianna Fail' were as eager to kill that sacred cow as they have been to do likewise with many others.

Republican leaders have for some time been involved in making it clearer that unity by consent was the position they sought to reach. This in spite of having told their membership for years that any such thing was a partitionist 'fudge'. Brendan O'Brien of RTE was one of the few commentators who noticed the trend when he wrote his book on the IRA and Sinn Fein in 1993. *An Phoblacht/Republican News*, sensitive to his insight, tampered with a review of O'Brien's book and added the sentence 'this is way off the mark' to refute O'Brien's thesis that Sinn Fein was a whisker away from accepting the realities of unionism, veto included.

All these transformations begin in a certain way. 'Consent' of the Unionists at first was mumbled almost inaudibly from behind five fingers. Only the most keenly attuned would pick it up. And then it was only 'desirable' to achieve it but was not a necessity. As years went by a finger would go down and 'consent' would sound less garbled, more decipherable. Eventually a point is reached, as in New York at the World Economic Forum, where the hand is removed and 'consent' rings out loud and clear so that every mover and shaker in the world of global capitalism is left in no doubt that another element in a once revolutionary ensemble has been laid to rest.

When Mitchell McLaughlin wrote what was viewed as a groundbreaking article for *Fingerpost* back in the summer of 1992 it was clear that the nettle of consent was being grasped albeit tentatively and in a gloved hand so that the leadership could deny to the rank and file that their fingerprints were actually on the 'Unionist veto'. McLaughlin did, however, sully his newfound commitment by adding in a 1994 article for the same publication that he knew of no one in the Republican movement who wished to coerce the Unionists into a united Ireland. It begged the question of how many in the movement he actually did know. After the signing of the Downing Street Declaration in 1993, based as it were on the principle of consent, Seamus Mallon of the SDLP was uncompromising in his assertion that virtually nothing separated it from the Hume-Adams document. Perhaps for that reason Republicans were asked to march through West Belfast in support of Hume-Adams but were not told what it meant.

In 1994 the Bobby Sands Discussion Group (later closed down by the IRA and Sinn Fein for asking difficult questions) hosted a debate in the West Belfast's Felons Club prompted in part by Mallon's comments. The late Pat McGeown argued passionately against others that Sinn Fein were about to accept the consent principle. Thirteen months later in Dublin he privately endorsed the comments he had heard made by some speakers at the Royal Dublin Society who claimed that accepting consent was the direction in which republicanism was going. By 1995 Pat Doherty was trying to divide the indivisible by separating the Unionist veto from Unionist consent. In an act of Orwellian slippage, Republican opposition to the 'veto' now meant only that the Unionists should have no power to block all political progress. Unionist power to block a united Ireland was now increasingly to be referred to as 'consent'.

When the Mitchell principles were signed up to by the Sinn Fein leadership in 1997, it was another marker on the road. The

Good Friday Agreement of 1998 was built on the immovable rock of the consent principle. So there should really be no surprise that the once hated unity by consent formula should be unambiguously articulated by the Sinn Fein president in New York. Everybody else was being told for years. The last people to find out, as usual, were the Republican grassroots. And even then some of them still think it is only a tactic.

But has the significance of the Republican abandonment of its opposition to unity by consent been fully grasped? When the Provisional IRA leaped out of the ashes of 1969 and began its war against the British state the organisation tapped into a reservoir of disaffection. Insurrection proved popular to people seeking civil and human rights. The only body doing anything against those seen to be denying such rights was the Provisional IRA. But the stated objectives of the IRA went well beyond the attainment of such rights. For its dynamic the IRA looked to the present, but for its proposed solution the organisation looked to the past and its own tradition. The goal of a united Ireland regardless of the Unionists was the aim. They were a nonelement in the equation as far as Republicans were concerned, something to be dealt with generously once the British had departed.

But the ill fit between proposed Republican solutions and the actual causes of the conflict were soon to be become apparent when the results of the 1973 assembly election confirmed an outstanding victory for constitutional nationalism and the SDLP who were unequivocally committed to unity only by consent. Sinn Fein's boycott campaign against the elections was effectively the only thing to be boycotted. The mass insurrectionary movement centred primarily in Belfast and Derry had dissipated and along with it fervour for Republican objectives. The IRA campaign went on the wane after that, with much fewer operations in the cities and a significant displacement of the Republican military machine to the rural areas where support for republicanism was more traditional. The trend was only effectively reversed when the present leadership of the Republican movement took control and pursued a

'Long War' strategy (significantly aided by support generated by the H-Block hunger strikes) that rejected totally any notion of Unionist consent or what was termed 'a sop to loyalism'.

The position of the British state was always clear—it never opposed the unity of Ireland. Rather, it laid down the terms on which the country would be united. A majority of people in the north would have to consent. Republicans for their part stated diametrically opposing terms. The British would leave through the coercive power of the IRA without any reference to the desires or thoughts of the Unionists. The acceptance by Mr. Adams in New York of the consent principle is an acknowledgment not only that the war is over but that the British won it.

Moreover, the acceptance calls into question the usefulness or purpose of the IRA campaign post-1974. Morally, how justified was armed opposition to a partition that Republicans now accept has a democratic validity? Strategically, despite the swing of the demographic pendulum toward Catholics in the last thirty years it seems remarkable that nationalism secured in the Good Friday Agreement a less substantive deal than it did through Sunningdale. Ultimately, after a sustained IRA campaign the British were in a position to offer less than they did in 1974.

A revolutionary body that settles for and then seeks to legitimise the very terms it fought against simultaneously delegitimises and arguably criminalizes its own existence. Consequently, historians of the conflict, now armed with the present Sinn Fein logic, will in all probability come to view the IRA campaign much more negatively than may previously have been the case—a sad denouement to an unnecessary war in which so many suffered needlessly.

From Good Friday to Easter Sunday: Two Days and Light Years

The Blanket, 11 April 2004

> *The frustrated follow a leader less because of their faith that he is leading them to a promised land than because of their immediate feeling that he is leading them away from their unwanted selves. Surrender to a leader is not a means to an end but a fulfilment. Whither they are led is of secondary importance.*
>
> —ERIC HOFFER

Easter Sunday, and all over Ireland various parties, militias, cults and sects were on the march. Even councillors who traipsed off to British war graves or cenotaphs would today put on their Republican false faces and pretend that their politics and those of the men and women in the graves they stood at were somehow similar. When I visit the Republican plot in Belfast the thing furthest from my mind is the politics of Sinn Fein, which sit like an ugly scar defiling the very sacrifice inscribed in each Republican grave. Even more nauseating is the sight of some Sinn Fein leaders who have risen to prominence on the backs of those who lost their lives recoiling in shame at suggestions that they may have been IRA comrades of the dead. How often must we listen to the cock crow?

I didn't attend any of today's events. It taxed me even to put out a tricolour. I am uncomfortable with flags and flag wavers. Too many of them and Nuremberg dawns on the horizon. Even when I fly the Palestinian flag, it is not a statement about Palestinian nationalism, but rather a protest about the murderous policies of the Israeli state directed against Palestinian people. As for the hoisting of the tricolour, my wife insisted on it. And as she can't reach from the bedroom to the flagpole holder, the task falls to me. She also flies the Stars and Stripes on 4 July and 11 September. She is a U.S. citizen and has a strong sense of identity with her homeland. Hanging that up falls to me as well. But people with sharply differing views can live together quite easily without feeling the need to stand on principle over such matters in the home. My friends in the Socialist Workers Party gently rib me about the U.S. flag. I suppose it gives a few knuckle shufflers elsewhere something to crow about, but who cares?

Tomorrow in Derry Marian Price will be the main speaker at a Republican commemoration. As it sits presently, I am tempted to take my daughter Firinne up there. We may then go on to Donegal after it and spend some time with Tommy Gorman. It would be a good way to tire the child out. By the time she is back in Belfast she will be ready for bed, if she hasn't already succumbed to sleep in Shando's car. The last time he and I went to Derry it was to a Socialist Environment Alliance conference and we broke down this side of Toome. But we got there eventually and almost had a mental breakdown listening to some of the conference speakers. A smoother journey and less cumbersome ideologues tomorrow, hopefully.

Why Derry and Marian Price? I suppose if it were not for the fact that we are personal friends, I would not go up. I do not subscribe to the philosophy of the 32 County Sovereignty Movement, and not just for its association with the Real IRA. Its blind adherence to a totalising nationalism that has no greater a right to call on our allegiance than Catholicism is odious and jars with my awkward intellectual and emotional attachment to the right to dissent. Nationalism attracts me only in proportion to the extent that it permits people to opt out of its schema for the nation. Priests, whether ideological or theological, when beyond my visual and audible range make life much more bearable.

But at least tomorrow, Marian and her movement will be honouring those who were alongside us during the conflict but fell as a result of it. And there is a certain poignancy involved in standing alongside others, even if fundamentally opposed to me, in silent and reflective tribute to those with whom we at one time shared arms.

There was no chance of my having gone over to Milltown today where there was a choice of two Stick parades. Years ago, as the Sinn Fein parade and the original Sticks met at the cemetery gates there would be abuse, mostly verbal, exchanged between the two. Today, the casual observer would experience difficulty distinguishing which is which, with both factions shouting, 'Up Stormont', at each other. A visitor attending a Workers Party commemoration in the mid-seventies and listening to Des O'Hagan would, were he to attend a Sinn Fein one today, be excused for thinking that Des had merely grown a few inches in the intervening years but had still retained the beard and glasses. What would Gerry Adams be saying today that O'Hagan hadn't said all those years ago and which we would uproariously laugh at? There is not much novel in a statement laced with references to the need to bring back Stormont, reform the police, secure a bill of rights, and oppose all who resist with arms. Small wonder that when a Sinn Fein parade was goose-stepping its way through Dublin today to the air of 'Take it down from the mast, Irish traitors', a woman confronted the marchers and shouted, 'Take it down from the mast yourselves, boys'. My sole thought was to recall the words of Cardinal Richelieu: 'Give me six lines written by the most honorable of men, and I will find an excuse in them to hang him'. Of the vocal woman I thought, *Watch they don't hang you from the mast in its stead, Mrs.* Their attitude toward those who disagree with them has won them few prizes for tolerance over the years.

Good Friday and Easter Sunday are a mere two days apart. But the gap between what Good Friday republicanism achieved and the objectives Easter Sunday Republicans died to secure can be understood only in light years.

Tame Bulls in the China Shop

Parliamentary Brief, December 2003

The recent elections in Northern Ireland have produced what many have long dreaded. The emergence of a DUP/Sinn Fein axis is considered viewing for over eighteens only, and never before dark, the supposed 'nightmare scenario'. For those gripped by such a doomsday vista, the Good Friday Agreement was a finely balanced piece of architecture purposely built to swivel on the centre ground, its construction designed largely with the needs and tastes of Mark Durkan's SDLP and David Trimble's UUP in mind. But with Ian Paisley's DUP and Gerry Adams' Sinn Fein now the principal deed holders, courtesy of a British government decision to call an election, the centre ground anchor has supposedly shattered. And a tense hushed breath awaits the anticipated tailspin.

Bleak as things may seem from the Camp Gloomy perspective, the real disarticulation lies not between the centre ground considered necessary to sustain the agreement and the new dominant but combustible combination of forces said to have the potential to destroy it. It is between those who worship the agreement and their own faith in it. Arguably, the robust nature of the agreement is such that rather than becoming a stage where the 'extremes' can strut their garish wares to the point of destroying their own theatre, the long-running play will in fact be performed by a new set of actors. Without doubt they will procrastinate, they may not be as pretty, they may have worked in the less salubrious side of the industry previously, but they have learned their lines. And when they have routinely settled into their performance, few in the audience—70 percent of whom still give a standing ovation—will care to remember that it was ever any different.

Whatever mutually exclusive tangents the 'twin peaks of extremism' veer off on, the journey will be temporary in duration. The centripetal pull will ultimately magnetise them back to base camp where waiting to greet them with a handshake—the free hand used to hold its nose—shall be the Good Friday Agreement. It might be called the Holy Thursday Arrangement or the Shrove Tuesday Accord, but that is mere packaging for the optics. Why else did the British government allow the election to take place when it could calculate with certainty the 'dreaded' result? Forget the moral imperative of it—realpolitik rather than ethics dictates. The way in which the publication of the Cory Report into collusion is being postponed, because the British are trying to censor it, tells us that imperatives other than moral ones determine London's intervention here.

The British more than most are hardly ignorant of the following laws of political gravity: The Sinn Fein leadership's craving for institutional power is stronger than its need to keep the IRA. The DUP's 'visceral hatred' of the IRA is firmer than its love for devolved government. Only one terminus leads from that.

Those fearful for the future trajectory of the agreement can, if they are so inclined, draw solace from the briefest glance at its past. Its twin foundations—cross border bodies combined with a power sharing executive—have since 1972, more than any other, been the preferred policy objectives of the British state. Not because it was the ethically decent thing to do but due to it being the most plausible alternative to provisional republicanism—Britain's most serious problem in Ireland. Rupture the link between those substantial sections of the northern nationalist population, which supported the IRA by means other than repressive, and an outcome light years short of a united Ireland would bring stability.

Up until the 1990s the British were much too absolutist in their strategy of marginalisation, seeking to exclude both Republicans and republicanism from any stabilising framework. It produced containment rather than victory. And then they hit on the notion of defeating the Provisionals through inclusion. They brought the Republicans in and left their republicanism out. Hence, what made the Good Friday Agreement a runner from the outset was the willingness of the

Provisionals to shed the core tenets of their belief system. John Kelly, a Sinn Fein MLA in the previous assembly, in recent days noted how the party was completing its journey from republicanism to constitutional nationalism—a journey it swore never to make, and one for which the British were prepared to cough up the price of a no return fare. That Gerry Adams should have been pushed from promising a united Ireland through Hume/Adams to seeking accommodation within Northern Ireland as part of some strange Paisley/Adams hybrid should in itself explain just how neutralised republicanism has become.

While David Trimble, the first durable strategic Unionist leader to emerge, appreciated that the longevity of the union with Britain coupled with partition had been secured, unionism in general has been very slow to acknowledge this. But the signs of change come as frequently as television commercials. There is absolutely no reason for seasoned observers to pay the scantest attention to the bluster of those already posturing in the respective camps. Although Gerry Adams has said that there will be no renegotiation of the GFA and Ian Paisley has threatened with expulsion any in 'his' party who talk to Sinn Fein, the agreement is going to reconstitute both of them in its own image, a task the government will find much easier with Sinn Fein, who already support the agreement.

Former Secretary of State Mo Mowlam appreciates instinctively what the parameters and contours are: 'Ian Paisley and his followers and Gerry Adams and the rest of Sinn Fein will have to face up to having to talk and negotiate with each other'—*negotiate* being the key word. And while the present incumbent, Paul Murphy, insists that the fundamental principles of the agreement such as power sharing and consent will not be changed, this is a vacuous truism. The DUP is not demanding that this type of change occur. What it will demand and eventually receive is the dissolution of the IRA.

Peter Robinson, deputy leader of the DUP, having accused senior members of the Sinn Fein leadership as serving on the IRA's Army Council, can hardly negotiate with them directly. But it is being speculated in the press that the party will put its views to Sinn Fein through a government intermediary. There are two elections in the offing—the European next year and the British general the following spring. While at present the Tories are unlikely to become the government, the DUP may take a leaf out of Sinn Fein's book and procrastinate long enough to get past the elections and then see what a much weaker Labour majority, feeling Michael Howard breathe down its neck, might do. And as long as they define renegotiation as meaning the end of the IRA on the grounds that the latter's existence undermines the working of any agreement, the force of their logic will, given their status as the most popular Unionist Party, be hard to withstand.

Whether a prolonged hiatus or one remembered for its brevity, two things are virtually certain: Republicans are not going back to war; the DUP is not returning to permanent 'splendid oppositionalism'. While rule from London suits Unionists much more than Republicans, wandering as nomads in the political desert of direct rule will amuse neither of them for long. They have drunk at the oasis of devolution and will come back for more, paying the asking fee as they step inside. And, ultimately, because they missed their chance with Trimble, Sinn Fein will pay more and receive less.

CHAPTER 2
Republican Dead

The Last Supper

The Blanket, 21 April 2002

*L*ast weekend's commemorative event in Dublin organised by Tirghra has given rise to much commentary and heated public discussion. As always in these situations there are those in the media who see themselves as sign readers, eager to interpret the latest revelation as definitively meaning the war is over, forgetting all the other occasions on which they told us the same thing. Unable to resist the lure of sensationalism, they endlessly search for that one event rather than look at the end of the war as a process akin to paint drying.

Sinn Fein like publicity but not public discussion, particularly if it comes at a difficult time for the party. Republican involvement or not, public discussion of the Castlereagh theft, the alleged existence of IRA intelligence files on Tory Party MPs, the murder of Barney McDonald, and alleged Sinn Fein participation in vigilantism in the republic all help to reinforce an uncomfortable political climate for the Republican Party as it prepares for the southern general election after which, according to Pat Doherty, it expects to hold the balance of power.

And particularly since the Colombian debacle the seemingly polished performances by its spokespeople have given way to inept, bungling affairs—reminiscent of that *London Times* drunk 'marching the wrong way on an escalator'. Those who gulp are admonished for not swallowing the incredible: 'We sat up all night making up these fictions and you have the temerity not to believe them'. Despite Eoghan Harris in the *Sunday Independent* querying the ability of Miriam O'Callaghan, her interview with Gerry Adams for *Prime Time* brought out among other things a dark side the spin doctors have long since sought to exorcise. As one *Sunday Tribune* columnist put it, O'Callaghan's eyes grew wider as the nose of Adams grew longer.

The presence of so many families in Dublin's Citywest Hotel underlined the terrible price IRA volunteers and Sinn Fein members paid in the course of the Provisional IRA's war against the British. Many died unsuspectingly. Others saw death coming and faced it with tremendous courage. Enough died willingly but none easily. And it is sanctimonious attitudinising for political commentator Ruth Dudley Edwards to claim that those being honoured were 'poor idiots'. They were 'poor' but the 'idiot' side of the equation is hardly borne out by the above average educational achievements of their equally poor comrades at university level in the prisons and elsewhere.

The deaths of hundreds of IRA volunteers, for the most part on active service, illustrates the social insurrectionary nature of the conflict. The subsequent IRA funeral rituals referred to by Seamus Mettress in his short study of Republican eschatology illustrated a community solidarity with the armed Republican body. All of it ruptured the myths and propaganda of both unionism and the London/Dublin political axis who for long enough sought to explain armed resistance as some form of aggravated crime wave. Small wonder that the reaction from unionism to the Tirghra organised commemoration was predictable. Its self-righteous inability to bear any responsibility for a conflict that its own rigidity helped produce was so strikingly vivid in Jeffrey Donaldson's comment that Republicans wanted to 'dine out on their stories of terrorist deeds' at a 'feast of IRA members celebrating their so-called comrades, who were involved in some of the most terrible atrocities that occurred in the last thirty years'.

The body of the Unionist critique saw the commemoration as a deification of warlike activity. William Fraser, who, according to media reports, lost a father and four other family members to the IRA, said understandably that he was disgusted 'that so many terrorists are going to be celebrating what they call a war'. In a sense this mirrored and complemented some dissident Republican thinking that saw the event as an exploitation of the dead for further electoral gain. But there is another way to view the occasion that would identify a need on the part of the Sinn Fein leadership not to take the Republican dead forward with them but to lay them and all that they represented to rest.

Therefore, it was not as Susan McKay claimed in today's *Sunday Tribune*, a celebration of the link between Sinn Fein and the IRA, but a step in the process of dissolving it. The dead were being legitimised, true, but more importantly the dead were legitimising the establishment politicians of Sinn Fein in the eyes of their most loyal supporters as they march on into the establishment, where the activities of the dead who unknowingly put them there will become a thing of the past. Despite Joe Cahill's ludicrous claim that had Tom Williams been alive 'he would be very much in favour of the course we're taking now', has there been one trace found in the records of a single IRA volunteer who died on active service that he or she anticipated or endorsed anything remotely approaching what Sinn Fein have settled for today? Westcity was a melding of separate projects, necessary to maintain the pretence that one was the outgrowth of, rather than a break with, the other—a revisiting of the 'sacred' ground by a 'profane' leadership for one last time in order to complete a rite of passage to a completely new world.

While the families in attendance were treated with great courtesy and consideration, each being allocated their own personal 'chaperone', their motivation was hardly the same as that of the Sinn Fein leadership. Paul Kavanagh, whose brother Albert was one of the earliest volunteers to join the roll of honour said, 'From the families' standpoint it is important that they, the relatives, are seen as equal victims. This is a tribute to the fallen dead, but to the families as well'. Many of the bereaved were said to be both deeply moved by the occasion and honoured to receive the sculptured tribute designed by Dublin artist Robert Ballagh.

Gerry Adams offered a reason why the gathering took place: 'This event has been a number of years in the making and actually came about as the peace process developed and we saw this huge group of people, who do come together quite regularly in commemorations'. A critic would point to the fact that many of the bereaved families in Belfast were, up until recently at any rate, given the paltry sum of three pounds a week by the Republican movement. One bereaved relative is said to have commented that it would cost her more to pay the taxi to go and collect it. Adams spoke of being proud of the volunteers who 'were ordinary men and women, some little more than boys and girls, who saw injustice and who struck for freedom'. Perhaps, but not so proud as to permit them any input into decision making at crucial points in the leadership's peace strategy the origins of which now—if press reports of an interview given by Father Alex Reid to a Basque journalist are to be believed—may go back as far as 1981 and was never designed to achieve a united Ireland. How many went to their graves knowing that? Those who at times were little more than boys and girls could die for their country but were not allowed an army convention to consider the first cease-fire of 1994. Moreover, they suffered the indignity of being snubbed by the leadership on the question of decommissioning.

The Tirghra body, which Sean McManus, father of the dead volunteer Joe, explained was comprised of elements much wider than Sinn Fein, in one sense functioned like a modern day Gethsemane group, organising the 'first and only' event of its kind where St. Peter—always willing to praise the sacrifice of the volunteers so long as he can deny ever having been part of their ranks—took it upon himself to administer the Judas kiss to the IRA. There is a certain irony in hosting what one writer termed a 'U.S.-style tribute dinner'. Few of the dead, unlike their leaders, ever saw the inside of a banquet hall. That the Westcity is used both by Fianna Fail and Fine Gael to stage their ard fheisanna is hardly without symbolic significance. The subliminal message: The anti-establishment sacrifices of the Republican dead have brought us here into the bosom of the establishment.

Despite the furor, there will be no price to pay for Sinn Fein. Wiser heads in the political establishment will think strategically, viewing Adams presiding over the ceremony as Albert Reynolds did when he lectured John Major after the Sinn Fein president had carried the coffin of IRA volunteer Thomas Begley. Reynolds said to the British prime minister, 'If this man didn't carry that coffin, he couldn't deliver that movement. He's no good to you or me if he didn't carry that coffin'. And in terms of having delivered the movement, the Tirghra event indicates that the IRA expects no more of its volunteers to die officially on active service. If they do it shall be unofficial—they shall be disowned just like those now expected to criminalise themselves if caught for IRA activity. The cruel irony is that some of those being honoured in Westcity gave their lives to ensure that the IRA would not be criminalised. What a way for the worm to turn—about.

The British State Murder of Pearse Jordan

The Blanket, 26 November 2002

> *The best manner of avenging ourselves is by not resembling*
> *him who has injured us.*
>
> —JANE PORTER

When Pearse Jordan died at the hands of the RUC ten years ago this month, I and other Republican prisoners were on the work-out scheme from Maghaberry Prison where it was customary for Long Kesh lifers to serve out the last three months of their sentences in a sort of half-board existence. Sleeping in the prison—usually aided by a few pints—four nights a week, the rest of the time was our own or nominally that of whatever employer we were supposed to be working for as part of our smooth transition to becoming 'normal' citizens again.

After almost two decades in prison and now faced with decisions that would determine whether imprisonment would feature as part of our lives again, the killing of Pearse Jordan was a wake-up call. It brought home to any of us considering reporting back to the IRA in any active capacity that life in the organisation for serious volunteers was devoid of frills. While there were plenty of areas within the structures in which to hide, there seemed no reason other than pseudo ones for choosing them as an option. For active volunteers a pitiless existence was what lay ahead. For those of us pondering such a path the seriousness of the matter was etched ever deeper in our minds as we felt a sense of eeriness descend upon us while visiting the flower-marked scene of Pearse Jordan's death at the front of the City Cemetery facing St. John's Chapel. Each time I passed in a black taxi on my way to the bus to return to jail on dark December evenings the thought that a new life was awaiting me while his had ended so soon proved turbulent to any peace of mind I expected to have as a result of imminent release.

Two decades earlier we had promised to end it and now volunteers born into it were dying with still no end in sight.

Pearse Jordan graced the ranks of the IRA at a time when membership of the body had a purpose other than lording it over neighbours or maintaining some disembodied sense of esprit de corps. He was no cease-fire volunteer or Good Friday soldier, the manner of his end underscoring the point. Some of those who strut our streets and ex-prisoner centres today would not have opened the door to him or his comrades during the course of an IRA operation. Militant Republicans of the verbal type, their homes were IRA-free zones when the IRA needed houses most, a point often made with understandable bitterness by those who risked their lives and freedom alongside Pearse.

On the morning of his funeral I travelled to South Derry to visit friends whom I had been in prison with. I had not known him and a year would elapse before I attended my first IRA funeral in over twenty years, that of volunteer Thomas Begley in Ardoyne. Later I would live in Ballymurphy, the home territory of the IRA squad that Pearse belonged to. Through the prism of bereavement it could be seen that a generational change had occurred within the IRA. Although Ballymurphy had lost a number of volunteers during the conflict, Pearse more than any other was revered amongst his comrades. Their respect for him mirrored that of the Blanketmen for Bobby Sands. For many of them he was the only dead volunteer they had served alongside. Some local Republicans named their children in honour of Pearse's memory. His framed photo adorns the walls in the halls and living rooms of others. On Monday many of them congregated in Milltown Cemetery to pay their respects.

His death hurt them. It still does. The number of times his name has come up in conversation over the years is testimony to his status within local Republican iconography. His father Hugh summed up what many of them feel: 'Every anniversary is difficult. You wonder what he would have been doing now, would he have had children'? He died as a Provisional IRA volunteer in a war that could not be won, although he was not told that at the time. Had he survived a mere two years, like his comrades, he would have been denied any input into the 1994 leadership decision to halt the war—an event being planned as he was losing his life while prosecuting the same war. In the minds of the leadership he was sound enough to risk and ultimately lose his life for the war but strangely, like the rest of us, not sound enough to decide on either ending or persevering with it.

Arguably the greatest tribute that could have been paid to his Provisional Republican memory was in the end not paid at all. A simple display of the moral courage required to say 'no' to a leadership determined to go Stick would have been more fitting than anything else and at the same time less incongruous with both the etiology and formative ideology of the Provisional Republican movement.

In terms of republicanism as distinct from the political ambitions of this or that individual Republican, very little was gained from this war. But that can never take away from the enormity of the sacrifice made by people like Pearse Jordan. A young New Barnsley IRA volunteer with his life in front of him, he gave it all up out of a sense of something wider than himself. And as the Belfast drizzle pounds his grave of ten years people will pause to reflect that his sightless eyes once blazed with a vision of something better, much better than what we have now.

Loughall—A Truth to Remain Untold

The Blanket, 23 August 2004

The decision by Mairead Kelly to meet PSNI boss Hugh Orde in a bid to acquire more information about the death of her brother Paddy has generated a certain amount of public discourse. Paddy Kelly died at Loughall in 1987 while on active service with the Provisional IRA. He and seven comrades were ambushed by the SAS and RUC in a carefully constructed 'killing zone' and finished off. It was as merciless as it was premeditated.

There is no doubting the lethal intent of the eight Republican volunteers who set out that May evening. They were on a mission against an enemy installation and personnel and knew the risks involved. They were heavily armed and some did manage to fire the weapons they held at their British state attackers, presumably with a view to killing them, before being felled themselves. Many in the Unionist community have subsequently protested that they got what they deserved and that should be the end of the matter. On today's BBC *Talkback*, Jeffrey Donaldson of the DUP articulated such sentiments, arguing that Republicans like myself who feel further exploration of the issue is purposeful are being inconsistent. Many of those who later contacted *Talkback* went further and accused Republicans of downright hypocrisy.

The main contention of the Unionists is that Provisional IRA volunteers claim to have been involved in a war and could not therefore expect to have benefited from the niceties of arrest. Conveniently ignoring the state interception—when it suited—and arrest of heavily armed UDA killers en route to kill unarmed nationalists, Jeffrey Donaldson persists in the myth that death before detention is the only plausible option open to British state security personnel monitoring Republican active service units equipped with modern weaponry.

In a war it is anticipated that there are rules of engagement. While the Provisional IRA has violated them incessantly it was certainly not alone. The British can ill afford to stand on some moral plateau and wax ethical to others on these things. Seamus McIlwaine was administered the coup de grâce by a member of the SAS while he lay on the ground injured, having been earlier shot and then interrogated by his captors. At least one of the Loughall volunteers had covered some distance on foot before being captured unarmed and then shot at point-blank range.

In justifying this, the Unionists provide an unwitting justification for the war waged by the Provisional IRA. If the British were not involved, as their advocates and apologists over the past thirty-five years have insisted, in prosecuting a war but were merely responding to an 'aggregated crime wave', then warlike measures have no part to play in that response. State murder of those involved in 'crime' is precisely that—murder. And if the state murders those it claims are its own citizens, it hardly encourages others to desist from responding in kind. Those seeking an insight into the origins and development of the Provisional IRA campaign need look no further than 1969 and subsequent state policy. British indifference created the organisation; British repression sustained it. Its volunteers did not carry some genetic code dating back to 1916 predisposing them toward physical force. How otherwise can it be explained that the settlement of Good Friday 1998, so readily embraced and celebrated by those volunteers, does not vaguely resemble the objectives of Easter Sunday 1916?

Unionists such as Jeffrey Donaldson wish to place their bets each way. On the one hand, the IRA was not at war and was a mere criminal enterprise. On the other, because it claimed it was at war its volunteers could therefore be subjected to the merciless rigours of the battlefield with no means of legal recourse. And the war measures used to suppress the IRA of course absolves the British state of any culpability for human rights violations, which it would most certainly have to answer for in circumstances other than war. Quintessential Unionist cant, both self-serving and pompous.

The Loughall massacre certainly throws up a range of challenges.

But unionism is not alone in facing them. One avenue that will never be fully explored, no matter how many meetings take place between Mairead Kelly and Hugh Orde, is the possibility that IRA volunteers were deliberately targeted at Loughall after the British government was made aware by a key element within the Republican leadership that it was willing to parley and settle for considerably less than those who died that night were intent on securing, something they might have revolted against had they not been slain, something that in order to succeed necessitated their removal. Whether the British killed those volunteers to facilitate what later became known as the peace process may be the real story of the Loughall massacre.

Joe Cahill—Provisional Republican Veteran

The Blanket, 26 July 2004

> *Once it's an extended truce, then it's detrimental to the*
> *Republican movement.*
>
> —JOE CAHILL

J oe Cahill, who died at the weekend, was the Provisional IRA's second chief of staff. The organisation fielded nine such supremos throughout its thirty-five year existence and Cahill's incumbency proved to be the shortest but one. With his passing the first four Provisional IRA chiefs of staff are now dead, all from natural causes. Cahill lived longer than the others, succumbing at the age of eighty-four. Although he is noted as saying that he was born in a united Ireland and hoped to die in one, had he lived to be 104 he would not have realised that ambition. His fellow leaders ensured that much by agreeing to the partition principle of consent.

Joe Cahill hailed from West Belfast. That one Westminster constituency alone provided the Provisional IRA with four of its chiefs of staff. The three Belfast Brigade delegates who attended the London talks at the Chelsea home of British minister Paul Channon in July 1972 all went on to hold down the position as did two of the other three London negotiators. Dave O'Conaill alone of the six who made up the IRA talks team never assumed the top spot. Although Cahill, perhaps due to a brief spell of imprisonment in Dublin under the Offences Against the State Act and a subsequent hunger strike, was not at these talks, he twice met with Harold Wilson and Merlyn Rees of the British Labour Party in 1972 as part of an IRA delegation.

Of the five surviving former and current chiefs of staff, none will see fifty again. Consequently, if the organisation dissolves before appointing another CS none of those who commanded the Provisional

IRA will live in the united Ireland they waged war to achieve, testimony in itself to the utter failure of the campaign.

Joe Cahill was described by Gerry Adams as 'the father of this generation of Republicans'. This is not a view shared by all those who were contemporaries of the former Crumlin Road Prison condemned cell prisoner. While it would be inaccurate to dismiss the role of Cahill in the formative years of the Provisional IRA, including his work in helping to build the organisation up outside the northern capital, authentic parentage in the eyes of many rests with Billy McKee, the first leader of the Provisional IRA in Belfast, who was succeeded by Cahill after his arrest in March 1971. McKee has stayed robustly loyal to the tenets upon which the Provisionals were founded. This adds a touch of the bizarre to the eulogy to Cahill proffered by Martin McGuinness:

> When people look back on his role, they will come to the conclusion that Joe Cahill was rock solid and he will stand alongside the likes of Robert Emmet, Wolfe Tone, Padraig Pearse, Maire Drumm, Bobby Sands, and Mairead Farrell.

Had Joe Cahill died in his sixties and not his eighties this account would have chimed more easily with the trajectory then covered by his Republican odyssey. But by the time of his death that trajectory had veered sharply to the point where the politics Cahill embraced resembled nothing of the organisation he helped establish in 1969 and had everything in common with those in the Official IRA from which he broke. It is more straightforward to make the case that he stands alongside Cathal Goulding, Malachy McGurran, and Liam McMillan, all who gave a lifetime of service to their particular brand of republicanism including the peace process they kick-started in May 1972. This lends a cruel irony to Cahill's role in the IRA split of 1969. The army he built, in sharp opposition to the latter three leaders of the Official IRA, came to embrace everything those 'hated reformists' stood for.

The role of Joe Cahill within provisional republicanism resembled more that of continuity presenter than main anchorman. He provided the veneer of Republican continuity that helped mask the ugly joints created by Gerry Adams' reformist strategy and acceptance of an internal solution. His presence served to disguise what in essence were major strategic departures. A year ago Joe Cahill made the extraordinary comment that the IRA had won the war, leaving his colleagues looking awkward when subsequently pushed by media interviewers to state if the war was indeed won, then why could they not say it was over.

Like many youngsters growing up in militarised Belfast streets, my first memory of Joe Cahill dates back to August 1971 when he fronted an IRA press conference in Ballymurphy a couple of days after internment to announce that the IRA was intact. My mother's acerbic intervention on seeing him thwarted any designs I might have had toward lionising him. Although he headed for Dublin once the conference was over, those who remained in Belfast under the command of the late Seamus Twomey proved Cahill's assessment of the IRA correct. They prosecuted the war with a ferocity that would ultimately help force the British government to ditch the Stormont parliament.

I last saw Joe Cahill two years ago at a funeral in Belfast. I greeted him but he ignored me. In that he was no different from others in the leadership coterie: willing to direct but never to answer to those fortunate enough to have survived with their lives from the debacle the leadership so ineptly oversaw, and who sought to ask those questions dead volunteers never had the chance to.

Joe Cahill lived a long life. I am glad that he did. His longevity helped compensate for the numerous years taken from him by British and Free State penal systems. So many others didn't make it out of their teens. They are the real tragedies of the conflict.

Padraic Paisley

The Blanket, 5 December 2004

*L*ast week we took two American friends who stopped overnight with us to see some of the political artistry that adorns the gable walls of the area in which we live. The community here suffered greatly for its resistance to the British state. The walls pictorially narrate something of its experience. Their powerfully evocative imagery always holds an attraction for visitors, who never cease to marvel at the dexterity of the artists. Last week, same as this week, such was the talk of the deal of all deals being struck between the DUP theocrat and the Sinn Fein autocrat that I suggested to our New York friends that they should not be surprised if we come across a mural of Connolly, Pearse, and Paisley. Those who would see nothing untoward about it would be the same people who still believe that decommissioning never took place, and who would happily assemble at Dunville Park for the three o'clock spacecraft to take them to a united Ireland simply because it had been advertised in the local party front paper.

Once the murals had been photographed—thankfully, none of which were of Padraic Paisley or Peadar Mac Robin—our loquacious and exceptionally witty taxi driver sped us over to Milltown Cemetery and the burial place of IRA volunteers. At the grave of Bobby Sands our three-year-old daughter skipped and laughed. She had only recently been told the story of 'Brave Bobby Sands, the wicked witch Maggie Thatcher, and the H-Blocks'. No matter how much I dress it up she insists it is a 'terrible story' and demands to be told Dora the Explorer instead. Nevertheless, she advocates that we should get a rope and 'pull poor Bobby out from the bury hole'. In response to her toddler-style graveside laughter, my wife reminded me of Bobby's revenge being the laughter of our children. His place of rest seemed a fitting spot for Firinne to be laughing, in some small way unintentionally providing the only revenge he achieved.

For this reason, my daughter's laughter offered but small consolation. Standing at the grave and thinking back over the terrible suffering that Bobby endured before his comrades placed him in the clay one dank, dismal Thursday afternoon, I gritted my teeth at the sheer futility of the sacrifices made by the men and women lying beneath our feet. They gave up everything they had, every last shred of a personal future in the belief that others would be rewarded with a victory over the British state in Ireland. They fought and died for a free Ireland and now their leaders discuss giving them free presbyterianism.

When we took part in the Adams war we did so with a view to getting the British out. We deluded ourselves that we were fighting for Ireland when all we were doing was fighting for Adams. He became the author of our meaning, distorting it into a wholly fictionalised account. He succeeded so well because most of us preferred belief to reason; our involvement was reduced to a question of faith, defined by Nietzsche as 'not wanting to know what is true'. Were I to have suggested a course of action during my H-Block days that would lead republicanism to where it is today I would have found myself residing in a loyalist wing.

None of us know what way the Republican dead, had they survived, would have viewed events of today. We do know, however, were they not beneath the damp clay of Milltown, they would be allowed no input into decision making. That is the prerogative of a small leadership clique. IRA volunteers empowered the clique so that it in turn could disempower them. Defrauded of any rightful return on the investment they made in terms of emotional energy, personal liberty, and lives, their reward is one of deception and lies, not to mention marginalisation if they opt not to nod their heads obediently every time they are fed some rubbish by the leadership lie machine. They are allowed to mould strategy and objectives the same way that a cow shapes the journey of the train it watches from a field. They can give freely of their lives for the cause but not of their opinions. They would be hounded if they publicly spoke out against a process leading to an outcome that would leave the north being compared with Iran. Courtesy of Sinn Fein, a western European state or statelet—supposedly situated in the intellectual tradition of the Enlightenment—faces the prospect that a theocratic fundamentalist may at some point lead it.

Paisley has told the world of his plans to humiliate the current IRA. Its volunteers must publicly wear sackcloth and ashes to sate his vengeful urges. When we were told the same thing in 1976, the first Blanketman Kieran Nugent defied the British. He threw down the gauntlet, challenging them that if they wanted him to wear the sackcloth called 'prison uniform' they would have to nail it to his back. He emerged from the prison three years later with scars on his back but no sackcloth. He was a volunteer in an undefeated IRA. There is no chance of the current IRA taking such a stand. It is a defeated IRA. Many years ago it began to eat the elephant of total failure one bite at a time, not remembering the previous bite and never seeing the next one being served up. Ultimately, there is nothing else it can do other than eventually ask for two pieces of sackcloth so that those who populate its ranks shall have a fresh one for Sundays. No amount of nonsense about the greatest leadership ever and the undefeated army can explain how a combination of both, in return for our toil and the ultimate sacrifice of our comrades, brought us to a point where, in the words of Gerry Adams, 'Sinn Fein will be putting Ian Paisley into power'.

Bravo the undefeated army!
Bravo the greatest leadership ever!
Bollix to both of you.

CHAPTER 3
The Colombia Three

An Ambiguity That Corrupts

The Observer, 2 September 2001

> *Three political prisoners in Colombia show how Sinn Fein*
> *bow to the politics of compromise.*

In West Belfast black flags still adorn the streets in fluttering memory to the ten Republican volunteers who lost their lives on the 1981 hunger strike. This year has added poignancy, being the twentieth anniversary of that awesomely selfless act.

A world away from West Belfast, three Irish Republicans are imprisoned in a country with an atrocious human rights record. Culpable or not, the three detained in Colombia's Modelo Prison remain political prisoners. Their arrest occurred only because they were Republicans, conveniently positioned when a range of powerful forces in London, Dublin, Bogotá, and Washington found it purposeful to move as one on strategic matters of mutual interest.

The party that benefited most from the suffering of Republican prisoners seems to have little to say in their defence. 'Never seen them before in our lives' is the apparent refrain from Sinn Fein. The party's obsession with suppressing adverse public discussion of the obvious—reflected in claims that the Colombian affair is in fact a 'nonstory'—has merely led many to conclude that the 'obvious' in this case is the guilt of the three men. The British media, exultantly adhering to the principle that everybody is innocent until proven Irish, has been eager to facilitate each Sinn Fein faux pas on the matter. If Sinn Fein is to be believed on the anodyne matter of the men's alleged links to the party, then not only are the British and Americans lying through their teeth—an eminently reasonable proposition at the best of times—but so too are the Cuban and FARC leaders.

It is not that Sinn Fein is embarrassed only by the existence of alleged IRA links with FARC. Indeed, it seems that on strict evidential grounds there is little to link merely alleged IRA volunteers to the Marxist guerrillas in a manner that would constitute serious illegality. Sinn Fein do not even want it said that the men are totally innocent but linked to the party and were in Colombia on a whatever-the-euphemism-of-the-day mission. Hence its willingness to make liars of both the Cubans and FARC. The right-wing palate of corporate America must be assuaged even if it means behaving as St. Peter no matter how often the cock crows.

Perhaps things may not have been so distasteful had the men been arrested leaving a camp run by right-wing paramilitary groups. It is hard to imagine the Bush administration upsetting itself over that despite the fact that the right rather than the left are the main players in the drugs trade. Sinn Fein may even have sighed with relief.

In a semi-explanation to a local daily newspaper Sinn Fein Chair Mitchell McLaughlin alluded to Republicans having internal management problems that he dated back to October last year when, coincidentally, Real IRA member Joseph O'Connor was assassinated, which the Provisional IRA denied, causing people to reflect that the 'P' in 'P. O'Neill' must have stood for Pinocchio. McLaughlin had earlier told the *Observer* that only a fool believed that IRA guns are totally silent. Perhaps he should have added that only a fool would use IRA guns and then be disowned by Sinn Fein if arrested for having them.

Once the British had laid down the ground rules pertaining to the circumstances in which sanctions would be employed for breaking the silence of those guns it was always inevitable that IRA armed activity against some members of the nationalist community would continue pretty much as before and that there was always the possibility that IRA volunteers would be arrested, thrown into a criminal environment—and subsequently deserted. When Mo Mowlam bizarrely rationalised in 1999 that young Belfast man Charles Bennett was legally dead but somehow politically alive so that the IRA cease-fire could not be determined as having been breached, she nourished the 'constructive fudge' and 'creative ambiguity' that has made the peace process the intellectual farce that it is. Its foundation is a nonsensical consensus that is presently blind to UDA attacks on Catholics and their homes.

That consensus was revealed at a 1998 Oxford conference on the need for a Truth and Reconciliation Commission when a leading Irish participant proffered the following wisdom on the Good Friday Agreement—'a delicately balanced compromise that can be destroyed by truth . . . honesty and straightforward talking must be avoided at all costs'.

Twenty years ago as prisoners died and people trudged the streets in a bid to save them, who would have thought that Sinn Fein, gorged on fudge and ambiguity, would dismiss Irish political prisoners as a 'nonstory'?

Sinn Fein should have no reason to be embarrassed over Republican prisoners. But such prisoners may now have every reason to be embarrassed over Sinn Fein.

A Spotlight on Evidence Not There

The Blanket, 18 October 2001

*B*BC's *Spotlight* team found itself in Colombia in recent weeks on the trail of evidence regarding the ongoing detention of Jim Monaghan, Niall Connolly, and Martin McCauley. Tuesday night's broadcast of the findings demonstrates that the really interesting evidence in this case is not that supposedly linking the three Republicans to illegal activity but in fact relates to the nature of the operation staged for the purposes of trapping the men. Those intent on effecting the arrests seemed unconcerned with the guilt or innocence of the trio. Evidence was hardly a consideration, given that little effort was expended in collating any. The overriding concern seems to have been one of making a big media splash for the purposes of political leverage. Regardless of the facts of the case, who was going to listen to three Irish Republicans, two of whom had previous convictions stemming directly from their involvement in armed Republican activity?

Spotlight, aided by the time that had elapsed since the arrests coupled with its acquisition of agenda-setting documentation emanating from British diplomats and the RUC, managed to conduct a considerably more focused investigation than that of the UTV *Insight* team a number of weeks previously. The major difference between the two documentaries lay in the highlighting of culpability. *Insight* suggested, plausibly enough in the views of most people, that the three Republicans were not out on holiday. Conversely, *Spotlight* drew the attention of the audience to the total lack of evidence against the three accused and succeeded in refracting attention onto probable spook involvement. In one piece of footage a female attorney for the Colombian state came across as a blathering idiot, rendered speechless when asked the simplest of questions in relation to evidence. While Sinn Fein's incoherent babbling in the wake of the arrests merely persuaded people that the men had some case to answer, the Colombian attorney pitched the pendulum firmly in the other direction. The men may not be innocent but the case for their guilt appears unlikely ever to be made.

It now seems clear that from the outset the Colombian operation to detain the three Republicans was not the outcome of legal or judicial process. Attributing political culpability to the Provisional Republican movement at a significant moment in the north's political process was the determining factor. Events in Belfast rather than Bogotá sealed the fate of the accused.

This is not to excuse Sinn Fein or its abysmal management of the fallout from the episode. It is not even to suggest that the men were not out in Colombia on IRA activity. Sinn Fein's willingness for a number of years to tread the quagmire of decommissioning and then try to play it long through delaying the logical inevitability most likely spurred powerful agencies in London, Dublin and Washington to move against it and close off all remaining options to the party. The three men, guilty or innocent, were useful patsies in the matter.

What emerges from the *Spotlight* investigation is that three Republicans are being held in dangerous and less than humane conditions in Colombia. The case against them is political rather than legal. It is not nearly as strong as the case for their immediate release.

Sinn Fein and the Embarrassing Three

The Blanket, 1 May 2002

S inn Fein have not had an easy week. Hounded from many different directions, the party exudes the appearance that it is tottering and struggling to maintain its balance. Given the pounding it has sustained, that it is not punch drunk by now is testament to its considerable cunning in the ring. From the moment Henry Hyde, chair of the U.S. International Relations Committee, sent his letter to Sinn Fein asking Gerry Adams to 'appear and help us determine what the Sinn Fein leadership knew about the IRA activities with the FARC narcoterrorists in Colombia and when did Sinn Fein learn of them', it was clear that the knotted tie of the IRA was being moved uncomfortably close to the party windpipe. Sinn Fein denied receiving any letter. But things in relation to Colombia can move very slowly within the party. It was months, we are led to believe, before its leadership learned that Niall Connolly was in fact a member. And according to Gerry Adams on *Hearts and Minds* the leadership went to Cuba rather than Belfast to learn this. Presumably Hyde's letter went via Cuba also.

A Sinn Fein spokesperson made it clear that the party 'do not have a case to answer'. Nevertheless, its Washington office did not rest on this and as part of what David McKittrick called 'a major damage limitation exercise' went to formidable lengths to pull out all the stops in order to create plenty of wiggle room designed to allow the leadership to dodge the flak certain to come its way. And where it landed the objective of Congressman Peter King and colleagues was to ensure it missed the main target, Sinn Fein president Gerry Adams. With a senior Bush official saying of seven alleged IRA members supposedly in Colombia, 'If these people are who we think they are, then it beggars belief that the Sinn Fein leadership did not sanction what was going on', the stakes were higher than they had been for some time.

If media coverage this side of the Atlantic is accurate Sinn Fein emerged somewhat unscathed. However, if this is so, and given the party's assurance that there was no case against it, it seems strange that Mr. Adams did not avail himself of the opportunity to go to the congressional hearing. Comfort himself as he might that the hearing's outcome 'vindicates the position that we took in relation to all of this', his 'snub', as many Americans view it, could have been avoided and he would have secured a moral victory. That the Americans would view it as a snub can be gleaned from *The Philadelphia Inquirer*:

> Perhaps Mr. Adams doesn't appreciate what is at stake. Snubbing the House International Relations Committee . . . may play well with Irish Republicans back home in Northern Ireland. But the Americans who support Sinn Fein—literally, by donating the bulk of its political contributions—may have serious qualms about giving money to an IRA-aligned Sinn Fein now that three men with IRA connections are accused of aiding Colombian rebels who thrive off America's drug addictions.

Gerry Adams—who says he accepts the claim of the three imprisoned Irish Republicans that they were only studying the Colombian peace process—in maintaining that the hearing would have jeopardised their trial is raising a few eyebrows. It would only have done so if Sinn Fein had a case to answer, went out, and were brought to book. There is much to be said for the *Guardian* leader (a paper that by no means gives the Republican Party a rough ride) when it observed that if the Sinn Fein president was able to show that the three Republicans in a Colombian jail 'were not involved in a network with the Colombian FARC rebels, then he would surely have done so. It would have helped, not prejudiced, the three defendants'. There was little possibility that the Colombian authorities would have flagrantly dissented from a verdict reached in open session in the American Congress. There was a much better chance of obtaining a de facto acquittal in Washington than in Bogotá. A Colombian de jure acquittal would surely have followed.

Despite Cass Ballenger, a Republican from North Carolina, having attempted to prejudice the outcome by stating before the Subcommittee on the Western Hemisphere on 11 April that 'the IRA has been in Colombia providing the FARC narco-terrorists with urban terrorist expertise and training', the *Irish Echo* informed its readers that the forty-seven member House International Relations Committee represented a broad cross-section of congressional political opinion. Some of the constituencies represented had 'a strong Irish-American makeup. A substantial core of these have been identified over the years with Irish issues'. As well as Ben Gilman, there were:

> Peter King, a New York Republican; Robert Menendez, a New Jersey Democrat; Joe Crowley, a New York Democrat; Christopher Smith, a New Jersey Republican; Eliot Engel, a New York Democrat, and Gary Ackerman, also a New York Democrat. All have been sympathetic to Sinn Fein and the Irish nationalist agenda in general . . . and can be expected to lend a sympathetic ear to any plausible explanation from Sinn Fein as to what the three Republicans were doing in Bogotá, should the party choose to send a representative to the hearing.

And as Mark Davenport of the BBC reported, 'In the past, the International Relations Committee has debated allegations of human rights abuses in Northern Ireland and called for reforms in policing'.

On the other hand, the Sinn Fein president was armed with professional legal advice that his presence at the hearing could have jeopardised the trial. And that must be taken in conjunction with other motives that may have been influencing the investigation. Adams claimed that 'investigating counsel told me and Martin McGuinness separately that he had been pressed by British representatives'. True or not, unlike Britain's relationship to the north, where it is hard to conceive of any strategic interest that would hold it here, the United States sees Colombia as being central to America's hemispherical interests. Assistance for FARC from whatever quarter is, in the words of the BBC, 'seen as impinging on U.S. national interests'. According to the *Observer*, President Bush wants to send an extra $98 million to train the Colombian army to defend a controversial oil pipeline. Not surprisingly, several members of the International Relations Committee see a benefit in establishing a link between FARC and the IRA so that Plan Colombia can be extended to fight FARC on the grounds that such links indicate that the Marxist guerrillas are part of an 'international terror network'. Davenport, therefore, concedes that 'Gerry Adams has a point when he says that both he and the three Republicans still in custody in Colombia are pawns in a bigger game'. And the *Irish Independent* allowed room for the opinion to be expressed that Sinn Fein just 'happened to be the meat in the sandwich'.

In all of this Adams found a staunch ally in Peter King, who argued that nothing new would emerge from a pointless hearing. In addition, Father Sean McManus, who had called for many inquiries over the years, found himself in the rare position of opposing this one on the grounds that it 'will be seen as an open invitation by right-wing extremists in Colombia to assassinate the three Irishmen'. And U.S. Congressman Bill Delahunt who was described by the *Irish Independent* as 'one of the committee members who appeared most determined to nail Sinn Fein' dismissed the findings of the committee's investigation as 'short on facts and replete with surmise and opinions'. He further opined that it was sitting 'not to determine facts, but to rubber stamp' conclusions already drawn.

Nevertheless, all of this has not tipped the scales in favour of a generally benign interpretation of Sinn Fein's refusal to attend the hearings. *The Guardian* is close to the mark when it said of Adams, 'Many will assume the worst from his failure . . . the reality is that he faced a big challenge to his political credibility and bottled it'. This hardly reflects on Adams' personal courage. Over the years he has batted at the crease for Republicans in the most difficult of circumstances. This time he made a political choice, arguably quite independent of any concerns for the three men in Colombia. Had Mr. Adams chosen to go out, the prospects for those three may have improved dramatically.

But the overall game plan of the congressional hearing was to allow matters to unfold in a manner that would allow the Sinn Fein leadership to be exonerated from having prior knowledge of the activities, whatever they were, of the three arrested men. Such a get-out-of-jail card, however, was to be denied the imprisoned Republicans. The price of exoneration for the Sinn Fein leadership was leaving the men victim to a growing belief in the United States that they were linked to the IRA, and it in turn to FARC-related activity. The lifeline to Adams was the anchor pulling the detained Republicans ever deeper into the mire. Seemingly the campaign 'to let them rot' has begun in earnest.

It did not have to be like this. Rather than Gerry Adams briefing the media that it was quite legitimate for the human rights–defiling Colombian government to lobby Washington over the coming days for extra U.S. aid to combat FARC, he could have informed the International Relations Committee that the behaviour of its own government in relation to support for the war criminal Ariel Sharon, its refusal to allow Henry Kissinger to stand trial for war crimes, and its interference in the internal affairs of Venezuela are all matters of infinitely more gravity than the presence of three Irish Republicans in the Colombian jungles. He could have used the congressional hearings as a platform to argue that were U.S. government–backed Colombian state repression and human rights abuses not as pronounced as they are the three Republicans would never have been in the country to begin with. But he chose not to do this. And as a trade-off the International Relations Committee chose not to do him.

Does anyone believe that had Hugo Chavez been the subject of the inquiry he would have walked away unscathed? The American state has never gone over to the side of revolution and has no tradition of helping revolutionary leaderships. It only helps those who are of use to them. These hearings have ensured that its record of consistency on this matter remains unblemished.

A South American Verdict

The Blanket, 3 May 2004

*T*hree summers ago I received a phone call from a radio station in Bogotá. On the other end, a female journalist seemed excitable and her voice conveyed a pleading tone. It is hard to mistake an elongated 'please' for anything else. Three Irish men had been arrested in Colombia and were being accused of having illicit links with FARC guerrillas. Understandably, she wanted the scoop for her station and felt her endeavours would be beefed up a bit if she could add an 'authentic' voice to the narrative. Since I had previously done South American broadcasting, the task seemed straightforward enough for me.

She wanted to know what the IRA was doing in Colombia. I probed her as to how we could be sure it was the IRA. Yes, one of the men at least was a Republican well known to everybody but Sinn Fein seemingly, and he had functioned as a senior party education officer. The one time I had spoken with him was at a 1990s Ard Fheis and the only thing we discussed was education, or the thwarting of it within the party. A decade later, he had just left a demilitarised zone controlled by FARC that had been ceded to the guerrillas by the then Colombian president Andres Pastrana, who was looking at ways of developing a peace deal. So while the detained man's voice had not yet managed to make it into public discourse explaining why he was in the conflict-riven South American state, at the time it seemed plausible to me that he had been there for what he later claimed—looking at the peace process. The interviewing journalist, while probably not convinced, was happy enough to have a voice even if it was highly perspectival. Despite the plausibility I wasn't entirely persuaded myself but had no way of knowing and did not want to say anything that would enhance the potential risks facing the men detained. My sympathies invariably lie with the jailed, never the jailers.

Their innocence or guilt did not primarily concern me. It still doesn't. For having wreaked terrorist havoc in South America, it was easy to argue that there were other more suitable candidates to spend decades locked in a Bogotá jail than these three, Henry Kissinger heading the queue. In a country with an atrocious human rights record, it is straightforward enough to think of worse things than helping guerrillas fight the government.

Although the *Irish Times* has argued that why the three men were in Colombia in the first place has still not been satisfactorily explained, this is more a political concern than a judicial one. Legally the men had only to stand mute and the onus after that was on the prosecution to prove its case. As far back as 2002 it was clear that such provability was determined to remain elusive. The verdict, when pronounced, merely reflected the evidence before the court. The defence case was much the stronger.

What helped persuade many that the men had a case to answer was not the shoddy evidence presented against them but that Sinn Fein, true to form, immediately sought to lie about any links to the arrested men. Worse still, reports of party representatives telling U.S. officials and media people in off-the-record briefings that it was all the work of a Marxist on the Army Council who 'Gerry can't control' hardly tipped the credibility scales in favour of the account offered by the arrested men. If the latter were, as claimed, out examining the peace process and nothing else, then all critics and adversaries could be told to get lost and there was no need for the party to wax flabbergasted. But as the Sinn Fein leadership lie so routinely about events, a suspicious public suspects the party of something underhanded even when it is wholly blameless.

In Ireland the verdict has been treated with the usual congenital instinctive responses. Sinn Fein, always comfortable when sporting a brass neck, will now seek to exploit the return of the men, greeting them with open arms despite having done a St. Peter on them three years ago. The staggering in sentences suggests that the Colombian judiciary is seeking to deny Sinn Fein any propaganda victory, which may mean the three men do not arrive in Ireland as a group. The Unionists, for their part, never learn and have been spewing venom about the acquittal. Much better, in their view, had the men been shot when arrested and then all this pesky business of human rights and due process would just go the Argentinean way—up against a wall alongside those about to be despatched. Unionism seems both PR and justice blind: always willing to play by the rules until wrongfooted. When things don't go its way it reverts to type. David Trimble hits out at human rights agencies and Pat Finucane suddenly becomes an IRA member despite all the evidence to the contrary.

And as if to confirm nationalist scepticism about Unionist intentions, the Unionists had nothing to say when thirteen British cavers, many of them British military, were found in Mexico in March, forcing the country's leader Vincente Fox to ask the British government to explain what its soldiers had been doing in Mexican caves. Under the country's law a special visa for scientific explorations is required and foreign military exercises are outlawed. The cavers' refusal of local assistance coupled with demands that British specialists be flown in to rescue them led to speculation that the group had been exploring the caves on a secret military mission. But none of that matters—there is no mileage to be squeezed from it in the battle to kick opponents out of Stormont.

While the three Irish Republicans were found not guilty in a court of law, Sinn Fein has already been judged complicit in the court of political interests where legalities play second fiddle to geo-strategic considerations. That the United States played a role in building the case against the arrested men will ensure that. And there is no get-out-of-jail-free card in the deck shuffled on the bench there. There will be no appeal against the judgement of Mitchell Reiss.

Political columnist James Davis suggested in *Counterpunch* that it may be even more difficult for Sinn Fein's leadership to explain why, were it not for a grassroots family campaign, the three men might be looking at a very long time away from home.

Don't hold your breath waiting on answers.

CHAPTER 4
Decommissioning

Follow Me—I'm Right Behind You

Irish Republican Writers Group, 1 February 2000

'Jumping together' is a phrase that Gerry Adams probably wishes he had never used. Issued in Washington last year as a means to either entice David Trimble or temporarily wrongfoot him, the phrase has come back to haunt Mr. Adams as the Unionist deadline for some verifiable form of decommissioning of IRA weaponry steadily approaches. Trimble has jumped and in the process has made Adams' offer sound ridiculously like 'Follow me—I'm right behind you'.

The logic of jumping together was that both leaders needed the other to cushion the fall of each. Trimble has landed at the bottom and simply has nowhere else to go. Not surprisingly, a media and political cacophony has erupted, demanding that Gerry Adams joins David Trimble, which, at present, he shows no sign of doing, advising the Unionist leader instead to be patient and that 'together' may mean two years apart. But is the Sinn Fein leader being insincere? Probably not.

Gerry Adams is an astute enough politician to realise that the argument on decommissioning had been lost some time ago. For this reason he conceded that it was an essential part of the Good Friday Agreement. Sinn Fein by even taking the bait and agreeing to discuss the matter effectively kept the ball on the field of play and at no time did the party manage to kick it into touch. Once the British got Sinn Fein to play the constitutional game it was inconceivable that the party could for long serve in government without serious questions being posed by the IRA's retention of arms. As I write, serious opposition is being generated throughout the European Union against the possible participation in government in Austria by the Freedom Party. The ideas of its far right leader Jorg Haider are the problem. What position would London and Dublin adopt within Europe if he also had guns?

In recent days Mitchell McLaughlin and others have attempted to claim that the IRA had decommissioned because the guns were not being used. While intellectually valid it is a weak negotiating position. If true, what was the Mitchell review all about? Are we to believe that this logic was conveyed to Trimble during the review and that he agreed to jump first on that basis? And that the IRA interlocutor has been explaining precisely this to General De Chastelain ever since? Hardly likely.

That said, Trimble has made the leap but crucially has held his party together. Adams has not made the leap presumably because he feels he could not hold republicanism intact. Therefore both men have made what moves were possible for them. Trimble is now stuck at the bottom and Adams is likewise stuck at the top. It is not a question of choice. Indeed, if it were, there is the likelihood that Adams would accept decommissioning (although not necessarily a handover to the British) while Trimble would not demand it. Ultimately the leaders do what they can get away with before their respective bases pull them back into line.

Of course it will be argued by those who believe that Adams is conning the Unionists that if the leadership were ever sincere on the matter it would have begun conditioning the Republican base for some 'seismic shift', something it seems not yet to have done. But this state of affairs suggests that Adams and his colleagues have not yet won the battle within leadership. And at that level it is not a question of merely defeating opponents—it is one of bringing them wholly on board. Given the virulent opposition of the Republican base to any form of decommissioning, one key leader breaking ranks and launching a public assault on the leadership's position may be the catalyst that could lead to a divide from which could emerge a new force with more credibility than either the Real or Continuity IRAs.

Consequently, any leadership assault on the belief system of the Republican base could not take place prior to leadership unanimity on the question of decommissioning. The British found provisional republicanism a difficult old beast to tame and threw it a few sweeteners. Some in the Republican leadership are now finding that even those have failed to rot all its teeth.

Sinn Feign

Parliamentary Brief, December 2001

When does an act of surrender become an act of patriotism? Seemingly, when the IRA decommissions some of its weapons—an event the Republican leadership reassured its grassroots would never happen precisely because it would be surrender. Not even in one thousand years, insisted one commentator. Just how wrong can you get?

The leadership is now engaged in 'organised lying' to its grassroots by claiming that De Chastelain was a fool who had been conned, that no decommissioning had in fact taken place. Indeed it might. Because the grassroots have reason to feel particularly aggrieved. Not only were they not consulted, they were insulted—London, Dublin, Washington and, of course, the Unionists had all been told in advance. The Republican support base was urged to go out ignominiously and think about a decision already made.

Hence the need to tell the membership that De Chastelain had been duped. It helps to take the sting out of the humiliation for a Republican rank and file who sense that their critics are laughing at them in nationalist ghettos. The references to DIRA (Decommissioned IRA) and 'No More Lies' have left them uncomfortable. They now have to face those they deemed 'stupid' or 'mischievous' for having predicted the inevitability of decommissioning. They had even painted walls in West Belfast brightly proclaiming 'Not an ounce not a round' and 'Decommission?—no mission'. Now the walls have to be painted over just as they were a number of years ago. Then the occasion was to obliterate the 'No return to Stormont' slogans.

While that act of decommissioning was always inevitable, equally so was the fact that Republicans would seek to manage the event in such a way as to mollify the British, Irish, and American governments but cause uncertainty and fractiousness within unionism. Seepage from Republican ranks sullying the substance of De Chastelain's integrity would nurture doubt in some Unionist minds. This would allow the Republican leadership to claim that unionism was all at sea and had been destabilised by the 'courageous and imaginative' IRA initiative (Sinn Fein recommended words of the week according to the writer Eamonn McCann). Victory through only appearing to decommission would be the whispered rationale. But both inside and outside the ranks of republicanism it is only the incorrigibly faithful who believe such nonsense. The type who would readily believe the same leadership pronounce that the British are no longer really here but are only pretending to be just to fool the Unionists. Those more prudent know the enormity of what has happened and wisely give a philosophical shrug when asked to explain.

The ease with which the Republican leadership took the decision indicates just how devitalised antisystemic tendencies within provisional republicanism have become. As they are moved muttering from one slain sacred cow to defend another before it too is slaughtered, their numbers are fewer. Their reputations as defenders of sacred beasts in tatters, they inhabit an increasingly isolated and self-referential world.

Some commentators and politicians, while accepting the bona fides of the Sinn Fein leadership regarding its commitment to getting rid of IRA weaponry, nevertheless felt that the grassroots acted as a constraint on the leadership's freedom to manoeuvre. But how could such an intellectually cauterised and strategically moribund body of people act as a brake? The let-them-eat-cake attitude of their leadership did not illustrate even disdain for their opposition. It simply acknowledged that there was no opposition. For quite some time the Adams leadership had been free of any internal constraint. Determined to decommission, it was aided in its purely tactical procrastination by the practice pursued by London and Dublin of imposing ultimate deadlines by endless postponement. It was merely waiting on the opportune juncture to cash in the guns. In the view of some writers the most likely moment was in the run up to the republic's general election. Guns for votes and parliamentary seats would seem a nice trade-off in Sinn Fein's view.

DECOMMISSIONING

What changed everything was the September 11th attacks on the United States. The pressure of the new constraint—American opprobrium compounded by the Colombian debacle in which three Republicans were arrested—proved stronger than the lure of any opportunity. And like the tragic victims on the roof of New York's World Trade Centre Sinn Fein could do little other than jump. Despite its denials and its unalloyed self-praise that it only moved to save the peace process, the latter was no longer dependent on Sinn Fein support. The Good Friday Agreement certainly was. Prior to September 11th the Good Friday Agreement was considered essential for the peace process; the latter could now stand alone. Could the IRA bomb the financial heart of London to allow Sinn Fein to continue administering British rule? Highly unlikely. It would be administered with or without them. Sinn Fein moved to save itself—nothing else.

And for that reason De Chastelain has not been conned. Such is the emphasis on maintaining American approval that American demands for real product in terms of arms decommissioning are not going to be subverted by trickery and fake weapons.

'Oh, what a complex web we weave when first we practice to deceive'. But it is Irish Republicans rather than Americans who are on the receiving end of that strategy of deception.

Go to Sleep, My Weary Provo

Fortnight, December 2001/January 2002

At a time when the UDA is disbanding its political wing Sinn Fein seems headed in the opposite direction by dissolving the IRA. But is the organisation that fought so hard to secure a British declaration of intent to withdraw being put uncomplainingly to bed without even the slightest sign of the lights going out for Britain in Ireland? It was said recently that medieval Catholics, about to tuck into the Friday steak, would address it 'I baptise thee carp'. The Sinn Fein leadership, with little or no internal fuss, having done likewise by baptising a defeat 'transitional', could quite easily wind up the IRA. The latter is now a mere extension of Sinn Fein policy, and if the new exigencies of such policy require yet another 'courageous and imaginative' summersault, do not be surprised.

By early summer the Provisionals seemed to be cruising. They had just doubled their representation at Westminster and had, against even their own expectations, usurped the SDLP as the leading nationalist party. Glenbryn loyalists guided by the strategic equivalent of Mr. Bean and Basil Fawlty were beginning their PR suicide campaign. This enabled Sinn Fein's most pompous performer to swan round the television studios condescendingly admonishing the Unionists for kicking up such a fuss about silent IRA guns while a colleague told a British newspaper that only a fool would believe that IRA weapons were completely silent.

Then all of these linguistic mazes, doublespeak, gobbledygook, and jabberwocky that had helped sustain the leadership throughout its prolonged dance of deceit, caught up with it. Three Republicans were arrested in Colombia. The evidence against them was so terribly deficient that in its defence a prosecuting attorney in Bogotá interviewed by BBC *Spotlight* was reduced to incoherent babbling. Yet even she appeared articulate compared to the Sinn Fein spokespeople who denounced any suggested links between the party and the three arrested Republicans. Media lie detectors that for so long had lain idle began to buzz frantically each time a Sinn Fein spokesperson appeared on television. Even *Sinn Fein on Sunday* found their evasions hard to stomach.

Of course, it all depended on who were being told the lies. If it were the Republican grassroots the media would tolerate that, even facilitate it in some cases. But the American government was a big no-no. The president of the United States can lie to you. And you can even jump up and down and wave your hands in the air to boot while he is doing it, a la Mexican wave for Clinton in the Odyssey last year. But you cannot lie to the president.

The September 11th attacks on the United States further compounded matters for the Provisionals. With the spectre of FARC haunting every refuge, Bin Lying pontificated in his eagerness to denounce Bin Laden. There was no comparison between the IRA and Al-Qaida, the growing band of sceptics was assured. The awkward question produced the evasive response. Only media mischief makers would suggest that, for Sinn Fein, human bombs in Derry were implicitly ethically defensible in a way that similar vehicles of civilian death in New York were not. But it was all a face-saving charade. Just as in the title of a Christopher Hitchens book there was no one left to lie to—except the Republican grassroots of course. And they could be ignored. Loyalty to them mattered little when Big Brother had to be appeased.

When the decision was announced by the Sinn Fein leadership that it would move to secure decommissioning, the fact that it could so contemptuously ignore the input of those who had fought, killed, maimed, and served time to help put the leadership where it is, demonstrated just how easy it would be to send the IRA packing if external pressure necessitated it. A grassroots quite prepared to allow the leadership to reach a point where its objectives had been reduced to debating what version of a partitionist police force it would accept—

GOOD FRIDAY

Mandleson's or Patten's RUC—could scarcely celebrate shutting the gate once the horse, long since bolted, was off grazing, fat and prosperous, on Stormont's four green fields.

It Never Happened—Again

The Blanket, 9 April 2002

What would never happen has happened again. The strategy of 'never but will' trundles on oblivious to the silent well of sensitivity and layers of sacrifice abandoned as mere backwash in its wake. The IRA leadership has opted for a further round of decommissioning and has effusively praised itself for having done so. According to the official version, this is only the second time in the history of the Republican tradition that such an action has occurred. But like many other 'truths' on republicanism a mythological virus has crept into the account. And it has nudged into the shade the evidence presented by County Inspector Gelston of the Clare Royal Irish Constabulary who, when giving his evidence to the Royal Commission of Inquiry investigating the events of Easter Week 1916, informed it that 'in one case a parish priest addressed the Sinn Feiners and asked them to give up their rifles to us. That was the only case in which rifles were given up to any extent'.

There will be those in the Republican leadership who will in the days ahead troop around the Republican family meetings in West Belfast and elsewhere to perform a little pirouette of prevarication. They will tell anyone who will listen that nothing was decommissioned, that De Chastelain—who yesterday in a Freudian slip described how he wished to 'recapitulate' again—made it all up; London, Dublin, and Washington went along with it to keep the peace process alive. There are even some who will swear to having been there when decommissioning didn't happen—again. 'Honest, that's the second time I saw it not being done'.

A common thread running through the queries of observers, somewhat perplexed at the incredible ease with which the bulk of Republicans accept what would only recently have occurred over their 'dead bodies', is whether there really is anybody other than the 'terminally stupid' within the Republican base who believe such nonsense. But this is to come at it in the wrong way. No one should be so arrogant as to presume that the entire Republican grassroots are gullible fools. Yes, as elsewhere, there are those a la Sean O'Faolain who labour without 'a spare sixpence of an idea to fumble for'. And their numbers are indeed reinforced by fawning acolytes who know better than to believe any of it but who, wanting to maintain what power they have by dint of being apparatchiks, seek to emulate Lord Copper's sycophantic gofer in Evelyn Waugh's *Scoop* who remained incurably anxious never to contradict his boss. Yet there are others who are disgruntled but 'pragmatically acquiesce' out of a sense of impotence, concluding that the leadership have it all sown up and that open opposition will only bring the green shirts to their door.

Even in the middle level bureaucracies—a comfortable home in every organisation for the flunkeys and sycophants who disproportionately populate the functionary niches—there are to be found some who steadfastly refuse to celebrate what only the week before they condemned; who are not to be seen tearing through the dictionary in search of new ways to say 'courageous and imaginative'; who make no pretence that patriotism is a synonym for surrender; and who will run a million miles from humiliating Mexican waves aimed at pleasing U.S. presidents who have just signed the latest cheque for the child-murdering Israeli government. But even if they never read him nor heard of his name they are instinctively alert to the perception of Alexis de Tocqueville that people are more afraid of being marginalised than of being wrong. Experience has left its mark. Those who wish to think differently learn quickly that critical questioning can lead to social suicide. Ostracism is a powerful tool carefully honed to exert maximum pressure upon those who decline to conform. For the place seeker with ambition, leading the mob of social banishers may help improve the political career CV. There is no shortage of would-be councillors to be found when it comes to waging campaigns of intimidation against those who speak out. And to add sinister muscle the 'Kray Twins', Mug & Thug—the leadership's thought police—are all too willing to visit homes and ominously wag the trigger finger.

So, at best the stupid thesis remains unproven, at worst demeaning. It is more credible to contend that the grassroots have been subjected to a prolonged campaign of attrition strategically designed to intellectually cauterise them by managing and filtering information. Advised not to listen to or, worse, speak with the 'enemy press', the bulk of their take was formed by what the leadership—who have no qualms about speaking to the 'anti-Republican media'—tell them.

That leadership, inebriated on the arrogance of power, rarely managed to conceal a rabid hatred of anyone disagreeing with it. Committed to zero tolerance of alternative viewpoints it ensured the Republican movement would be a cold house for other voices. Even in supposedly democratic Sinn Fein, the hidden centre of power in republicanism—the prosperous men of the Army Council—sought to rule the party with the ethos of the army. Under its domination, dissent—initially promoted by it for its own sectional ends against the O'Bradaigh/O'Conaill axis—was viewed as a contagious disease. Those who displayed the symptoms were quarantined by being either marginalised out of the movement entirely or banished to some remote corner within it. Heads raised above the parapet would immediately draw the attention and surveillance of thought traffic control and the fire of the verbal snipers, their weapons loaded with vitriol, eager to impose silence and prevent republicanism from becoming more democratic.

For long enough most could be expected to acquiesce in this, given that there was a war to be prosecuted that helped generate an imperative to protect the struggle from anything that could be presented as divisive. There was an acceptance that the civilian values of democratic rights and equality had no place in an army. Hierarchy was what was needed—and plenty of it. Those at the top sought to dangerously totalise intellectual life. And that fierce self-serving ambition of leaders to empower themselves while disempowering followers was best served by suppressing any sign of independent thinking, which might lead to a rupturing of the banks of conformity and an irrigation of that barren terrain where previously little in the way of new ideas sprang to life.

Yet when the war wound down matters did not improve. With no obvious need to consent to leadership demands for quiet, the institutional imperative for self-preservation kicked in and leaders coerced silence. Consequently, dissenting views were ignored or explained away through the illogic articulated by the hounding hacks. Those who believed that the leadership would sign up to a partitionist arrangement no different from Sunningdale describe strategic failures as new phases of struggle, invent idiotic phrases like 'a transition to a transition', sit in Stormont, join centre-right coalition governments north or south, administer British rule, accept the consent principle, settle for no abolition of the RUC, endorse a new status as an establishment party, criminalise the armed struggle of other physical force groups, murder members of alternative Republican organisations and decommission weapons were dismissed as mentally ill, alcoholics, whores, self-publicists, and egotists. If a party member opposed to the leadership strategy drank three nights a week they were automatically consigned to the doghouse. Strangely, though, if on the other hand, your tipple ran to thirty-one days a month but you supported the strategy, you could cruise comfortably at leadership level, even arriving to speak at commemorative events blocked.

A regime of truth was being constructed. It didn't matter if it was all false—just that people believed it to be true, or at least said as much. And yet the pervasive culture of conformity has failed to subdue everyone. There are still Republicans both inside the movement and without who reject and resist the repressive concept of Section 31 regardless of who wields it; who remain determined that a sanitised and revisionist account shall not monopolise the historical record; who feel they have every right to ask the difficult question. Why should we have to rely on the probing of Seamus McKee, Noel Thompson, or Mike Nesbitt to elicit answers that make the leadership look foolish and fumbling, seeking the cover of the nearest stone from under which to complain 'but that is not helpful to the peace process'? We invested considerably more in this struggle than any media interviewer so why should we not be able to publicly confront these leadership figures in a bid to satisfy ourselves that we have not been defrauded of a rightful return on that investment?

The leadership of course would not agree. They want only Stalinist clones with an ability to reiterate someone else's cloned phrases. The type who when told, metaphorically, that everybody needs shoes, thinks size sevens all round is the solution—and off to the social gulag with anybody possessing the ungrateful temerity to complain that their feet hurt.

The Republican struggle is over. The energies expended in it and the structures moulded through it are now being used for a different project entirely. Republicans without republicanism are little different from constitutional nationalists. The blood spilt was a costly fuel with which to power the ambitions of self-proclaimed establishment politicians. The ends have corrupted the means. Genuinely taking the gun out of Irish politics would be a step forward. Taking the dignity and defiance out of Irish republicanism is a step too far.

Pulling the Guns Over Their Eyes

The Blanket, 27 October 2003

> *Pathological liars are brilliant at deception. They know how to*
> *make a story sparkle, they breezily proffer instant explanations*
> *for any little inconsistency, they're scheming all the time while*
> *you, their mark, are preoccupied with a hundred other things.*
> *Besides, you want to believe them—they're so charming,*
> *attentive, and flattering.*
>
> —KATHA POLLITT

Nobody knows for certain just what was surrendered to John De Chastelain last week except of course the general himself and elements of the IRA leadership, but not all elements of the leadership. Nothing new in this—Ed Moloney in his *Secret History of the IRA* left few in doubt that the 'big lad' had been pulling the wool over the eyes of other leadership figures for years. It is said, even today, that after almost two decades of a 'never but will' strategy there are some as senior as the GHQ staff who will continue to believe it is all a con—thinking that everybody other than themselves had been duped—and who have been trying to convince anyone who will listen rather than laugh that 'not an ounce, not a round' has ever been destroyed. Some of these people and their associates would like to pass themselves off as the intellectuals of the movement. Each time they speak or write I am mindful of a worry that gnawed at the mind of Christopher Hitchens: 'the willingness of intellectuals and academics to become worshipers of whomever is in power, or passers-on of whatever the reigning idea is. Conformity, in other words'.

Perhaps part of the job description for being a senior loyal gofer for the Army Council is agreeing to sell the ridiculous. And when the spaceship lands in Dunville Park on Sunday at three o'clock to take all true believers to a united Ireland, the gofers can go first class—if the

74

securocrats and rejectionists don't sabotage matters just to undermine the peace process, that is. Why they would undermine a process that secures the long-term strategic objectives of the British state is never explained. Only those mischievous types unhelpful to the peace process ask that.

Whatever the absurd beliefs that people hold, estimates of the amount of weaponry surrendered vary. The *Daily Telegraph* reported the DUP's claim that just 1 percent of weapons may have been destroyed. According to Tom Clonan, a former Irish soldier, De Chastelain may have overseen the decommissioning of 400 rifles. Henry McDonald in the *Observer* suggested it was 'massive', perhaps as high as 100 tonnes. The *Irish Independent* claimed its sources had revealed that the IRA had destroyed all of its heavy machine guns imported in the Libyan shipments in the mid-1980s. A British government source said: 'The irony is that we now have more than we've ever had from Republicans, a very serious act of decommissioning, but we can't tell people why we believe that is the case. People need to know how many AK-47s, how many rocket launchers'. Tony Blair beefed it up even further by stating that the arms were not simply 'old World War One rifles'.

These last two statements raised eyebrows. A Republican, who has long given up believing any utterance from the Sinn Fein leadership, yesterday raised the question of how did the government of Tony Blair know this? Was the prime minister lying as claimed by the DUP? Or do the British have another agent somewhere near the top of the IRA who told them? Does it really matter? No informer throughout the course of the conflict has been able to deal such a blow to the military capacity of the IRA as its own leadership has. Yet the very people who gave up the IRA's weapons have sat in judgment of others and sent them to their graves for 'informing' on IRA munitions. Charles Bennett, blasted in the face with a shotgun about a quarter of a mile from where I write—during the cease-fire—was never as culpable in the field of betraying weaponry as those who ordered him killed.

This is one reason that the leadership is determined to engage in falsehoods to the end. It cannot join the dots between killing people for giving guns up and then giving up considerably more themselves. Even the nefarious activities of Frank Hegarty, killed in 1986 for compromising 100 or so weapons, pales out of focus when judged against the actions of those who ordered him killed. When Sinn Fein president Gerry Adams rejected calls for disclosure, his reasoning was 'one man's transparency is another man's humiliation'. Indeed it should be, because that is as close as we have come to wrenching a public acknowledgment out of them that they have shafted their own base yet again.

A galling aspect about the leadership deception is that Republican activists always prided themselves on having a high level of political savvy. That sophistication, they would inform people, rather than emotion or reaction, motivated, governed, and sustained their participation in Republican life—quite often a dangerous exercise with its omnipresent threat of death or imprisonment. They considered their 'political awareness' to be higher than that of the average punter on the street. That myth at least has been debunked. The only people lacking the ability to work out that the IRA has decommissioned its weaponry are to be found within the Republican movement. Nobody outside the ranks is running around whispering, 'It never happened'. Over a drink in a club in Turf Lodge a couple of years ago, we sat as a local Republican explained to us how decommissioning would never happen. When he left to buy a round, the 'civilian' company burst out laughing. One commented, 'Just like he told us in 1998 they would never sign up to the Good Friday Agreement and would never see the inside of Stormont. The 'Ra should rename itself the IBA for people like him: 'I Believe Anything'. Perhaps it is the dynamic of groupthink at work. The punter on the street, not being subject to the strange logic of the group, is able to arrive at their own eminently sensible conclusions.

Although the 'I Believe Anything' people consider themselves to be the most politicised in our communities, this is belied by their ability to defend every new twist on the basis that it is somehow revolutionary, which contrasts sharply with their inability to see such twists coming. Maybe only days before they had outlined in great detail to a sceptical but wiser audience that only a heretic could anticipate the leadership making the 'heretical' move. Yet the heresy has taken place, and those highly politicised types who denounced predictions of it as an 'appalling vista' now defend it and would burn at the stake those who question it.

Of course they think they are the recipients of some secret knowledge that their special relationship with the leadership gives them access to. And because they labour under the misapprehension that the leadership treats them with respect rather than contempt they believe that theirs is the only constituency being told the truth. Everybody else, including the U.S., British, and Irish governments, are all being taken for a ride. Brian Cowen is talking nonsense when he says the IRA leadership insist on confidentiality because to do otherwise would, in its view, 'damage rather than enhance the process of resolving the arms issue within its organisation'. Martin Mansergh likewise has fallen victim to the grand stratagem leading him to claim that the absence of transparency is 'to shelter volunteers as long as possible from the radical changes of role and behaviour that completion of the peace process will inevitably require'.

History is, of course, replete with people being conned. In 1971, Dee Brown, author of *Bury My Heart at Wounded Knee*, said that what pained him the most was 'how much the Indians believed the white man over and over again. Their trust in authority was amazing. They just never seemed to believe anyone could lie'.

How the grassroots ever promised to move mountains in order to prevent decommissioning and yet acceded to a leadership demand that it should take control of the weapons is one of the outstanding lessons in internal management to emerge from the peace process. After all, this is a leadership with such a reputation for evasiveness that allowing it to control the guns is akin to transferring responsibility for your life savings to Charlie Haughey.

What has unfolded in front of our eyes is organised lying by organised liars. Half a century from now pilgrims, patriots, and prevaricators alike will flock to the graves of the Provisional Republican leadership to be greeted by an inscription meticulously inscribed into a headstone: 'Here they are—lying still'. The rule of thumb in analysing announcements from the Provisional leadership is this: What any of them tell you is possibly true but probably not. Until independent verification of their 'truth-claims' emerge, search for an alternative. Otherwise, you too will be at Dunville Park at three this Sunday wondering what is delaying the spacecraft.

CHAPTER 5
Hunger Strikes

Burying Republicans and Republicanism

The Blanket, 15 October 2001

*Y*esterday saw the reinterment of ten Republican volunteers from the War of Independence era. Kevin Barry, Thomas Whelan, Patrick Moran, Patrick Doyle, Bernard Ryan, Frank Flood, Thomas Bryan, Thomas Traynor, Edmond Foley, and Patrick Maher were all tried by British military tribunal and sentenced to death. Few expected clemency. The British were not renowned for that type of thing.

Many have expressed disappointment that the reinterment took so long in happening. Few seem to doubt that one motive in the Fianna Fail–dominated government's calculations has been the perceived need to confront Sinn Fein with a little shroud waving. On the twentieth anniversary of the H-Block hunger strikes Fianna Fail must find it apt to say, 'Our ten men dead are better than yours'. An election looms in the not-too-distant future and Fianna Fail, aware that Sinn Fein will hardly be standing idly by when there are votes at stake, are intent on decreasing the likelihood that such votes will come from any new emerging constituency of Republican sentiment.

Sinn Fein too is aware of the electoral implications. And so nothing registered on the shock seismograph when Sean Crowe appeared firmly squeezed in between party leaders Martin McGuinness and Gerry Adams. Crowe believes he is comfortably placed to take one of the capital's seats in the Dail next time around. A whiff of Dublin Republican cordite from the 1920s, safely removed in time from a similar whiff from Bogotá 2001, would not go amiss.

There is a strange irony in what Fianna Fail is doing. Bertie Ahern and colleagues are obviously apprehensive about the Sinn Fein challenge eating into their majority status in the Dail. Yet the Sinn Fein vote seems to increase as the party ditches more and more of its Republican baggage. Why then should Fianna Fail challenge Sinn Fein on ground that is rapidly thinning out under the feet of the latter?

One explanation is that in burying the ten volunteers Fianna Fail were not engaged in a vote-grabbing exercise alone by laying to rest Republicans. They were also engaged in a symbolic act of burying any republicanism other than their own. This act of reinterment could have occurred in 1971, 1981, or 1991. Better not to arouse a sleeping dog of presumed latent southern Republican sentiment in those years. Provisional republicanism was on the go and, as they say, armed and extremely dangerous.

The very act of inviting the most articulately vociferous anti-Provisional cleric of his day, Cahal Daly, to act as celebrant for the requiem Mass combined with the tricolour-clad coffins actually being allowed to enter the church was a statement by the political establishment that its 'constitutional' republicanism had won the day, that it and it alone was the heir to those being buried yesterday. Added to this was the fact that the leaders of provisional republicanism—who at one time would have shunned any attempt through a ritualistic ceremony by Fianna Fail or Cahal Daly to claim the mantle of republicanism—felt compelled to sit in subdued silence as their republicanism was mocked, sneered at, and dismissed.

At the symbolic level the burying of the ten dead volunteers was a victory celebration for constitutional nationalism. Unlike 1971, 1981, or 1991, the sleeping dog of latent republicanism can be stirred. Who is it going to bite? What home has it other than a safe constitutional one? It is safe now for the constitutional to bury the unconstitutional. It is safe because in the act of interment an unconstitutional philosophy was being laid to rest. And its chief philosophers were summoned to watch the act, their words of protest as silent as the graves into which their philosophy was being lowered.

The Blanket Meets Blanketmen

The Blanket, 16 May 2006

Anthony McIntyre speaks with Richard O'Rawe

> *All truth passes through three stages. First, it is ridiculed.*
> *Second, it is violently opposed. Third, it is accepted as being*
> *self-evident.*
>
> —ARTHUR SCHOPENHAUER

Q: This month marks the twenty-fifth anniversary of the death of Bobby Sands, Frank Hughes, Raymond McCreesh, and Patsy O'Hara. How has it been for you emotionally?

A: Terrible. It has been terrible.

Q: Can you elaborate?

A: Bob has been in my thoughts all the time. He left from our wing. The others were in different blocks. And I just get this vision of him. I see him in the wing canteen for Mass just before he went up to the prison hospital. He was smiling at me. He knew he was going up there to die. I knew it too. It was just so unbelievably heartrending and it has never left me. That smile has been with me for over a week, that smile of pathos. I went over to his grave and just looked around me. There was Joe and Big Doc, Bryson and our Mundo, wee Paddy Mul, Todler, and all the dead volunteers. It was just horrific.

Q: Bobby was very much the master of his own destiny once he decided that he would face down the Brits in the sure knowledge that Thatcher was determined to see him to the grave. And in a sense you and the jail leadership had less control over the first four hunger strikers than you had over the rest. There was effectively little you could do. But the real story of the hunger strike for you begins with Joe McDonnell. You claim that in the final days of Joe's hunger strike the British made an offer substantive enough to end the protest and save the lives of Joe and the other men. In your account the prison leadership recommended accepting this but the Republican leadership outside the prison effectively overruled you. The hunger strike continued and six other men lost their lives. This is what makes your book *Blanketmen* so important and in the eyes of many critics controversial. What prompted you to write it?

A: I saw a wrong here. It was a gut-wrenching wrong.

Q: Despite attempts by Jim Gibney to pull the wool over the eyes of people with his spurious claim in *The Irish News* that you never raised your concerns with any ex-prisoners until last year, it is well known within the Republican constituency that you had been giving off on the matter for years—long before the book came out. In fact, Brendan Hughes would often rib about it—a 'quick, hide, here he comes again, complaining about the hunger strike' type thing. You actually claim to have raised the matter with Danny Morrison in the Rock Bar while he was in the company of Gibney.

A: I remember that. Danny and Jim had just finished a game of squash in the Beechmount Leisure Centre and had come in for a pint. I was only in a couple of minutes before them and I joined them in one of the wee boxes. During our conversation, Danny said that he was writing a book about the hunger strikes. I then asked him to write 'the truth'.

Q: That must have sounded like a foreign language to him. How did he respond?

A: When he asked me what I meant, I told him about us accepting the deal. You know, his mouth dropped open. I was left with the impression that he didn't know about this. Either that or he's a better actor than Robert De Niro.

Q: Or he was amazed that you knew about it. He may have thought up until the Rock Bar discussion that only one person in the prison knew—the camp OC.

A: A possibility.

Q: One that may place him in the frame as being complicit in the events, whatever they were, during the final days of Joe McDonnell's life?

A: It is a way of looking at it.

Q: What happened that his book wasn't published?

A: I don't know. An interesting question, though.

Q: Do you think the leadership told him to bin it?

A: I don't know. One thing's for sure, if he had been writing anything contentious and been silly enough to show it to them, they'd have put the squeeze on him to pull the book. We're talking in the conditional tense here, but it takes a bit of balls to publish and be damned—especially when those who might be criticised are the IRA leadership. One criticism that was directed at me was that no one knew *Blanketmen* was coming. In fact, a member of the GHQ staff, a former Blanketman, visited me about a year before the publication date, and asked me about it. Specifically, he asked me if I was going to 'hurt Gerry Adams'. I told him I was going to 'tell the truth'. I asked him if he knew the real story of the hunger strike, that we had accepted the Mountain Climber offer, and he nodded his head. Do you know what he said? 'Sometimes hard decisions have to be taken in times of war, Ricky'. Well, fuck that. I don't mind hard, strategic decisions being taken. I mean, who would want to be a general? They have a thankless task. But when brave men die needlessly—that's crossing the line; that's not on, as far as I'm concerned anyway. You know, the GHQ staffer wired me off not to be influenced by yourself!

Q: Despite all their nonsense that you never told anyone about your concerns, he must have suspected that you had vented them to me. Why else say that? How did he learn you were publishing a book if you didn't tell anyone?

A: That's a point.

Q: And of course I'm the advisocrat working tirelessly to undermine the peace process! Maybe myself and Catherine McCartney wrote the book in the month after her brother was butchered just to wreck Gerry Adams' chances of getting a knighthood!

A: Anyway, I told the GHQ staffer I was my own man, that neither you nor anyone else would force me to do something that my conscience didn't feel was right. Then he asked if I'd like to speak to Gerry Adams. I said no. Now, in fairness, this guy didn't threaten me in any way, nor did I feel threatened. What he was trying to do was to start a process that was aimed at persuading me to pull the book.

Q: This is the book that no one including themselves knew about until it appeared on the shelves?

A: I wasn't going to allow that to happen.

Q: If I can take it back to Jim Gibney. He was there in the Rock Bar, yet he put out that dissembling cant in his column that you never raised the issue with anyone over a twenty-four year period?

A: I've answered that in Monday's *Irish News*. You know as well as anybody else the status of Gibney's *Irish News* column.

Q: I take it you are referring to it being widely viewed as the 'I love my leader' column?

A: Homer Simpson! Do you ever read it?

Q: I wouldn't make a point of looking for it. But every now and then somebody points to something in it where he seems to reveal something he shouldn't have. He wrote one time that the peace process does not want truth and cannot function with it. Another time he claimed that Bobby Sands wrote out on the evening of the end of the 1980 hunger strike that he would begin a new hunger strike on the 1st of January. Which meant the Brits had no time to renege on the offer they supposedly made to end the first strike. This was an admission that the first strike collapsed and the Brits did not renege. It also means that Gibney is contradicting himself when he wrote in *The Irish News* that 'the document could have been the basis' to end the protest. Why otherwise would Bobby have written out stating his intention to start a new strike when there was absolutely no time to test the Brits for sincerity? I look for the faux pas rather than the intent in what he writes. I am waiting on you to be labelled a securocrat in that column. The problem is that you support the peace process.

A: Firstly, let's look at what Gibney said in the first part of his 11 May article. In relation to the Brit document that was delivered to the hunger strikers after they had come off the 1980 strike, he said, 'Hours before the document arrived the strike was ended rather than let Sean McKenna die. The document could have been the basis on which the prison protests ended. However, the document was an offer from the British to the prisoners, not an agreement. There is a huge difference'. How right he is! But if there was no 'agreement' between the two parties at the end of the first hunger strike, then how could the Brits be accused of 'reneging' on an agreement? That's why Bob immediately wanted a second hunger strike. He knew there was no agreement. We all did. The first hunger strike collapsed. The Dark told *The Daily Mirror* that the boys had indicated they were not prepared to die. So all this stuff that Big Laurny McKeown is going on about, you know, the 'we wanted to avoid a repetition of what happened at the end of the first hunger strike, when the Brits reneged on an agreement/deal', is pure bullshit. Understanding that is crucial to removing the gobbledygook that Laurny, Morrison, and Co. have thrown up to cloud the issue in the second hunger strike. They are talking what Mick Collins called 'ballsology'.

Q: It seems that you are right and that once again Gibney has put his foot in it. I have written elsewhere that the need to have firm guarantees on any offer from the Brits was understandable but not because of what happened at the end of the first hunger strike. The year 1980 failed before the Brits made any offer that needed to be guaranteed. If the leadership is inaccurate about the ending of the 1980 hunger strike, then its account of the 1981 hunger strike depreciates in value.

A: To answer the second part of your question, of course I support the peace process. Like or dislike Gerry Adams, he has to be given credit for ending the unwinnable war.

Q: I think there is some confusion that you could help clear up. It relates to the decision-making process during the hunger strikes. What was the chain of command and what say, if any, had the prisoners in the decision-making process?

A: Anyone listening to the likes of Laurny would think that the hunger strikers had the ultimate say in this. Let's get real here. Laurny is trying to protect Big Gerry. The foot soldiers in the trenches never dictate strategy. Why, even the majors and the colonels—in this case, Bik and myself—didn't have that power. Tactics come from afar, from people who are removed from the field of conflict but who have the power to determine strategy. People should read Bik's comm to Adams on page 336, *Ten Men Dead*. On that page Bik told the hunger strikers, 'I explained the position about my presence being essential at any negotiations . . .'

Q: What is the significance of this? Would Bik not have a right, even an obligation, to be there?

A: Let me give you an example that shows the real purpose served by Bik's presence. It also illustrates their tactic of dictating the ground on which the debate will take place—and they've done this rather successfully, I think. Right, they have restricted the whole debate to the four days before Joe died. But eleven days later, the Mountain Climber came back with the same offer. Adams was on the blower to him. Adams told the hunger strikers about this offer when he visited the camp hospital on 29 July, so there is no disputing that this offer was genuine. Yet when the Mountain Climber came off the mountain for the second and last time, Bik didn't even know what had been rejected on his behalf. This is evident from Bik's comm to Adams, dated 22 July 1981, written after the Mountain Climber had gone. Bik said, 'You can give me a run-down on exactly how far the Brits went' (page 330, *Ten Men Dead*).

Q: This seems to suggest that the prison leadership had a very tenuous grip on the actual negotiations. They left it to outside leaders.

A: Outside was always in control. Whoever claims otherwise is talking bullshit.

Q: It certainly reveals the true nature of the balance of power between the leadership and prisoners. I consistently argued within the prison in the mid-1980s that the jail leadership was a mere extension of the outside leadership into the ranks of the prisoners. Its primary function was to represent the interests of the leadership against the prisoners and then only to represent the interests of the prisoners against the regime. They did both quite well.

A: Bik was Adams' man. When Bik spoke, Adams spoke. Everybody knew that. The hunger strike was in safe hands when Bik was in control. The frustrating part in all of this is that the likes of Laurny and Bik know the score. But rather than confront the leadership and ask for an account as to why their last six comrades died, they feel a perverse duty to defend that leadership. It's part of the shameful cover-up to protect the leadership from acute questioning. The first four lads knew the score. They accepted that there was little chance of them surviving. But Joe reaching critical point was different. And this was eating away at me. What made it all the worse was that people were running around as if the history of the hunger strike was a beautiful box of chocolates wrapped in roses. I knew that the roses were nettles, there to jag your finger if you tried to open the box. Everyone could look at and admire the chocolate box but no one was ever really allowed to open it up and look inside to see what was really there.

Q: You took massive criticism for your book from Sinn Fein apologists. To rework a phrase from the Czech writer Milan Kundera, they all lined up against you, right from the president of lies to the idiots of writing. They vilified you, tried to demonise you and to this day they are vitriolic in their condemnation of you. Can you explain the type of tactics that have been employed against you?

A: Nobody knows more about demonisation than Sinn Fein. For decades Republicans have been demonized and marginalised and made out to be the ghouls of society. Now they are doing the same thing with me.

Q: Such as?

A: They needed to bring me down from the status of former Blanketman to the level of the gutter, where it would be all the easier for people to kick me as they passed by. They had to ensure that I was something people would kick off their shoe. Right from publication day, I was persona non grata, someone who was to be ostracised. The smears started. People who I had been friends with avoided me. A former cellmate on the blanket refused to speak to me. Friends I had all my life blanked me out and made it clear when I went in to a pub that I was not welcome in their company. All the president's men cut the tripe out of me on television, radio, newspapers—anywhere they had the chance. They tried to attribute false motives to me. They said it was about money. All of this was bullshit. As Danny could testify there is hardly a washer to be made from books.

Q: Especially the type of books he writes.

A: That's another matter. They even accuse me of taking a position of being close to those who supported Thatcher during the hunger strike.

Q: It's ironic then that Thatcher's colleague Michael Portillo should turn up at a play by Danny Morrison and not at your book launch. And no one has heard you call, in true Thatcheresque manner, for the comrades of Bobby Sands to hand themselves into the Diplock courts like common criminals in order that they may be whisked off on the conveyor belt to Maghaberry Prison by the British justice system. The IRA chief of staff and adjutant general at the time of Bobby's death have been doing just that in the past week.

A: Enough said.

Q: But you must have known that this is what you would face. It is their form. They have tried it on John Kelly, Brendan Hughes, Brendan Shannon, Tommy Gorman, Martin Cunningham, Marion and Dolours Price—the list is endless. And these Republicans were not challenging the most sacred cow of Adams-style republicanism in the way that you were. You knew that there was little in the way of reward in what you were pursuing, only grief.

A: Some times in life you need to stand up and tell the truth. When the lack of truth is used to camouflage the facts surrounding the deaths of the most sacred of comrades we all need to take stock. These are our kith and kin. These six men should have been enjoying a life with their families like the rest of us; maybe the unmarried ones would have found wives and had the pleasure of enjoying watching their kids grow up. No, there is a wrong here and it has no respect for creed, ideology, tradition, or simple humanity. Six people need not have died. They should never have died. Human life is important. So is humility. I see no humility at all from those who made the crucial decisions, not an ounce of it. I see no contrition or adequate explanation given to the families as to why their sons died. What we get instead is the jackboot on our necks. Why?

Q: You know why. They cannot stand the slightest modicum of dissent. They view any alternative idea as some sort of dangerous illness, the spread of which must be halted by a range of means. Some people, including former members of the movement, think they are fascistic. But you emerged robust. Every TV studio or radio station that I happened to be at in the wake of the book's publication—usually for discussions about the murder of Robert McCartney—I heard comments that you must have a point, given the track record for unreliability of some of those who attacked you. The morning your book hit the shelves you featured on *Talkback*. Danny Morrison came in heavily but unpersuasively against you. His performance in a sense won the argument for you or at least gave you the space to develop your argument. The following Sunday I was in the BBC in Belfast and all the talk was of how unconvincing Morrison sounded. This week at a book launch just after the RTE documentary, it was the same thing, essentially: 'O'Rawe must have a point as Morrison simply does not sound credible'. In essence, without Morrison protesting too much you would not have made the impact you did.

A: I don't think that is correct. People have difficulty believing Danny at the best of times but . . .

Q: Ed Moloney recently wrote that he 'had caught Danny telling so many lies' that he could believe him about nothing.

A: . . . but my book has to stand on its own. I think it has done that.

Q: There are many memorable pages in your book. It is a moving account of how naked men for years defied a vicious and brutalising prison management working for the British government to brand the mark of the criminal on republicanism. But the real point of controversy is your assertion that the Army Council stopped a deal being reached that would have delivered to the prisoners the substance of the five demands. Army Council people of the time seem to dispute this. Ruairi O'Bradaigh, for example, is on record as saying that the council did no such thing, although he does state that your claims must be explored further. It seems clear that he suspects you are right in what you say but wrong in whose door you lay the blame at. What have you to say to this?

A: At the time we had no reason to believe we were dealing with anybody other than the Army Council of the IRA. What reason was there to think otherwise?

Q: And not a subcommittee specifically tasked with running the hunger strike?

A: Whether they called it a subcommittee or not, we were of the view that everything went to the Army Council. Nobody led us to believe any different. Did you think any different?

Q: At the time, no.

A: We all felt it was the Council. Brownie was representing the Council and he wrote the comms. Why would we think we were dealing with anything less than the Council when he was the man communicating with us?

Q: You might not wish to say it but for the purpose of the reader—and this has been publicly documented in copious quantities—Brownie is

Gerry Adams, who was a member of the Army Council and the IRA adjutant general during the hunger strike.

A: I have nothing to add to that.

Q: But do you still hold to the view, despite the protests from O'Bradaigh, that the Council actually prevented a satisfactory outcome from being reached?

A: No, I do not. Army Council was the general term I used to describe the decision makers on the outside handling the hunger strike. I was not privy to Army Council deliberations. But I believed they were the only people who had the authority to manage the hunger strike from the outside. So it seemed safe then to presume that when we received a comm from Brownie it was from the Army Council as a collective.

Q: But what has happened to lead you to change your mind and accept that the Council may have been bypassed on this matter by Gerry Adams?

A: I have since found out that people on the Army Council at the time have, after my book came out, rejected my thesis and refused to accept that the Council had directed the prisoners to refuse the offer.

Q: Bypassing the Council as a means to shafting it and ultimately getting his own way would seem to be a trait of Gerry Adams. Do you believe then that the bulk of the Council did not approve blocking an end to the hunger strike before Joe McDonnell died?

A: Absolutely. The subcommittee managed and monitored the hunger strike. Given that comms were coming in two and three times a day it is simply not possible to believe that the Council could have been kept informed of all the developments. Could the Council even have met regularly during that turbulent period?

Q: Could they not be covering for their own role?

A: I have not spoken to any of the council of the day. But those that have claimed that, appeared genuinely shocked that my book should implicate them. And they do allow for the possibility that the wool was pulled over their eyes by the subcommittee handling the strike.

Q: So what do you think did happen?

A: As I said in my book, Adams was at the top of the pyramid. He sent the comms in. He read the comms that came out. He talked to the Mountain Climber. As I said earlier, we know that he, and possibly the clique around him, decided to reject the second offer, at least, without telling Bik what was in it. Nobody knows the hunger strike like Adams knows it. And yet he is maintaining the silence of the mouse, the odd squeak from him when confronted. Here's what he said in relation to the Mountain Climber in the RTE hunger strikes documentary, 'There had been a contact which the British had activated. It became known as the Mountain Climber. Basically, I didn't learn this until after the hunger strike ended'. He didn't learn what? About the contact and the offers, or the Mountain Climber euphemism? If he's saying he didn't know about the offers, then why did he show the offer to Father Crilly and Hugh Logue in Andersonstown on 6 July 1981? And if he's saying he didn't know of the Mountain Climber euphemism, I'd refer your readers to Bik's comm to Adams on pages 301–302, *Ten Men Dead*, where Bik tells Brownie, who is Adams, that Morrison had told the hunger strikers about the Mountain Climber: 'Pennies has already informed them of Mountain Climber angle . . .' So he knew about the Mountain Climber euphemism, and he knew of the offers. As a defensive strategy, this lurking in the shadows, this proceeding through ambiguity, can only work for so long. At some point academics and investigative journalists are going to ask the searching questions and Gerry Adams is not going to be up to them.

Q: Are you now suggesting that Adams may have withheld crucial details from the Army Council?

A: I don't know the procedural detail of the relationship between Adams and the Army Council. What I do know is that my account of events is absolutely spot-on. You said yourself on RTE on Tuesday that there was independent verification of the conversation between myself and Bik McFarlane.

Q: Indeed. I think you realise there is a bit more than that. As you know I have enormous time for Bik. It goes back to the days before the blanket. But I can only state what I uncovered. I am not saying that it is conclusive. These things can always be contested. But it certainly shades the debate your way. If Morrison and Gibney continue to mislead people that there is no evidence supporting your claim from that wing on H3 I can always allow prominent journalists and academics to access what is there and arrive at whatever conclusions they feel appropriate. That should settle matters and cause a few red faces to boot. We know how devious and unscrupulous these people have been in their handling of this. They simply did not reckon on what would fall the way of *The Blanket.* Nor did I, for that matter—a blunder on their part.

A: If the Army Council say they received no comm from us accepting the deal, and also say that they sent in no word telling us effectively to refuse the deal, then I think the only plausible explanation is that those who sent in the 'instruction' to reject the Mountain Climber's offer were doing so without the knowledge or approval of the Army Council.

Q: When you say 'those' you presumably mean Adams and Liam Og who was also sending in comms coming to the prison leadership?

A: Yes.

Q: Liam Og has been identified by Denis O'Hearn, author of the biography of Bobby Sands, as Tom Hartley. It appears that Hartley was privy to every comm between the leadership and the prisoners.

A: That would be the case.

Q: How can we be sure that Adams rather than Liam Og was responsible for withholding information from the Army Council?

A: Because while we might not know the procedural detail, Adams had a relationship with the Army Council that was vastly different from Liam Og. You point out that this is well recorded in public.

Q: Despite Jim Gibney's assertions in the *Irish News* that you never discussed your concerns with anyone prior to the publication of the book, you claim to have raised them with Hartley in 1991.

A: I did. He didn't think pursuing it was the wisest course of action. Immediately after the conversation with him I told my wife Bernadette about it. She recalls it to this day.

Q: Was he a gofer?

A: Not at all. He was a major player.

Q: If his role in the hunger strike was so central and he is aware of your concerns but has chosen to say nothing he leaves himself open to the allegation that his main concern lies in protecting his master and his own role in what seems to have been a sordid exercise in manipulation and deception. Why were you still expressing your doubts to people like him ten years after the hunger strike?

A: I liked Tom. And it wasn't just him. I had serious reservations about our boys dying on hunger strike. I didn't like the way the Army Council, as I believed it then was, had handled the matter. I was angry. I just felt that the six boys had been used and abused. I felt that my six buddies had died on hunger strike for nothing. I raised it with a lot of people, some of whom have admitted to you that this is so. And nobody could tell me why the boys died. They became pawns in a wider battle. These were people who had lives, feelings, and families. They did not deserve this.

Q: There is an irreconcilable tension between your account of the days prior to the death of Joe McDonnell and Brendan McFarlane's. Can you take us through that?

A: Bik was called up to the camp hospital on Sunday the 5th of July to meet Danny Morrison. I knew nothing about what was happening up there. He returned and sent me up a comm telling me that there was some guy called the Mountain Climber on board. He was from the British government and he had offered us a package of concessions.

Q: Which in your estimation was sufficient to end the hunger strike?
A: Absolutely.

Q: How close were they to the five demands?
A: We had eight men on hunger strike. To go beyond Joe took us into an abyss that I could see no way out of. I looked at the Mountain Climber offer for three hours. It was a fantastic offer. I never expected it. Remember, Danny Morrison told RTE's *Good Morning* show on 5 May, Bobby's anniversary, that what the Brits 'were offering us was more than they were, publicly or privately, offering the Irish Commission for Justice and Peace . . .'

Q: Was the fact that you were desperate to prevent your colleagues from dying not colouring your judgment and allowing you to overstate what was on offer?
A: Obviously not, if we're to believe Danny's account of the offer. No. I repeat that what was on offer was enough to honourably end the

hunger strike. We had our own clothes—we didn't care if the ordinary prisoners had their own clothes as well. We had made this crystal clear in our fourth of July statement, written by myself. It was a bit like Eamon de Valera—he deleted the idea of a republic in order to break the deadlock with the Brits during the War of Independence, and we took out the term 'political status' to also break the deadlock with the Brits during the hunger strike. After that everything was possible.

Q: Then why has Bik McFarlane held to his position that there was no offer?

A: I don't know why he started out from this position in the first place given that Morrison contradicted him so thoroughly. Since his initial claim that there was no offer he has shifted his position, though, to try to come into line with Morrison. He is now saying there was no deal. They want to river dance between deal and offer and blur the issue.

Q: Yet he knew that a deal was on offer?

A: Morrison told him the offer was made. In the RTE hunger strikes documentary, Danny said he visited the prison hospital on 5 July 1981. 'I went in and I think there were eight people there. Joe McDonnell was brought in as well. Joe was blind and was in a wheelchair. We told him what they were offering at that stage . . .' Is it possible that Morrison didn't tell the OC of the prisoners about this Brit offer? Come on!

Q: It seems clear that Adams was the main point of contact with the Mountain Climber. Why do you think he has been so reticent in responding to your charges? While trying to dismiss you his intervention has nevertheless been minimalist. He has preferred to leave it to the sandbags—people like Morrison and Gibney.

A: Because he has got so much to hide. He pretended on the RTE documentary that he only found out who the Mountain Climber was after the event. He was the man who was talking directly to the Mountain Climber on the phone. He was the man who was making the decisions as to what was a good deal and what wasn't. And what was good for him was by no means good for the boys. And he has avoided this like the plague. It is about time we knew exactly who the Mountain Climber was, the nature of the contacts, and the detail of the offer that he made. Was that offer sent into the prisoners? Twenty-five years on, and we still don't know the detail!

Q: Which would invalidate Morrison's point that if the leadership had prevented a deal the Brits would have been trumpeting it from the rooftops. The Mountain Climber was presumably told that the prisoners had rejected it. And Thatcher, with her reputation for facing down rather than parleying with opponents, was hardly going to let it out that she was making offers to the deadly enemy, the IRA.

A: Of course.

Q: Is it your view that the offer from the Mountain Climber was relayed to the jail leadership by Morrison in the hope that the prisoners would reject it and that when they decided to accept it elements within the leadership had to effectively overrule yourself and Brendan McFarlane?

A: Yes. We accepted the deal. Why would we not? We were offered a way out that meant comrades would not have to die. Who in their right mind would not take it?

Q: It has been a difficult time for the Sinn Fein leadership. Instead of arriving like conquering heroes carrying the flame lit by the hunger strikers they now have to answer media questions implying that they may have had a hand in killing the hunger strikers. No matter what answer they give it is swamped in the tidal wave of reverberations caused by the question. The leadership has been less than sure-footed in its media management.

A: All they have done from day one is stick the knife in me. And that is not a successful PR strategy. At the end of the day for all these guys who know what happened I have one thing to say to them: You should have some contrition and acknowledge that we deserve the truth. That is the least our dead comrades deserve.

Q: Truth from them?—some would say you are losing it.

A: We have a right to know.

Q: If you absolve the Army Council of the day, as a collective, of responsibility for sabotaging a conclusion to the hunger strike that would have saved the lives of six men, who do you hold responsible?

A: Maggie Thatcher had the responsibility for bringing this all to an end.

Q: But given that she made an offer, which would have brought it to an end and which was sabotaged, who then on the Republican side, if not the Council, was responsible?

A: You are trying to tie me down.

Q: I should not have to. You should be telling us directly if as you say you believe in our right to know.

A: Let's put it like this. The iron lady was not so steely at the end. She wanted a way out. The Army Council, I now believe, as a collective were kept in the dark about developments. The subcommittee ran the hunger strike. Draw your own conclusions from the facts.

Q: What could be the possible motive for Adams and the subcommittee wanting to prolong the hunger strike?

A: I don't know for sure. I can only speculate and this time it would be wrong for you to try to nail me down on what is only opinion.

Q: Yet one way of reading your book is to see the decision to sabotage a successful conclusion to the hunger strike in the context of Sinn Fein needing to strike while the electoral iron was hot.

A: I floated it as a possibility, yes.

Q: John Nixon from the 1980 hunger strike team was very forthright in asserting this perspective on the RTE documentary.

A: John Nixon demonstrated that it is probably the most persuasive argument made in relation to the longevity of the hunger strike. The absence of an army order to end the hunger strike, when it was blatantly obvious that nothing more was to be got from the Mountain Climber, reinforces this opinion. It is impossible to believe that Gerry Adams did not see the bigger picture and did not realise how omni-important Owen Carron's election was to the future of Republican strategy. He would have been a fool not to. And Gerry Adams is no fool.

Q: But being a fool not to see the electoral opportunity does not mean that it is ethical to follow such a premise to the point of allowing six comrades to die in order to fulfil the potential of that opportunity?

A: It would be an absolute disgrace if it were the case that six men were sacrificed to bring Sinn Fein onto the constitutional altar. I just find it impossible to believe that any Republican would let six of their comrades die so they could work partition.

Q: But the logic of your book is precisely that?

A: It is one of a range of possibilities. I am not going to be dogmatic on it. I can only state what I know and anything after that is speculation. I know that there was an offer made and somebody outside rejected it.

Q: I have always seen Bik as a very humane and compassionate guy. I know this may jar with the way the media often depicted him. But I knew him well. To me he loved his comrades. The image of him as someone who would not fight to save the lives of the hunger strikers against the wishes of a malign and ambitious leadership element jars with my experience of him.

A: I feel sorry for Bik. He has been thrown to the wolves. And he is hoping that this dies out before any more serious questioning takes place. I can live with that. He did what he did at the time and that's it. The problem he has is that he has never learned to question; he has never learned to think outside of the movement structure. And that is a tragedy.

Q: Do you as a leading Republican strategist during the hunger strike feel any sense of guilt over what happened?

A: Well, yes. I feel guilty that I didn't call for it to end sooner. But I did try to prevent the last six men dying, to save lives. I did put out the conciliatory fourth of July statement. Bik had about 5 percent input into that. I tried to stop the thing. But it was patently clear that it didn't matter what I said. It just did not matter. The leadership called the shots.

Q: How do you feel when former hunger strikers like John Pickering and Laurny McKeown try to minimise your role in the hunger strike?

A: It's not nice, not nice at all. In fact, some of the attacks on me have bordered on the fascist. It's as if no one else is allowed to express a view contrary to the leadership's line. Their sole intent—not just them, but Morrison, Gibney, and cohorts—is to de-intellectualise the discussion, engage in name calling and smearing and that way either drag the debate down into the gutter where people will switch off, or force me off the field so they can continue to have it to themselves. I'll tell you one thing, they are wasting their time. I'll always oppose those who try to suppress truth, whether from inside the Republican movement or outside of it.

Q: What does the future hold in terms of where this debate is going?

A: The leadership had better get used to the idea that this debate is going to expose them. Their troubles won't soon blow away, you know. The debate will explain how they have got to where they are. Did you ever think back then, as we debated socialism and republicanism, that we'd see the day Republicans would be nominating Ian Paisley for first minister in a Stormont Assembly? Jesus, what a debacle! Bobby Sands, socialist, secularist, Republican bears no resemblance to any of this. None of the boys did.

Q: Thanks for your time. What you have done is to remain consistent with the precept of Danny Morrison who urges Republicans not to let anyone else take authorship of our history. As you make clear in your *Irish News* 'Platform' piece it is a battle between your audacity and their mendacity. They have failed to intimidate you. You are right never to yield to these leadership screws, any more than you did to the blanket screws, the self-appointed custodians of a hideous and terrible secret. To give way would allow them to prohibit you from expressing now what you expressed during the blanket protest—in the immortal words of Bobby Sands:

the undauntable thought, my friend
that thought that says 'I'm right'!

Looking Back on 1981

Forum Magazine, June/July 2006

I t should have been Sinn Fein's year. The ninetieth anniversary of the Easter Rising and the twenty-fifth anniversary of the hunger strikes were destined to merge as one seamless thread of continuous resistance and struggle, and send the party strutting along the stage of Irish nationalism bathed in the light of adulation; the carriers of the eternal flame fuelled by the blood of the 1916 leaders and the ten men who died in 1981. It has hardly turned out that way. The Easter Rising thunder was siphoned off by Bertie Ahern and Fianna Fail. Not too hard to do. The choice was between Real Fianna Fail and Provisional Fianna Fail at a point when the latter could no longer expect to benefit from a sleaze-free image. Sinn Fein since 1998 have more than sufficiently demonstrated that they are Good Friday rather than Easter Sunday Republicans. It is inane to march past Dublin's GPO chanting, 'Administer British rule', and expect to win accolades.

As if that were not bad enough, the hunger strikes are proving to be a lot more thorny. The Sinn Fein leadership just can't grasp the baton passed on by ten dead men without recoiling from the prick of the barb. Rather than basking in reflected glory, they are facing questions in the media which, when stripped of their velvet sheath, sound ominously like 'did you help kill six of the hunger strikers'?

Anniversary years have not been kind to Sinn Fein. The party's centenary year, 2005, had already been destroyed by the killers of Robert McCartney. The year 2006, where such key anniversaries as 1916 and 1981 in other circumstances would have been a launching pad for greater things, has been overshadowed by the towering figure of Richard O'Rawe, resisting all the intimidating invective, slander, and innuendo that the diminutive party sandbags have thrown his way as they desperately try to protect their leader, the very source of their own status, with whom they have been complicit, their fates intertwined.

O'Rawe's charge is simple. The British government made an offer to end the hunger strike prior to the death of Joe McDonnell. The prison leadership said, 'Deal', informed key Republican leaders on the outside of their position, and sat back in nervous anticipation that the British would immediately proceed to initiate arrangements that would prevent further loss of life resulting from prison protest. To their chagrin the same leaders said, 'No deal'.

Since O'Rawe's book *Blanketmen* was published last year, much speculation has centred around the motives of the leadership element that was operating without the knowledge or approval of the bulk of those on the Army Council. Amongst those who find O'Rawe plausible there have emerged signs of a consensus that the guiding strategic objective of the then adjutant general of the IRA was to ensure that the hunger strike continued until at least the seat 'only borrowed' by Bobby Sands had been safely secured by a Sinn Fein member.

After the death of the sixth hunger striker, Martin Hurson, dark murmurings were beginning to simmer in the wing O'Rawe was held on. In conversation with one of the central figures on our own wing at the time I made the point that if the rumours coming out of O'Rawe's wing were true, then whoever repeated them might end up dead themselves. Since *Blanketmen* appeared on the shelves he has reminded me of the conversation each time we discuss O'Rawe's allegations.

Nevertheless, the jail was nothing if not a hotbed of distortion. Perspectives that would fly nowhere else would soar to great heights in that place. If gremlins were beginning to appear there would be enough conspiracy theorists to give them fair wind. But most people would have viewed untoward occurrences in the management of the hunger strike as the result of human error and miscalculation rather than Machiavellian manipulation in what was a precarious odyssey. No choice was easy; even less could it be guaranteed that success would follow. There certainly would have been few takers for the view that the foremost Provisional IRA leader for what was then the best part of a decade would be contemplating electoral glory at the cost of our comrades' lives.

To believe that prominent Republicans were capable of sabotaging a deal that would end the hunger strike to suit their own electoral ambitions, we would have had to entertain the seemingly absurd notion that those pursuing such an end would at some point seek to surrender IRA weapons, install Ian Paisley in a returned Stormont as leader of a partitioned Northern Ireland statelet, and call for Republicans to hand themselves over to the Diplock courts to experience the dubious merits of British justice. It is easy to conceive of such people as being endowed with characters of such malignancy that they would readily regard votes as more important than Republican lives.

Now who in their right minds in 1981 would ever have imagined that there was anyone like that in our ranks?

Death Brings Fr. Faul Vindication He Deserved

Irish News, 4 July 2006

After the conclusion of the 1981 Hunger Strike I and many other Republican prisoners came to reject Denis Faul. Although the bulk of us were not churchgoers we insisted that all Republicans boycott his Masses on our wings. Hooked on our own approved line, we blamed him for bringing the hunger strike to a premature end before it forced the hand of the Brits and the restoration of political status. It hurt him deeply.

Given the enormous support he afforded us throughout the years of prison protest, he must have felt let down at our hostility and our need to find a scapegoat. From that point on his criticisms of our movement seemed to be much more acerbic. He came to see us as fascists. Yet the true measure of the man was to be found in his incessant campaigning against those who treated us unjustly.

I first met Denis Faul in 1974 in cage 10 of Long Kesh when he was hearing confessions. Then he was an iconic figure in my mind as a result of the tremendous work he had done in bringing to light British injustices. And this great man was hearing the confession of a seventeen-year-old. I felt honoured.

When I returned to prison there he was again. By now I wasn't going to confession but he would be available for those who were and to preach the gospel.

During the blanket protest he was a regular on Sundays to celebrate Mass in the prison canteen. We all went. It was the only time we could associate with each other. Denis made no secret of the fact that he was an inveterate smuggler. Pulling clingfilm-clad tobacco from his socks, he ensured that Sunday nights were a source of relief for those who derived pleasure from a smoke.

An avid football fan, he told us the scores of all the games and it was from him that we first learned of that illustrious name Diego

Maradona. It was amazing how we could follow the football so avidly within the prison despite never reading a match report, watching a game on TV, or listening to it on radio. Denis was largely responsible for that.

The Sunday before Bobby Sands died he told us that our resilient comrade had fallen into a coma. We knew then it was over for Bobby.

Our hopes, which had been so built up by his capturing the Fermanagh/South Tyrone seat, crumbled as we listened to Denis. Nothing now was going to intervene and save the life of this preeminent IRA leader. Brendan Hughes' announcement two days later that Bobby had slipped away was something we were mentally prepared for. It was devastating nonetheless.

As the hunger strike ploughed forward it should have begun to look ominously like First World War soldiers storming trenches they could never hope to take. Ourselves alone failed to see it. Our emotions were bizarre. I had one punch-the-air moment during the entire thing, when Laurence McKeown's mother intervened to take him off it. Yet, absurdly, I continued to think that carrying on with the strike was the only option. There was neither rhyme nor reason to it at that point. We could not go forward and there was no going back.

I do not blame our determination on our own supposed recalcitrant personalities or any fanaticism that was then attributed to us. It was an attitude tempered in the vicious crucible of the H-Blocks. But something had to break the cycle of prisoner deaths and families' despair.

That something was a man called Denis. He moved to bring a halt to it. In doing so he saved the lives of many great men. It took some years to come to terms with, and some still have not. In many ways it took his death to bring him the vindication he so deeply deserved. It came in the form of an intensely moving letter to the *Irish News* from a relative of a dead hunger striker. The writer simply said: 'We asked Fr. Faul to help us bring an end to the dreadful and unnecessary hunger strike'.

GOOD FRIDAY

When first diagnosed with cancer he said he hoped he would reach the age of eighty-four, the innings his father achieved. I hoped it too. It was not to be.

Standing at his graveside last week in Carrickmore, one of three former Blanketmen, I felt that we had come to bury a fourth.

The Price of Our Memory

The Blanket, 26 August 2006

Speech given at the Annual H-Block Hunger Strike Commemoration,
twenty-fifth anniversary, Bundoran, Donegal

While sorrowful it is a deep honour to speak here today. To the organisers I would like to convey my appreciation for their having bestowed that honour upon me. It is also to the credit of the organisers and a measure of their integrity that they have not reduced this venerable event to a political rally. Their willingness to offer this platform to people who do not share their political outlook is admirable. It is clear that the sacrifice of the hunger strikers is the primary motivating spirit that guides them. The dark spectre of political opportunism may have stalked Casement Park two weeks ago but it is banished from here today as we gather to pay true homage to our fallen comrades rather than use their imagery and exploit their memory to add wind to the sails of political careers.

Today there are more than enough people claiming to be close friends of Bobby Sands. It is the price an icon of radical struggle pays. Some see only the celebrity dimension that is often generated by the life, works, or death of an incorruptible activist and tend to downplay the intense agony undergone by them and their families. While the hunger strikers never sought fame, perhaps the definition of a celebrity is apt for Bobby Sands in the current context if we accept the definition of a celebrity as someone who is known by many people he is glad he does not know.

I recall once acquiring a certain cynicism upon learning of a book about the late guerrilla fighter Che Guevara. Its title was *My Friend Che*. These things never fail to strike me as exploitative. Consequently, I was surprised to find in yesterday's *Guardian* that I too had joined the illustrious society of close friends of Bobby Sands. It was an honest mistake by the journalist who wrote the story. At the risk of depleting the membership of the society of friends, I was not one of Bobby's bosom buddies. I didn't know him well enough to acquire that status. Yet I am mindful of his own comment to Monsignor Denis Faul shortly before he died that man has no greater love than he who would lay down his life for his friends. On that basis we could all claim to be friends of Bobby and the other hunger strikers. They literally gave their lives for us and the Republican philosophy that animated us.

I take great pride from the fact that Bobby Sands, Frank Hughes, Patsy O'Hara, and the other volunteers who died were comrades and that I was on the blanket protest with them. We were young men, who along with young women in Armagh prison, pitted our one weapon, endurance, against the vile might of a state that had massacred an unarmed civilian population on the streets of Derry and would not balk at the thought of putting us to the sword. Blocks apart we were united, as all Blanketmen were, in our opposition to a British lie and the reassertion of a Republican truth. They, not we, were the criminals. Yes, the H-Blocks were filled with criminal types. They all belonged to the Northern Ireland Prison Service, who regularly beat Republican political prisoners and inflicted a regime of deprivation upon us in a futile attempt to break the spirit.

The British in 1981 demonstrated to the world the essence of their malign character. They gave in at the end but they exacted a terrible price for it. Had they delivered in March 1981 what they eventually conceded in October of the same year, there would have been no dead hunger strikers. But the vindictiveness of Britain is well known to Irish Republicans. One lesson to be learned from that terrible time is that all the force of British violence could not defeat the moral power of a peaceful Republican protest.

The H-Block hunger strike carried out by the volunteers of the IRA and INLA was a defining moment in Irish Republican history. It resonated globally and has led us here today to honour the memory of Raymond McCreesh, Kieran Doherty, and the eight men who never again were to wear their own clothes but who broke the will of the British to persist in their demand that republicanism walk the face of this earth wearing the criminal mark of Cain. Kevin Lynch and his comrades ensured that never again would Britain be able to succeed in characterising resistance to its rule as the work of common criminals.

There are some today who tell us that had Martin Hurson, Joe McDonnell, and the hunger strikers survived they would most likely support the corrupt peace process and back the Provisional leadership in its stewardship of that process. Perhaps. But how can we tell? The simple truth is that we cannot. To designate positions and perspectives to people who gave no license for such designation is every bit as dishonest as the attempts by the British to assign criminal motivation to the same people. It is to take a liberty where none was granted. It is theft. It is to steal a sacrifice and put it in a place other than its rightful one.

We can say absolutely nothing about where the hunger strikers would stand today. If we were of such a mind we could lie with statistics. We could infer that because some former hunger strikers stand ready to embrace the PSNI, then those that died would, had they survived, do likewise. But which ones? Who amongst us would dare pick one of the ten dead men and insult him by saying with any certainty, 'Yes—he would bust his gut today to support British peelers'?

To proclaim that the Republican dead would endorse Sinn Fein the Peelers Party is not to tell any truth about men such as Michael Devine and Tom McElwee. It is to provide cover for those who cannot walk erect, head held high to the partitionist destination that they have now chosen. They want to take the hunger strikers with them, to lean on them, use them as a crutch. We don't demand that they have the courage of the ten dead men. That comes to few. We simply ask that they have the honesty of the fallen. They would be better thought of. Perhaps, in a world governed by organised lying, methodical lying, where there are those who lie like the rest of us breathe, honesty is as rare as the courage of the hunger strikers. A fitting epitaph to be engraved on the headstones of those who would use the memory of the hunger strikers for their own scrofulous ends would be: 'Here they are, lying still'. The meaning would be clear to all.

Yet there are some things we can say with absolute certainty about the men who died on hunger strike within the corridors of steel and concrete that were the H-Blocks of Long Kesh. And the expression of that certainty in no way exploits the sacrifices made but on the contrary honours each and every life and death experienced by our ten comrades. As has been said, to the living we owe respect; to the dead we owe only truth. When the men lost their lives they died in opposition to a reformed Stormont; they died in opposition to acceptance of the Unionist veto dressed up in the language of the consent principle; they died in opposition to Leinster House; they died in opposition to a British police force enforcing the law of the British state in any part of Ireland. Whatever tradition inherits their legacy or lays claim to their suffering it is an absurdity to claim that such a tradition could be made up of all the component parts the hunger strikers died opposing.

It is important that we continue to reassert what we believe to be the truth. We live in a world where many are more afraid of being isolated than they are of being wrong. Consequently, they take the easy option and are content to be wrong. Recently, former Blanketman Richard O'Rawe, who I am pleased to say is standing with us here today, displayed enormous courage and went against the Provisional narrative of the hunger strike. To his credit, being wrong was more repulsive to him than being isolated. He did the right thing, faced down the isolation, and published the book *Blanketmen*. In it he levelled the charge that the lives of six of the hunger strikers could have been saved were it not for some elements in the Republican leadership machinating and manipulating events to further their own ambitions. Despite the assaults on his character and integrity, Richard O'Rawe, wearing the tenacity that made him one of the Blanketmen, persisted with his conviction. He withstood the whispers, the graffiti sprayers, the ostracism, the labelling of him as some sort of deviant who traded in his human decency for profit. What nonsense. Richard O'Rawe simply opted to bear witness. Given his knowledge of events, he feels it is the least he could do. What else but to establish truth were the blanket protest and hunger strikes waged?

The key questions asked by Richard O'Rawe remain unanswered. What did the offer made by the British through the Mountain Climber constitute? Where are the comms relating to the Mountain Climber? There has been a deathly silence on the part of some Provisional leaders in relation to these matters. There is only one place for a Republican to be silent: in the barracks. But even some prominent Provisionals managed to fail in this respect.

There is independent evidence to support the claims made by Richard O'Rawe in his book. That evidence has been made available to a small number of key leaders within the Irish Republican Socialist movement who feel obligated to explore the claims out of respect to their fallen comrades and their grieving families. It has prompted that movement to publicly state that it wants the matter further investigated.

Richard O'Rawe has faced accusations that his actions amount to launching a blasphemous assault on the most sacred cow within modern republicanism. The truth is that those making the accusations see in the hunger strikers a cash cow rather than a sacred one. And they are determined that it will graze in no field but their own. Blankets were being sold at the Casement Park political rally so that a corpulent crowd could march up the Falls Road and provoke the sarcasm of the press who lambasted it as resembling a Friar Tuck convention more than it did the austere era of the Blanket protest and hunger strikes. The contrast between the easy corpulence of today and the hard emaciation of twenty-five years ago was no more stark than it was on the Falls Road at that political rally. In a sense the imagery mirrored perfectly the ethical decay that has come to beset republicanism. The screws at least gave out the blankets for free.

Our dead hunger strikers are sacred to us. They occupy hallowed ground within our minds. The commercialisation of their memory is a travesty. It is a crime against Republican sensitivity and our own natural intellect.

But nothing else can be expected. Experience is a good teacher and we know only too well what happens when republicanism falls prey to the Stick virus. It becomes ravished and mutates beyond all recognition. Cast our memories back to 1981, our most intense ideological and emotional year as Irish Republicans. The people who today wish to transform the hunger strike into a profit-making industry do not with their politics remotely resemble the Republican spirit of that year. But they very much look like the Workers Party of 1981.

Cathal Goulding, the onetime Official IRA-Stick chief of staff, knew exactly how to strangle republicanism. The trick was to corrode it from within. Republicanism can withstand inordinate amounts of pressure from without. But it is always vulnerable to the false messiah, the leader who thinks we exist as playthings in his little dance of deceit. Such leaders prevail only where they go unchallenged.

Today the energy and sacrifice of the hunger strikers is in the service of a political project that at the time of their deaths they opposed. There is no need to go into the detail of a political analysis to see where things have ended up. Small human stories allow us to instinctively and intuitively grasp what is going down better than any amount of political treatises. Who would have thought that when Brendan Hughes lay in a bed in a prison hospital leading the 1980 hunger strike, fellow Blanketmen would two decades later visit him in the Royal Victoria hospital where he lay on a hospital trolley because there were no available beds? The British health minister at the time was a member of the Provisional movement.

It is in these little vignettes that we are able to see the collapse of the Provisional project, how little it actually achieved. And now it demands that Paisley be prime minister and that their own volunteers hand themselves over to a Diplock judge so that they may be jailed without political status for their role in the leadership-ordered kidnapping of Bobby Tohill.

During the Blanket protest one of our favourite acts of defiance was staged when the governor came around to impose punishment on us for refusing to wear the prison garb or do prison work. We would scream in his face, 'Up the RA'. Imagine had we shouted, 'Up Paisley; jail the RA'. The governor would have recommended our immediate release as the quickest possible way to secure the defeat of the Republican resistance.

In 1981 the British inflicted a terrible crime on Irish people. They scarred us deeply and its pain pulsates as we reflect on the lives and deaths of the H-Block volunteers on the twenty-fifth anniversary of that momentous occasion. As we leave here today we would do well to remember the words of two Czech novelists. Vaclav Havel urged people to speak truth to power. Milan Kundera said that 'the struggle of man against power is the struggle of memory against forgetting'. Let us memorise and never forget those who gave their everything; allow the awesome power of Republican memory to triumph over those who wish to forget what they inflicted and those who conveniently want us to forget what it was all about.

As Republicans who refused to wear the badge of criminality we will not commit the crime of forgetting. Always and everywhere, remember the hunger strikers.

CHAPTER 6
Suppressing Dissent

Out of the Ashes of Armed Struggle Arose the Stormontistas and They Fought . . . Ardoyne Youth

The Blanket, 5 September 2002

> *Nine times out of ten a revolutionary is just a social climber with a bomb in his pocket.*
>
> —GEORGE ORWELL

One of the certainties in politics is the certainty of egg on your face if you believe in too many of them. What certainty could be built on the foundations of a politician's word? It is a safer bet to find wisdom in the old joke that you can always tell a politician is lying when you see his or her lips move. Yet in spite of this there are some trends that have such consistency that they resemble the gravitational pull applied to Newton's apple. And nothing is more certain than that the pull of the RUC structure will prove irresistible to Sinn Fein, which will fall like an apple right into the rotten barrel it for so long railed against. The choice for the party merely lies in which model to opt for—Peter Mandleson's RUC or Chris Patten's RUC. Hardly a life or death choice that will cause party leaders serious hand wringing or deep soul searching into the small hours.

Danny Morrison writing in the *Sunday Tribune* shortly after the Patten report was published rightly contended that the RUC had not been disbanded, although he did not dismiss Patten, urging Republicans to move with caution after deep reflection before making decisions. In the intervening period as Patten has been diluted we are left even further short of anything vaguely resembling a disbanded RUC.

There is really no need to pursue an academic or philosophical discussion about what a police hat means as a method of testing the extent of change. Seven hundred forty-nine stitches across the peak rather than 750 stitches may serve as an indication for both the terminally clueless and the incurable gradualist that a stitch-up is less likely to happen and that it heralds improvement, albeit of a transitional kind; but those on the streets who have to deal with stitched heads as distinct from stitched hats know instinctively that the RUC has not been disbanded and that the baton and boot of Seamus and Padraic are just as unpleasant as those of Mervyn and Samuel. On every single core issue negotiated since the peace process began republicanism has lost out; from 'no' consent principle, 'no' Stormont, 'no' British declaration of intent to stay, 'no' internal settlement, 'no' decommissioning ad infinitum. It would be both futile and a bit late in the day for Sinn Fein to make a principled, rather than a verbal, stand on 'no' RUC. Toothpaste just doesn't go back into the tube.

Comments by the Sinn Fein president Gerry Adams that the experience of nationalists, in particular those living in the interface areas, meant that there was no chance of Sinn Fein signing up to the new RUC (Mr. Adams for reasons of tactical preparation of the grassroots prefers to call the not disbanded RUC the 'PSNI' or simply 'police') were mere wool pulling not designed in the slightest to thwart the momentum that is taking the party toward the RUC. 'Our position on this is very clear', Adams said. Someone not disabled by an ill-equipped memory might claim that it is as clear as it was when Martin McGuinness outlined the stance in relation to a cease-fire. His position too was 'very clear' and would 'never, never, never' change—it would simply not happen this side of a British declaration of intent to withdraw. The first cease-fire was called eight years ago—and the Brits, well, they haven't gone away you know.

Sinn Fein will become part of the structure of the RUC. Whatever change is made between now and the point at which they sign up, no matter how minimal—and described, no doubt, as a 'transition' to Patten—will be heralded as some qualitative improvement that caused a change of heart within the party, in effect the smokescreen used to camouflage a decision already taken. Declan Kearney speaking at the John Joe McGirl Commemorative Weekend made that much clear:

'In time, if and when the legislative, political, and practical conditions are fully met, we will have to assume roles in the oversight of the Six-County policing service'.

Mitchell McLaughlin too, in what was naively described by the *Daily Telegraph* as a 'direct challenge' to Tony Blair (when really it was the party chair responding to calls of 'your time is up Sinn Fein, you are coming in'), was engaging in a bit of kite flying when he said of the British prime minister 'when and if he gets round to making these necessary amendments to the legislation, and producing and delivering on his commitment to Patten, then Sinn Fein will step up to the mark. We will not shirk the very difficult challenge that will pose for us'. In other words, the party is about to be courageous and imaginative again.

Of equal significance to what Gerry Adams had to say was the location chosen in which to say it—Ardoyne. That area served as a window on the political fulcrum upon which pivots the Provisionals' ability to ease themselves into embracing the RUC. Two current obstacles were geographically distilled into one location or test site for Republican 'population management' strategies: Orange marches and interface tensions.

The North Belfast enclave—an interface from the first day of the conflict and long before the term became part of the political lexicon—situated at the top of the Crumlin Road was the site of serious disturbances in July as an Orange parade passed it. Earlier, Belfast's RUC supremo, Alan McQuillan, in what the *Observer* described as a 'preemptive propaganda strike', had warned that the IRA was planning a 'major attack', as marchers passed along the Crumlin Road on 12 July. Gerry Kelly complained that 'it was an outrageous piece of black propaganda, which has criminalised and demonised a whole area'. Why preparations for an aggressive defence of an area should be either criminal or demonic was left unexplained. The demonisation of the Official Republican movement became a central plank of Provisional mythology on the grounds that the behavior of the Officials was criminal for failing to prepare adequate defence. Equally puzzling was party colleague Martin McGuinness' claim that McQuillan's allegations represented the agenda of 'unreconstructed RUC elements' within the PSNI. The only surprise here is that anyone should be surprised that within an unreconstructed RUC there are to be found unreconstructed RUC members.

In our Orwellian little world of organised lying, where adversaries battle to have their own lie accepted as the 'truth' rather than actually believed per se, the only course to tread for those keen to interpret matters for themselves is to ignore both Sinn Fein and the RUC, neither of which would pass the lie detector test with any aplomb. Fortunately one Ardoyne resident agreed to be interviewed by *The Blanket*. A professed longtime supporter of the Republican movement, he so feared for his safety that he insisted on not being identified.

> People are afraid to speak out. I am only talking to you on the understanding that you won't sink me by letting them know who I am. You know what them boys are like. They don't like it if they think you mightn't let them shove their views down your throat. I don't want any comeback from them. Is that okay?

A grim reminder that Kanan Makiya's book *The Republic of Fear* had no reason to confine itself to Iraq.

His version of what happened in Ardoyne would exonerate Provisional Republicans from the allegations levelled by Alan McQuillan, but would indict them in the eyes of many within working-class communities who, like Michael Ignatieff's cynic, have a healthy awareness of the gulf between what provisional republicanism practices and what it preaches.

In his account, nationalists were physically beaten off the Crumlin Road not just on the twelfth but in the days coming up to it also. Tracing this type of behavior back to last year's Holy Cross dispute he claimed that some nationalist youths 'were beaten by the IRA as their mothers cried in despair'.

Regarding the controversial statement by Alan McQuillan, he claimed:

> The whole of Ardoyne was prepared for a riot. We had been putting bricks, bottles, and stones—anything that could be thrown—on the roofs of buildings for almost a week. We had no intention of using the antiburglar devices the cops showed on TV but we had to move them in order to get on to the roofs. The IRA knew what was going on and while they were not involved in it, they did nothing to stop it.

Why, then, the sudden Republican turn on people if they were so indifferent to the matter beforehand?

> McQuillan's statement changed the whole atmosphere in the area. The minute he opened his big mouth and said what he did the 'RA turned on the people. On the day of the march lots of 'RA from all over the city were drafted in to control the situation on the road. The people's blood was boiling at the idea of these Orangees walking up the road. There was a massive RUC presence but it wasn't needed. When the Orangees were only five minutes away many Republicans could be seen walking about using walkie-talkies. When the Orangemen were walking by, the 'RA turned on us. Young people were beaten on the Crumlin Road, behind the Star and in Balhome Drive. The RUC seen it all happen. They didn't have to draw their batons as Republicans did it for them. There were digs to the head and some of us were kicked like dogs.

When asked to quantify how robust the IRA policing of Ardoyne on 12 July was he alleged that thirty to forty people were beaten by Republicans, assaults that ranged from shoving and slapping to punching and kicking.

> Under threat we are supposed to stand with our hands in our pockets. The 'RA want to wind it up when it suits them but turn on the people if it doesn't. Now there is a major division in Ardoyne at the minute. The area has always felt the need for defence. But people are talking of being let down. It is no good. Sinn Fein come over at election time and then forget about us. There is whispering that they will not get as many votes next time they come round at election time. People have been sickened by what happened. We are now back to a situation like the 1970s where defence groups have to watch the area. People in West Belfast don't know how safe they are. It is very vulnerable over here.

The account of the resident would appear to be consistent with other reports. Supposedly senior IRA members named by the *Observer* 'were clearly seen defusing tension, pushing Catholic youths away from police lines and the loyalists . . . ' Alan McQuillan, according to the *Guardian*, 'praised leading members of the IRA'. The leading RUC figure was reported as having said, 'Very senior members of the Republican movement, Provisional IRA, were clearly involved in marshalling the protest. And when some young people did begin to throw missiles they moved in to stop it'. Mary Holland writing in the *Irish Times* claimed that 'PSNI' officers privately admitted the Provisionals' part in stabilizing the situation.

In reflecting on the behaviour of the Provisional IRA in all of this, the words used by Amanda Platell to describe some in the Tory Party spring to mind:

> With every crude attempt to appear normal and nice, these

people become more ludicrous. Their pursuit of niceness is like Michael Jackson's pursuit of whiteness: Everything they do to try to become that which they are not makes them slightly more grotesque.

The sense of a community being ill at ease with some aspects of Provisional behaviour was also indicated by a report from Suzanne Breen who claimed that 'Provisional IRA and Sinn Fein activists who arrived at Rosapenna Court after a Catholic man was shot in the thigh were given a hard time by some residents who claimed the Provos had left them undefended'.

This continuing tension in the area has further manifested itself in tensions between the Provisionals and the INLA. The *Irish Echo* reported that 'prominent members of the INLA were seen, in one case remonstrating with prominent members of the Provisional IRA who were restraining riotous youths'. Two writers who co-authored a book on the INLA and who obviously have sources within the organisation wrote separately in the *Observer* and *Irish Echo* that a meeting took place between the IRA and the INLA over the situation in Ardoyne. The Provisionals were allegedly furious at INLA involvement in the conflict, which they felt was destabilising the district, a major change in outlook for the Provisionals given that Ardoyne was at the forefront of a ruthless sectarian war prosecuted by the Provisional IRA over a two-year period from the end of 1974 to the beginning of 1977.

Other reports from Ardoyne suggest that Gerry Kelly was verbally harangued at a public meeting held in one of the local clubs. Some people allegedly went as far as to demand that he be removed from the platform of speakers.

One journalist privately posed the question what would the cops do if the IRA were to disband—who then would keep rebellion off the streets? In the view of one Provisional Republican it is the streets that are the key. 'The leadership is aware that it is from street confrontations that any alternative leadership may emerge'. In his view, before the leadership can embrace the RUC it needs to ultimately manage and defuse both the conflict at the interface areas and the problems that arise out of Orange marches.

> It is these two issues that bring nationalist youth into conflict with the RUC. We may see the leadership trying to take the heat out of matters by organizing street parties or cultural events within the areas to coincide with these marches. They would tell us some nonsense that this was a new form of protest.

The interface areas seem to be moving toward joint Republican-Loyalist management, already germinating from the Sinn Fein meetings with the Loyalist Commission, which knit the managerial strata from each camp closer together. The Provisional Republican continued:

> The leadership need to be able to show the Brits that they alone are the power within their communities and that their ability to deliver cannot be undermined by others. There are no circumstances in which they would allow any challenge to take place.

This reasoning would appear to go to the heart of the matter. The nature of the Provisional relationship to the nationalist community has evolved from one of loosely defending it to a position of tightly controlling it. Nonstifled and porous community self-expression whether on the streets or in print is treated as an anathema that needs to be blocked. Those who see republicanism as being something other than the property of a social climbing leadership clique maintaining itself through the power of patronage and crass nepotism, and eager to simply emulate those whom republicanism traditionally stood foursquare against could do much worse than ask, 'Who shall liberate us from our liberators'?

Hammering Dissent

The Blanket, 5 January 2003

It is not that often I would be in Downpatrick. The last time was almost ten years ago and then it was to visit lifelong Republican friends. This occasion saw me there to talk with other Republicans. Ten years back, whatever this or that difference between us all, we could at least complain or boast of belonging to a Republican community oppressed and harassed by the British. Things have moved on since then. Only some Republicans now face harassment. Most galling is that it is not at the hands of the British but instead is currently inflicted by other Republicans who once faced it themselves.

As a result of *The Blanket* having previously highlighted the plight of those Republicans still opposed to the administration of British rule in Ireland—regardless of who administers it—we had been asked to go to Downpatrick to speak with the parents of a young man who was the victim of a shooting carried out, we were informed, by Stormont republicanism. It was a familiar story. With nothing to show for the war other than an end to the war, those who ordered it waged react with violent fury to others who challenge their writ. Joe O'Connor in Belfast, Paddy Fox in Tyrone, Micky Donnelly in Derry—all these Republicans previously faced the wrath of the Green shirts; now the malevolence has spread to Downpatrick—its victim, Kevin Perry.

We arrived in the home of Francie and Geraldine Perry in the early afternoon. It was the first time that we had met either of the couple. We found them agitated and uneasy but determined. They were not going silently into the night while their son lay in the local hospital, incapacitated by five bullet wounds. They would have their say. And *The Blanket*—being a Section 31 free zone—would give them a platform from which to say it.

Geraldine Perry sat on a chair in her kitchen smoking while she spoke to us at the table. These were working-class people in a working-class home. The locality in which they lived reminded me more of Ballymurphy than Norfolk on the Glen Road. Few Armani suits would be found hanging in the wardrobes in these homes. She explained to me and my colleague that six days before Christmas her son Kevin was dragged from his house by five men into a back garden and shot in the shins, ankles and hands. He had also been subjected to ferocious attack, which involved the use of a hammer and a nail bar, leaving him with a hundred stitches. Before asking her what organisation was responsible, I smiled and commented that on another occasion when I asked a question like this and published the answer Sinn Fein sent a Glenbryn-type hate mob to my home to rant and rave, threaten and berate. Like the Holy Cross School parents, obviously undeterred—they can come back howling if they want—I proceeded with my business. Geraldine claimed that Kevin was adamant that the people who shot him were members of the Provisional IRA. The local Provisionals in the town were also said to be boasting that he was one of their victims. Word came back through the Republican grapevine to the family that the reason being put about for the shooting was that Kevin had threatened a senior member of the IRA, something the hospitalised man strenuously denies.

The backdrop to the shooting was laid out for us by Geraldine. In September 2001, her son Pat was attacked at a Sinn Fein function in Downpatrick by party members. 'The attack took place in the toilet of the premises where the function was being held. A prominent member of Sinn Fein held Pat down while party colleagues kicked him about the head and body'. Those who carried out the assault claimed that Pat had ties with an alternative Republican grouping. This was to prove the catalyst of a slander campaign. 'Since then a prominent member of Sinn Fein in South Down has criticised the family for over a year on the basis of anything he can. He has waged a campaign of slander and innuendo'. Geraldine fiercely disputed the allegation against Pat. In any event, it does seem strange that he would turn up at a Sinn Fein function if he was a member of an alternative Republican grouping.

Geraldine did point out, however, that the Christmas prior to the assault on Pat, his brother Kevin—now hospitalised—despite holding strong Republican beliefs had made enemies within the Provisional Republican movement. The latter told him he was persona non grata after he had the temerity to complain about malpractices being indulged in by some within that movement. In his view their activities were bringing republicanism into disrepute but the present leadership seemed prepared to let things go as it had lost its way.

In April 2002 there was an attempt to shoot Pat. At the time it was not clear who was behind it. The family readily admit to having differences of opinion over the likely perpetrators. But then local Provisionals began to boast in the town pubs that it was they who had targeted Pat. Geraldine, worried out of her mind, admits there are times when the thought occurs to her that the local Sinn Fein councillor has been in some way responsible for her house being subjected to RUC searches: 'Is it just to reassure themselves that there will never be anything in this house so that when they attack it they can do so in the knowledge that everyone here is defenceless'? She says, however, that she has no evidence that the councillor in question has done any such thing.

Geraldine complained bitterly of a sustained campaign in the local media waged against her and her two sons. Her husband Francie says, 'We have lived here all our lives and suddenly in the past year we have just become criminals'. Like his wife, he is in no doubt that the senior local Sinn Fein member has been feeding the local paper this line. He also claims that the same official has been trying to circulate a spurious story that 'dissident Republicans' carried out the attack on Kevin.

Geraldine added that a sign of the power the Provisionals are allowed to have is that such a spin can go unchallenged in the media and that the media virtually ignored the shooting to begin with. 'What chance have ordinary people in these estates when a gang can just shoot you and the media turns its back'?

The family's worries are compounded by an additional factor. Geraldine cares for her infirm seventy-two-year old mother Mary in the house. After the shooting incident involving Pat, the care workers were taken off as the location was now considered too dangerous for them to work in. Geraldine then tried to circumvent this problem by applying for a home in nearby Drumaness. While the Housing Executive claimed that the family had fulfilled all the necessary criteria for the application to be granted, the arrival of a bullet at Housing Executive premises led the Executive to conclude that the Perry family were at risk of death if they were allocated the house and the offer was subsequently withdrawn. That decision may now be subject to a judicial review.

As a result of the family's concerns over this type of friction they approached Sinn Fein. Two party officials visited the home and told them they would deal with the matter and would return within two weeks. According to Francie, before the two weeks had expired, 'We found out how they intended dealing with the matter—Kevin was beaten with hammers and shot'.

Francie concluded our discussion by saying that the family was really fearful for the safety of their sons:

> The police came last week and told us that Pat's life was under threat. While they refused to tell us who was behind the threat, it is clear that coming immediately after the shooting of Kevin the Provisionals are behind it. We call on Sinn Fein and the IRA to state publicly and clearly that neither organisation poses any threat to the safety or lives of our sons and that both will be allowed to get on with their daily lives.

We were not surprised by what the Perry family had to tell us. We had heard similar accounts all too often in the past. We had no reason to disbelieve their version of events but that did not prevent us from asking others what they thought. One former Republican prisoner, who no longer actively engages in political life, told us:

The Provos want to run the show and still any dissension arising out of opposition to their participation in the peace process and their future participation in the PSNI. Good people have been put out of the Republican movement as soon as they began to ask questions. Kevin Perry and his brother are no better or worse than any of the other young men in this town. Kevin's behaviour since he spoke out against the Sinn Fein setup is no different from what it was before he spoke up. Then he was a decent guy. The minute he disagreed with them he became 'antisocial'.

What really happened? The Provos decided to blacken him because they could not face criticism or dissent. The only way that the type of activity described in this article will end is for the Sinn Fein leadership to come clean about the limitations of its strategy. Republicans opposed to the present strategy know that the Provisional IRA lost the war. Rather than hounding those who wish to say just that, the Sinn Fein leadership should accept responsibility for leading us into a war that could not be won and that was ultimately ended on terms that were on offer in 1973. Persistently dissembling that the Republican struggle was somehow successful and that the present strategy is the continuation of it by other means rather than the abandonment of that struggle entirely fools only those who wish to be fooled and leads others to feel they were cheated rather than defeated. The ingredients for tension are built in to the process of denial. Tariq Ali complained recently about those with power treating citizens like children so that 'they can carry on spoon-feeding them lies'. A leadership not honest about its achievements will continuously feel the need to suppress those who are. The emperor has no clothes. What is so terrible about that? Denying it.

Living in Fear

The Blanket, 15 September 2003

rendan Shannon, or Shando, as he is more widely known through-out the Republican community, is a veteran Republican. Hailing from a West Belfast Republican family whose own involvement pre-dated the peculiar phenomenon of provisional republicanism, forty-seven-year-old Shando has a particular attachment to the values of traditional republicanism. Listening to him speak, it is impossible to ignore his passion, a fervent belief that republicanism is almost geneti-cally inherited, situated in and transmitted through the blood of his parents, both of whom were staunch Republicans of the old school. James Connolly stayed in his father's house on the Falls Road beside the Mill. He was there to talk to the workers. His paternal grand-mother kept the chair Connolly had stood upon from which to ad-dress his working-class audience. An aunt, unfortunately, later broke it up and burnt it, replacing it with a more fashionable one. Shando's father was attacked when he walked Leeson Street to court his future wife who lived in that area. That was the 'Devlin' era, when British imperialism ruled the roost and seemed to have no shortage of sup-porters in the Falls. Shando's father took to carrying his hurl from then on and often needed it. Republicanism seemed thin on the ground in those days and according to Shando it seems like the past is once again visiting itself upon West Belfast and making Republicans unwelcome in their own streets.

For many of us who were solely Provisional in constitution and out-look, 1916 and the values that traditional republicanism engendered, while honourable, are hardly what substantively shapes our political perception or activity. More anti-British policy than British presence, quite often Crumlin Road courthouse was as far as our attachment to the Republican tradition went. Once in the dock we were unable to curb our eagerness to shout, 'Guilty, your honour', loud enough so that the beak would be in no doubt that we meant it and would then go easy on us. All of the men and women of the GPO could not force us to turn our back on the cretin and face the spiritual direction of Pearse and the certain frugality that would accompany it. We were happy to be placed firmly outside the MacSwiney paradigm of enduring rather than inflicting. For those of us not attired in the holy grail there was little essentially wrong with that. Settling for a life sentence when ten years was on offer seemed to be taking republicanism a step—or a lot of extra years—too far.

Generally speaking, this lack of being baptised and schooled in the Republican tradition may go some way toward explaining why we ditched Republicanism so easily and ended up happily discussing what is the most effective way to administer British rule and what type of RUC would we put up with. For those carved from the quintessential Republican tradition such flexibility is a curse. It is tantamount to taking the white feather. In its dazzling white bosom there comfortably rests a fertile disdain for the type of compromises and capitulations that have come to characterise the republicanism of Sinn Fein. Fidelity to the Pearsean notion is very strong. For the 1916 icon any man who accepted:

> anything less by one fraction of an iota than separation from England . . . is guilty of so immense an infidelity, so immense a crime against the Irish nation, that one can only say of him that it were better for that man (as it were certainly better for his country) that he had not been born.

The Republican tradition demands a lot from its adherents. We may dismiss them, find them out of touch, not living in the modern world, glorifying the use of physical force, incapable of dialectically comprehending leadership-led revolutionary somersaultism and progressive censorship, but we cannot wish them away. We armed them with guns and legitimacy, we told them who it was legitimate to kill, that one Irish person alone had the inalienable right to kill all and sundry so long as it was predicated on the intention to remove the British from Ireland. And now they hang there as a mirror letting us know that they are what we promised to be forever. The image we see there is so unlike what we are now that on occasion the impulse to lash out with the power of Armani to obliterate the duffle coat is so strong that we might even kill or disappear them, all the while seeking to forget that each time we do so we kill and disappear part of ourselves. The Republican tradition visited us with a ready-made answer in 1969 and we embraced it. There is nothing we can do that will erase our fingerprints from it.

Shando professes loyalty to the Republican tradition that provisionalism wishes would go away. He was interned at the age of seventeen and remained under lock and key until twenty-one. In 1979 he was captured along with two others in possession of IRA weapons and received a twelve-year sentence. He joined the Blanket protest and stayed on it until its conclusion in 1981, living through the most intense and horrendous period in modern Republican jail history. He was released in 1986. He insists that regardless of his past he is not a member of any political or military organisation. His Republican activism these days is restricted to supporting Republican prisoners. For this reason he has attended rallies organised by the Irish Republican Prisoners Welfare Association, which is aligned to the 32 County Sovereignty Committee. However, he claims that his support is for all Republican prisoners, including those belonging to the Provisional IRA. 'I was in jail as a Provisional IRA volunteer. I am not going to turn my back on their volunteers who face a similar fate'. In that sense he will strike many as being both more honest and loyal than the Provisional leadership, who seem clearly embarrassed at the mention of Provisional IRA prisoners.

Despite being 'a lifelong Republican' he now lives in fear that he may be killed by the organisation to which he gave so much of his life merely because his political beliefs are no longer shared by his former comrades. A mere few hours before I interviewed him the PSNI had called to both his home and workplace to warn him of an imminent threat to his life. When I spoke with him he was articulate and witty. When I expressed my dismay at *The Blanket* having to meet him in a secret location, he quipped, 'Better than in a secret grave'.

The fact that we knocked around together in prison helped relax him but beneath the garrulous surface it was easy to detect an anxiety. He genuinely fears becoming one of the disappeared. He doubts that the practice has stopped as 'very few people are persuaded by Sinn Fein that the Provisional IRA did not disappear Gareth O'Connor'.

I put it to him that the Provisional IRA may be less concerned with attacking dissident Republicans per se and may be motivated as a result of the recent Real IRA killing of Danny McGurk in the Lower Falls. People are unhappy at the death and the Provisionals may be responding to local pressure. And while his name was certainly not amongst those doing the rounds with the dogs on the street as one of the culprits, the Provisionals may feel that with his standing within the Republican world lending weight to Real IRA prisoners, they should mop him up as part of the internal housekeeping for which the British state seems willing to provide a certain latitude. He responded by saying that this was nonsense. The animosity of the Provisionals toward him results solely from 'my refusal to agree with them anymore'. He illustrates this by detailing his history of harassment at the hands of the Provisional IRA.

> I was kidnapped by the Provos seven years ago and was ac-cused of being a member of a dissident organisation. They told me that if I became engaged in any military activity against the British they would kill me. Four years later I was summoned to meet them and when I agreed to go they told me that I was not to be seen in the company of more than four dissident Republicans at any one time, otherwise they would view this as evidence of membership and loyalty to such an organisation and they would kill me as a result.

You wouldn't get that type of law in South Africa under the apartheid regime. I take the Provisional threat very seriously. Gareth O'Connor is missing and Jo Jo O'Connor was murdered.

He claims that since 1995 he has more or less been at the receiving end of hassle from Provisional Republicans who find it impossible to tolerate Republicans who continue to hold the beliefs that the Provisionals themselves once killed and died for. I asked him when did he begin to have doubts about the direction in which the Provisionals were going.

When the peace process took off and the cease-fire was called I supported the strategy and was actually involved in heated exchanges at Republican family meetings with those who expressed reservations about the direction of the movement. I took part in one of the first Sinn Fein protests up at Stormont during the peace process so it is not as if I am opposed to politics. It is the type of politics that I call into question. When was this ever part of the Republican outlook? I will support solid and sound politics but not this farce. I was a staunch supporter of the peace process, but that was when it still had a semblance of republicanism about it and we could stretch ourselves to the point of believing that it might be possible to advance Republican objectives. Can anyone truly say that Republican objectives have been moved forward by all of this? It has become apparent that the leadership have been lying through their teeth. And now it has come to the point where they are prepared to kill and disappear those who refuse to accept the lies and are upfront about their opposition.

He did, however, at the time express concern to one senior Republican and was told that we either have everything or nothing. 'Give it six months'. Now, nine years on 'it is blatantly clear that we have nothing'. Not prepared to wait as long as many others, he severed his links with the Provisionals in 1995 when the six months passed and the only thing being discussed was the Framework document.

> I was a member of the Sticks at sixteen and I left them because they called a cease-fire and it was clear that they had got nothing. But I am not some rabid militarist. I actually supported the political strategy that the leadership promised would deliver. I did not leave the Provos because they gave up the war. I left because they gave up republicanism.

I mused to myself that he could now claim to have left the Sticks twice. Resentment also formed part of his narrative.

> My father brought guns in to the Falls in 1969. I remember him taking them out of a dirty oily bag. Then sound people got their hands on the weapons. Now that they are in the hands of dirty oily politicians, they are being given away and I am forced to ask why did my father ever bother bringing them in to begin with and why did I have to go to jail for possessing them? I missed my kids growing up as a result of being in jail, they missed their father—all because of holding on to guns the leadership have now given up. And to make matters worse, these people are prepared to let Scappaticci run about but kill me.

But could he not stand up and reject the physical force tradition as others including many of us at *The Blanket* have done? This might get the Provisionals off his back.

It hasn't got them off your back. My political beliefs are the same as they have always been. If the British state is here through force of arms, then the Irish people have the right to resist them through force of arms. This is the exact same sort of beliefs I had when I was with those who head Sinn Fein today.

But does that not mean that he is going to give succor and perhaps support to those groups that continue to wage armed campaigns that invariably result in defeat and leave a trail of human misery in their wake?

I merely want to get on with my life and bring up my kids. While I do not actively support any of those involved in physical force republicanism, I refuse to join in with all the hypocrites and condemn any Republican carrying on armed struggle. The position I hold on this was for long enough the position of Sinn Fein and I do not see why I should have to abandon it to suit the agenda of those who have given up their republicanism. Fascism is what characterises the Provos today. The war we fought was to secure democracy and now we are further away from democracy within these communities than ever. The very least I expected to obtain from this war was to be on equal terms with the Unionists. Now I am further down the food chain than anybody. Touts and drug dealers get a better deal in Republican communities than Republicans who oppose the present strategy. Druggies, thieves, and rapists can walk the streets unharmed but if you are a dissident Republican, then you are scum.

Would he not go to the mainstream media and try to highlight his case?

Are you serious? The media have been abominable. They simply do not want to upset the apple cart. The media are prepared to turn a blind eye while we have the absurd position whereby the Provos are prepared to kill so long as it is in defence of the peace process. What sort of process is it? We had the debacle at Stormont where the Alliance Party pretended to be Unionists for an hour to keep the whole farce up and running. And they are going to kill me—a Republican—to maintain that.

Is there no one in authority he can appeal to or put pressure on in order to get the situation resolved?

The British government stink. They are prepared to turn a blind eye to my murder. Tony Blair and Hugh Orde have both said that the IRA cease-fire is intact despite Orde conceding that they killed Gareth O'Connor. It means the IRA have a license to murder their own people but nobody else.

The British government not being the type of authority I had in mind, I asked him had he considered approaching his local MP?

Gerry Adams has the power to put a stop to this. He can call them off and prevent my murder and that of other Republicans who oppose the direction in which his movement had gone. At one time I saw myself getting up at six o'clock in the morning to go out on his election campaign to ensure that he would be elected. And to what end? If he wishes to he can ensure that I or no one else is murdered or disappeared. I have spent my life fighting injustice and I am in contact with others who feel badly let down by the way this has worked out. We cannot stay silent on these matters. People in authority just turn a blind eye to all of this. There is a need for those of us opposed to what is happening to come together and build a Republican group that will defend the rights of people in these communities. There are many problems in them but they cannot be solved by disappearing and killing people. If you are not in the Sinn Fein clique you are no better than human waste. Your life is of no value to Sinn Fein if you are not a member of the 'yes' gang. Sinn Fein have given up their beliefs and are now motivated by power. The ideals that lay behind our struggle are no longer sacrosanct.

It was with a large measure of regret that I left Shando to make the journey back home. We had spent many years in the H-Blocks winding, mixing, debating, backstabbing, furiously disagreeing with each other—myself and Tommy Gorman tortured him remorselessly as he lay in bed incapacitated by the flu. It was what he would have done to us given half a chance. It was simply all the usual things that prisoners do to put in the hours. Most of it was jovial. Our interview two days ago was the first time ever that sombreness dominated the exchanges. What saddened me most was that he was the same Shando from the jail, professing the same ideas and sentiments. And now he lived in the shadow of fear because in his view to succumb to groupthing was to succumb to some dictator ordaining that it should be so.

Shando holds to an analysis that I have long since abandoned. But on this I find common purpose with him: Whatever the problems that afflict these areas, capital punishment is infinitely worse than any of them. That more than anything else should be resisted. If the power structure is prepared to kill us for speaking out against it, all the more reason for speaking out.

The Rite of Passage

The Blanket, 3 October 2003

> *Those who can make you believe absurdities*
> *can make you commit atrocities.*
>
> —VOLTAIRE

Unfortunately but frequently *The Blanket* has, without hesitation, found itself in the position of giving voice to those whom wider and more powerful forces would seek to silence. Often these are the voices of 'dissident Republicans'. On occasion associates of the 'antisocial' fraternity too have had their say. In such cases *The Blanket* virtually never shares the perspective of those whose voices have broken free from the vow of silence imposed on them by more powerful institutions. But their right to speak is as inviolable as the desire to silence them is malevolent.

Few seriously dispute that for a number of years there has been an ongoing systematic campaign by the Provisional Republican movement to suppress those other Republicans who are opposed to the Provisionals' political project, which basically amounts to the naked pursuit of institutional power characterised by a willingness to ditch every tenet of republicanism in order to make the journey into officialdom easier. Rite of passage from a position of radical critique to one of conservative entrenchment invariably involves undergoing a certain ritual. Stamping on former comrades is like a symbolic public act of circumcision whereby the radical boy becomes a conservative man—the bloody and sharpened knife has to be brandished in order to demonstrate that the snip is complete.

For the most part the Provisional campaign of suppression is subtle and insidious. But from time to time the coercion is brutal and public as in the case of Gerry Adams' West Belfast constituent, Jo Jo O'Connor, who was left dead in the street in front of local people, including children. Only a matter of weeks ago the case of Brendan Shannon, who now lives under the burden of a death threat, was raised in the pages of this journal. So obsessed is provisional republicanism with emulating the strategy of the Workers Party that, with a measure of state and media complicity, there has been no abatement in its willingness to defend the process and disregard the peace. Seemingly, the peace process is not a peaceful process.

In the early hours of yesterday morning a member of the 32 County Sovereignty Movement was abducted by armed men in South Belfast. Although the 32 CSM contends that Stephen Moore's abductors claimed to be members of the Provisional IRA and that they had threatened his young girlfriend, the father of the girl has disputed this on both counts. Moore, who has in the past been the target of police pressure aimed at coercing him into becoming an informer, was, according to Marian Price, harangued by a senior Provisional late last month that if he did not hand himself over for interrogation at the hands of Sinn Fein's secret police he would face the same fate as Gareth O'Connor. The latter vanished while travelling from his Armagh home to Dundalk Garda station earlier this year. 'Members of the Provisionals told Stephen he had to hand himself in to them to be cleared by them. He refused, but the men told him if he didn't they would do a Gareth O'Connor on him'. Apart from being redolent of the arrogant triumphalism of the Argentine military (it too lost the war), this has added ballast to the already weighty suspicion that the Provisionals were behind the Armagh City man's disappearance. In a poignant twist, the mother of Gareth O'Connor last night rang Marian Price to inquire had Stephen turned up yet. In the view of Marian Price the deluge of relief that engulfed the woman was audible. Bernie O'Connor was uplifted to find that Stephen Moore's mother would not have to face the ordeal that the Armagh family has underwent since May. She expressed the wish to Marian Price that the Provisional IRA would disclose the location of her son's whereabouts.

Despite all its howling over the years about RUC and prison service ill treatment it seems that the Provisional movement, far from defeating those opponents, has been both outfoxed and influenced by their methods. People who try to excuse by way of contextualisation violently suppressing other voices through recourse to some grand meta-narrative—the peace process—have themselves become constituted by the very unequal power relations they profess to oppose. In a statement from the 32 County Sovereignty Movement it was claimed that:

> Stephen was stripped naked, had his head and face covered in duct tape, and then dressed in a white paper overall. His captors then bound his hands and feet behind his back and left him in a cold damp derelict house until this morning. He was then interrogated about antiagreement Republicans and told he was about to be shot. Apparently after a commotion outside Stephen was given his clothes and released.

Also, according to Marian Price, a woman visited friends of the kidnapped man in the Lower Ormeau Road and told them if the press or police were notified 'there would be serious repercussions'. Local people have told *The Blanket* that the woman in question was a member of Sinn Fein.

Stephen Moore is a West Belfast man. His constituency MP has on many occasions faced the accusation that he is also a member of the Provisional IRA's Army Council, an allegation the Sinn Fein president swats away with limp-wristed conviction, the Sinn Fein cumann in Outer Mongolia apparently alone in believing him. West Belfast Republicans who dissent from the current Sinn Fein leadership should not be cowered into a soundproof corner where their protestations go unheard. Nor should they play by the rules of the game the British and Irish governments are happy to host whereby all must acquiesce in the regime of deceit, which has become the lifeblood of the peace process. They should employ a counter discourse, which reverses and disrupts the linguistic falsities and niceties of the political class by publicly and vociferously stating that they want parity of esteem. This means openly demanding from every rooftop that, like other constituents governed by the British parliament, they cannot be murdered, mutilated, or abducted on the orders of their Westminster MP. Had Enoch Powell faced similar accusations in relation to his black constituents in Wolverhampton there would have been a public outcry. As Liam Kennedy observes, 'We inhabit a strange, deformed society'. Finchley, West Belfast definitely is not.

The Provisional Republican leadership could do worse than pay attention to the words of Danny Morrison who astutely addressed the matter of internecine bloodletting: 'Most feuds were initiated by leaderships who could not handle challenge and dissidence. It is important to persistently engage in dialogue, to listen, and to realise, above all, the humanity of the people who frustrate, anger, threaten, and even attack you'. Unfortunately, such a scenario seems as far away as the Provisional IRA Army Council becoming poverty-stricken.

Kidnapped

The Blanket, 2 November 2003

> *Mothers throughout Haiti threaten their children with the*
> *legend of Ton Ton Macoute, the malevolent spirit who comes*
> *in the night and steals bad children from their beds.*
> *What these women and their children do not realize is that the*
> *danger is very, very real, and it's not just the bad children*
> *who are taken.*

When Brendan Rice called to my home, it was the first time I had met him. He and a relative had made the journey from Newcastle, County Down. It is only an hour's drive from Belfast and the road between the two has been well covered by holidaymakers for as long as people care to remember. It's hardly surprising that Newcastle deservedly makes the news as a tourist attraction and not as a town at the hub of political controversy and violence. Throughout my time in prison, the amount of Newcastle men I met could just about be counted on the fingers of one foot. Well, there was one, possibly two.

I had previously spoken to one of the men, who now sat at my kitchen table, on the phone. Earlier, an approach had been made via a third party. I took the number and made a mental note to ring but it went clean out of my head. Within days the third party was back on the phone pressing me to contact the Rice family. The matter was urgent and it had escaped me. Perhaps it was because the type of incident that was to be raised had been dealt with so many times before that it had sort of become routine. Brendan Shannon, Stephen Moore, Kevin Perry, Danny McBrearty . . . and on it goes—totally unfair to those in search of help when those they seek it from file away their concerns as if it were yesterday's newspaper. I thought of other situations much worse than our own sordid and squalid bickering that we continue to dignify with the term 'conflict' and which we are in 'struggle' trying to resolve. I recalled Jacobo Timerman, meeting families of loved ones hauled off by the Argentinean military while he was a newspaper editor, before he too was hauled off and tortured for championing the cause of the disappeared. I wondered if he ever grew complacent. A momentary lapse in Buenos Aires could mean the difference between life and death, a roll on effect beginning with a call not made, an official paper authorising continued detention or release not signed, a helicopter journey for some drugged and tortured victim to a watery grave not aborted.

Our task here is immeasurably easier. While we do our utmost to protect those Republicans under threat from pro-state factions, there is no real comparison that can be drawn between the repression those Republicans experience and that undergone by Argentinean leftists. Since the cease-fires there have been at most two physical force Republicans murdered by forces loyal to the Stormont regime. We don't live in constant fear of Sinn Fein coming round to spirit us away in the middle of the night and ghost us off to an unmarked grave. When asked by people do I think the Sinn Fein leadership will ever order the murder of any of *The Blanket's* writers, I invariably respond, 'probably not'.

I rang the number passed on to me and after a short conversation arranged a meeting. When they arrived I was struck by the sense of anger they exuded. It was the anger of impotence in the face of abusive power. I had seen it before, felt it traverse through my veins while trying to prevent my face from making contact with the urine stained black floor of an H-Block corridor in the 1970s and 80s, during the mirror search while on blanket protest when solitariness, nakedness, and silence come face to face with organised teams, uniforms, and harsh commands.

Brendan Rice's story was simple. I could have narrated it myself by now. The experience is the same; only the names and locations are different. Around 10 o'clock on a Saturday evening a number of weeks ago he was about to enter his home when a group of men approached him and began to attack him. 'They used their fists and feet and threatened to shoot me if I did not stop resisting them'. Although they told Brendan they were armed, they did not produce any weapons. Once he was subdued they stated that they were members of the Provisional IRA and told him that he was under arrest. 'With or without their PSNI uniforms'? I enquired of him, sarcasm lacing my words.

Once his captors secured him by binding his wrists and ankles with plastic straps, he was kicked in the face and sustained a broken nose. The image of H-Block 4's senior officer letting me have his soft black boot full throttle in the face in September 1978 as I lay on the floor with my hands pinioned behind my back flooded my mind. Power loves to kick in the face when its victim is sprawling and defenceless. It is enamoured of the notion that its target can actually see the boot coming but is helpless to deflect it.

Brendan Rice was then bundled into a van, trussed up and blindfolded, and driven for some distance. He was taken out of the vehicle and then put in an outbuilding for approximately fifteen minutes before being transported to a car and then to the roads once again. At the end of this second journey he was taken to another outbuilding and was questioned throughout the night by three men taking it in turns to be his interrogator. The allegations they levelled at him were that he was involved in extortion. 'Did you answer them'? I asked, hoping that his reply would have been that he told them his name, address, and that he was over twenty-one. That's what we always told cops and nothing could induce us to volunteer anything more than what was required by law. Why treat Sinn Fein's cops any differently?

> I couldn't answer questions I knew nothing about. Yet they continued to beat me about the head with their fists and they kicked me also. They threatened to shoot me or put me in a barrel of water and hold me under until I told them what they wanted to hear. They then asked if I was a member of the Real IRA. They said if I was I was only a small fish. They

made allegations against other people, including members
of my family and said they would get them. They also tried
to frighten me by suggesting I could be disappeared, that I
was a single fella—who would know what had happened to
me? After a while they told me they knew I was not involved
in extortion and that they believed I had a drink problem. I
would be released. After securing a promise from me not to
attack them they cut me free.

Brendan was then put into a car, all the time blindfolded. The car
was driven for a while before drawing to a halt. He was then taken out
and put facedown on the ground where his blindfold was removed.

Then they started to give me a third kicking. All of this happened after they told me I had a drink problem and was not
involved in extortion of any kind. I was pointed in the direction of what they said was a phone box and told to get on
my way. I did as they ordered and eventually I met a woman
who made a call for me. A relative came and picked me up.

The relative of Brendan Rice who sat with him throughout the interview for *The Blanket* said that he felt the kidnapping of Brendan was
in response to work a family member had done in support of Republican prisoners in Maghaberry. He claimed that it was not the first time
a member of the Rice family had been kidnapped. In 1975, a brother
of Brendan, Frankie, was abducted and murdered by loyalists.

It took place on a Saturday night. Throughout Sunday morning
the family had to sit undergoing terrible anxiety before they finally
learned that Frankie was dead. Now on this occasion the family had to
go through a similar experience. Thankfully, Brendan returned home
but these people who did this to him have the cheek to call themselves
Republicans and claim to be protecting us.

During Brendan's ordeal other family members went to a Sinn Fein councillor to see if he could secure Brendan's release. While he went off to find out what he could, he stressed that he believed it might have been the work of dissident Republicans. This was nonsense and he must have realised it himself. The question that the Rice family now ask is this: Are the people who carried this out behaving with the approval of the Provisional Republican leadership? If not, then does that leadership accept that the community can now regard the kidnappers as common criminals?

> Our family has been heavily involved with the Republican movement over three decades. Our door was always open. Now we find that those who call themselves Republican are stooping to the levels of loyalists, kidnapping, terrorising, threatening, and beating other Republicans they don't like.

Brendan asked: 'Are people willing to vote for these thugs? Is this the vision of the new police force they have been promising to achieve for years? Do we really need a police force that is worse than the RUC ever were'?

They left my home to make their way back to Newcastle. The path they beat to and from my front door had been well trodden by others who came here to put on public record their experiences at the hands of Stormont republicanism. Later in the day as I reflected on our exchange, it struck me that in the discourse of those they seek to repress, Provisional IRA volunteers feature ever more frequently as some sort of right-wing militia eager to defend whatever reactionary position the leadership adopts in its lurch for respectability. Some observers try to explain it away in terms of the ranks being populated by former joyriders and ex-hoods determined never to be caught in possession of a political idea and who see value in having some political cover for their otherwise self-serving activities. Other commentators have noticed that a common refrain in working-class nationalist areas is 'big house, big car, and big wallet', although from what I can see, those on the ground who fought the war seem to have little in the way of material assets to show for it. Many eke out just enough to get by on the margins of the economy, struggle daily with poverty, live frugally, are not revellers on the junket circuit, and do not own the latest model Jeep or 'houses on the hill'—a form of destitution that cannot be said to extend to their leaders. Perhaps there are some around grassroots level who do feel that if the leadership's idea of knitting both parts of Ireland together is for leaders to own houses on each side of the border, then they too should have a slice of the cake. But they, like the former hoods and joyriders, are a minority amongst volunteers and can hardly be considered the primary determinant governing the strong-arm behaviour and political thought policing that IRA activists are increasingly associated with.

A more sustainable explanation is that the Sinn Fein leadership, which admires alternative ideas as a vampire does sunrises, is determined to muffle, if not effectively silence, those who oppose its writ. The merest hint of dissent infuriates it by publicly reminding it, in spite of its narcissism, of how little it actually achieved in return for all the people it both put to and sent to their deaths. As John Kenneth Galbraith said, 'Nothing is so admirable in politics as a short memory'. The realpolitik of the peace process, however, means that the leadership cannot murder 'the opposition' at will, but like a bully will operate on the principle of instilling fear in those considered less powerful—an insidious activity that both British and Irish governments pretend not to see. Who was the last cop to face a punishment attack?

IRA volunteers, who today support the opposite of what they supported yesterday, would have little internal difficulty persuading themselves that if the Sinn Fein leadership want somebody roughed up or worse, then there must be a good reason for it. And in their hopelessly apolitical way they are willing to serve as the cutting edge: an Irish version of the Ton Ton Macoute determined to protect the venal power structure that sponsors it. As I persistently remind a black friend, gays and blacks living in these communities may hope the Sinn Fein leadership does not come to view them as they do guns—something to be gotten rid of in the hope of increasing the vote. On past form, who in the ranks of the IRA would say 'no'?

CHAPTER 7
Robert McCartney

Burdens Unbearable

The Blanket, 4 February 2005

The Short Strand in Belfast is a mere four miles from where I live. Still, it took about thirty minutes to get there this evening in a taxi as a result of a detour to the south of the city to pick up a friend. St. Matthew's Chapel, which sits on the edge of the district, has a central place in the narrative of provisional republicanism. It was there thirty-five years ago that the leader of the IRA in this city was injured by armed loyalists as he and a couple of comrades, one of whom died, were the only ones preventing the small nationalist enclave to the rear of their position from being overrun and the residents from possibly being murdered and most certainly burned out of their homes. The British army had cut off the two main bridges from the city centre leading into the Short Strand. They had orders not to go in. The IRA leader, a seasoned volunteer with over thirty years experience, had managed to get in ahead of them in time to coordinate a defence effort, which he led from the front. The IRA's own blood on 27 June 1970 marked the line across which the murderous mobs of sectarian hatred would not pass.

Thoughts of an IRA driven by a commitment to protect its own community passed through my mind this evening as I stood in the shadow of St. Matthew's. But it was an IRA far removed from the sentiments of many of those who had gathered to pay tribute to Bert McCartney, who was murdered last weekend by knife wielding psychopaths as dextrous in their slashing and cutting as anyone belonging to the Shankill butchers. People in the crowd with whom I spoke were scathing of Bert McCartney's killers. 'Animals' and 'scum of the earth' were terms used to convey their sense of outrage.

Standing amongst a crowd of what a friend estimated as 1,000 to 1,500 I sensed that this was more than a vigil for a murdered man. It was also a political protest. No statements or political denunciations were necessary. No one carried placards or chanted slogans. A local priest spoke through prayer rather than political critique. It was the conversation in the crowd that said it all. They want their community cleansed of the viciousness that led to Bert McCartney's killing. They seek the apprehension of those who cut short his life. They oppose obstacles placed in the way of police investigations. They implore the Provisional Republican movement—which many of them continue to support—to offer no sanctuary to his killers. They want the many genuine members of that movement to state clearly, 'Not in our name'.

Some Provisionals were there. Others were not. Those who treated Bert McCartney with the same inhuman disdain that Lenny Murphy would have been proud of would hardly be welcome at a vigil in his memory. The Provisionals who were there, by all accounts, were genuinely angry, angry with some of their colleagues for having visited this despicable crime on a member of a community they work to represent. They were at pains to point out that 'the movement' had nothing to do with the murder; that those who had brought so much grief to the community were a disgrace.

Although some Unionists have called this an IRA murder, it was anything but. The IRA was not an accomplice to this killing. If, however, reports from the residents and Republicans of all hues are accurate, then most people believe that thugs associated with the IRA were responsible. While the IRA was not complicit in the murder, the organisation runs the risk of being an accomplice after the fact. Numerous reports are coming out of 'the east' about intimidation of witnesses. People claim to have been threatened by known Republicans trying to impose the code of omerta. One report has it that the local IRA marched into a club less than twenty-four hours before tonight's vigil and demanded that all criticism of 'the movement' cease.

If any of this is true, it paints a picture of an organisation so absorbed in the labyrinthine pursuit of power that it has lost all sight of its own origins. Communities become mere strategic pawns in the wider power play. When justice is a hindrance that stands in the way of the struggle, then the value of the struggle itself must be questioned.

After the vigil we made our way to the home of the deceased man. His body was released today for burial. His cut face told its own story. Gazing on his lifeless form, I wondered if my own thoughts were shared by others: Had the IRA, which selflessly spilt its blood to defend this area, become a home for the worst possible elements in this society—sadistic blackguards who had stepped across that defensive line of IRA blood at St. Matthew's to plunge their knives into the chest of a man from the community the IRA had come into being in order to protect?

Bert McCarthy leaves a wife and two young sons. The grief that weighed down his mother's shoulders was palpable as we offered our sympathies, self-consciously aware of an 'unbearable lightness of being' occasioned by the knowledge that her unbearable sorrow was not on our shoulders. We left the house to an equally unbearable silence that screamed for justice.

Oderint dum Metuant

The Blanket, 9 February 2005

> *Some said the vigil was a sign of the growing unease at the*
> *criminal activities of what one person called a 'Goodfellas'*
> *gang of IRA 'peacetime' paramilitaries. People complained of*
> *IRA punishment beatings, racketeering, intimidation, and*
> *sexual violence over recent years.*
>
> —ANGELIQUE CHRISAFIS, *THE GUARDIAN*

Whatever the time of the year funerals are invariably cold occasions. At least that is how they are stored in and replayed from the memory bank. Looking back over those that I have attended, I cannot think of any that were without chill. The least bit of warmth in the body is involuntarily pushed out by the first peel of the chapel bell, which tolls for the deceased as they begin that final journey to the grave. Even if the day in question was sunny nothing of the sun bursts through when later the mind's playback button is pressed.

Yesterday's funeral in East Belfast for Bert McCartney was a cold occasion in every sense of the word. Those of us who stood outside St. Matthew's Chapel shifted from foot to foot as the funeral Mass took place inside. I watched a senior PSNI member leave the church toward the end and walk by us. The previous day he had appeared on television outlining the progress in the investigation of Bert McCartney's murder. Having been at odds with the cops all my life, I was somewhat surprised and confused by a desire welling up inside me to bid him 'good luck' in his effort to remove the cutthroat killers of Bert McCartney from the streets of Belfast. While I said nothing, the thought that he should have good luck remained with me all day. Watching the victim's distraught loved ones, his tiny children, and anguished friends and neighbours walk in the cortege that winded its way through damp streets, hindered me from wishing failure on the cops. To do so on this one would simply deny justice to everyone who shed tears yesterday. The butchers of Bert McCartney are no different from Mark Wright and James Fisher, the two Scots Guards members who plied their murderous trade to end the life of Peter McBride. Why should the cops be denied the luck needed to ensure Bert's killers no longer stalk Belfast streets?

Watching news coverage of the funeral later in the day, the comments of the officiating priest may have passed me by as eulogising words sincerely offered as a balm to his family were it not for the observation of my wife. She said that the sentiment 'greater love hath no man than this, that a man lay down his life for his friends' showed that Bert had more in common with Bobby Sands than those who murdered him. An image flashed through my mind of Bobby, defenceless and naked in the H-Blocks, surrounded by screws ready to tear into him. Reading Brendan Devine's account in the *Irish News* of how his friend was confronted with thugs reinforced such imagery. Bert had stood, hopelessly outnumbered, holding up his hands as he reasoned with his would-be killers, 'Nobody deserved this. We didn't do anything'. Reason died and hate slithered away to cover up the evidence of its crime.

Talking to locals as the funeral procession weaved its way along the Mountpottinger Road, I listened as they spoke not only of their abhorrence but also their fear. And the source of their fear were members of the organisation that had sprang into existence as their defenders. I teased this out, suggesting that the IRA had never been populated by Shankill Butcher types and would hardly want them about the organisation now. They accepted the logic but protested that some Republicans had visited homes in the area telling people to stop discussing the events surrounding the murder. One longtime Sinn Fein voter mentioned one of those named in the grapevine as having plunged the knife into the two drinking buddies and said, 'You know yourself he is a sadistic scumbag and has been so all his days'. I could hardly dispute it, mentally recalling complaints that came through regularly about the same person when prior to the Good Friday Agreement I had staffed a Sinn Fein office in the Lower Ormeau Road. Had I failed to sufficiently flag it up years ago?

If there is to be any consistency or justice, then the same affront felt within the wider nationalist community when Fisher and Wright were readmitted to the British army needs to be on public display today. If the long stated opposition to a hierarchy of victims is genuine, then there can be no hierarchy of murderers.

Despite what has been said of the IRA in recent weeks, or what motivates its leadership, it is still very difficult to conceive of the body of its membership as being motivated by criminal self-aggrandisement. Some of those named as being suspects in the Northern Bank robbery would have ability in abundance to plan and execute the raid but they would be clueless when it comes to thinking like criminals. The minds they are equipped with lack criminal intent. Yet it is indisputable that a strain of vicious criminality does lurk within the IRA, a parasite feeding off the legitimacy that association with the IRA provides. Its one attitude toward the community it feeds upon is that of the emperor Caligula, 'Oderint dum Metuant' (Let them hate as long as they fear).

In such circumstances it is futile to resort to platitudes and advise those who are frightened that there is nothing to fear but fear itself. That will hardly dissuade the knife plungers from coming to the door. Today's *Guardian* graphically described the fear that grips the community. Yet, if the butchers are not tackled the tyranny of the knife will rule over the lives of the most vulnerable in areas like the Short Strand. There the community has been robbed of one of its most decent members. It cannot be fitting that those who murdered him should find any solace or succour from within that community. No organisation or group should shield them. Bert McCartney's killers have no right to a hiding place. They should be cast to the tender mercies of the Northern Ireland Prison Service, where together with the screws they can share common cause as having participated in the murder of Irishmen willing to lay down their lives for their friends.

Time to Go

The Blanket, 21 February 2005

When I visited the Short Strand home of one of the sisters of the late Robert McCartney, it was the third time in a week that I had been drawn to the area. The previous evening, while travelling through Belfast city centre in a friend's car, a call came through from a member of the McCartney family circle. I was asked would I be able to call over and see Robert's sisters. They had buried their brother two days earlier and were concerned that the sound of the earth that had thudded onto his coffin was uncannily like the sound of Provisional movement attempts to cover up for the crime of murder carried out by an element of its membership. With each crack of its intimidatory rod a further piece of the evidence was pushed under the surface, never to see the light of day again.

Then the courageous intervention of Gerard Quinn, a cousin of the murdered man, who had asked in the letters page of the *Irish News*, 'How does murdering the innocent "protector" of a "respected family" in the local community build an Ireland of equals'? defied the rod. Two journalists in major newspapers picked up on the story and the lucid reporting that appeared in their subsequent coverage thrust the issue centre stage. Throughout the following week the name Robert McCartney blazed like a flaming torch, as his sisters and partner, with incredible dignity and composure, held it aloft, bringing light to areas and matters that have been concealed for years.

Three decades ago, as a young IRA volunteer I had stayed in the Short Strand area while 'on the run'. The community was tough, resilient, and generous. There was never any difficulty in finding a bed, a meal, or a bath. The owner of one of the homes I stayed in was later murdered by loyalists as he went about providing for his young family. The son of another couple met a similar fate. These people were outstanding, their hospitality always something to be remembered. They were a people worthy of nothing less than the highest regard.

The tiny enclave's IRA membership was a determined lot. Their ranks, much depleted by the constant attrition of the British state forces, always managed to be replenished by teenagers willing to defend but never to torment their own community. Some of the area's volunteers never experienced life beyond their teens. Their lives were wrenched violently away from them, 'killed in action' in the ranks of an army for which active service meant service to the community and not service to one's own sense of power over that community.

As a sign of the rapid arrest rate, many of those I met in the Strand would later end up in prison by my side. They had a tendency to clannishness but this had its roots in the sense of siege an isolated community experiences when cut off from its wider hinterland. Their collective stand, many of them mere teenagers, in the face of terrible deprivation and prison management brutality, was driven by a raw courage and a total anathema to any attempt to portray them as criminal, or the community they hailed from. Kicked, beaten, tortured, hosed, starved, they were always first to the door to shout 'up the RA' after every wing shift.

When I sojourned in the Strand it was part of the Belfast Brigade's Third Battalion, which covered virtually all areas outside of West Belfast. The latter had two battalions all to itself. Later, during the 1975 cease-fire the Third Battalion would be split up. The Strand, Markets, and Lower Ormeau Road became the spine of the new Fourth Battalion. Within it, the Strand assumed the greatest importance. Battalion or battalion council meetings were invariably held in the Strand. Most operational matters had to go through it. In 1976, it was one of the areas in which volunteers lost their lives along with a brigade staff volunteer in leading a major attack on a British army installation in the Gasworks.

Republicanism in the Short Strand was robust and always had a good relationship with its support base. As elsewhere much of this was borne out of necessity. During the armed conflict with the British state, IRA volunteers could never have endured were it not for access to myriad resources provided by the local population. The community had to be treated with respect, otherwise it would never have taken the risks that it did to help sustain the armed struggle. The IRA was home to a large body of people willing to use force. It was never populated by shrinking violets and pacifists. But the aggression that its volunteers were all too able and willing to display was never directed against its own community. People can debate the rights and wrongs of punishment attacks, but these actions were never viewed by IRA volunteers as attacks on the community. Nor were they the work of sadists only too eager to give vent to their urges by thrashing wayward kids.

Today many in the IRA have lost their way. The need for immediate community support is not pressing. There is no quid pro quo between IRA volunteers and the community dictated by necessity. Certainly, Sinn Fein need votes and cannot afford to have Republicans standing on the toes of the electoral base. But a vote in a year or two's time does not have the same disciplinary or constraining effect on an IRA volunteer as would the need to have access to someone's kitchen or wall cavity within which a weapon can be concealed.

When members of the IRA and Sinn Fein election workers thrashed Robert McCartney with sewer rods and stabbed him, they plunged their knives not only into his body but also into the hard-earned legitimacy and rich history of republicanism within the Strand. Their vicious criminality has placed clear blue water between them and the Short Strand volunteers of the Blanket protest. There would be no need to nail a prison uniform to their backs. It should fit them like a glove.

While the Sinn Fein and IRA leadership have given the public appearance of distancing themselves from such thugs, many are coming to view this as a cynical ploy. Robert McCartney's killers walk the streets of the Short Strand without a word of protest from the Provisional movement—a potent reminder to any who might think of testifying. RTE's Tommie Gorman, reporting on a Sinn Fein rally held at the Hilton Hotel in the shadow of the Short Strand, tonight informed viewers that neither Sinn Fein nor the IRA showed any sign of expelling the killers from their ranks. When independent Republican councillor Martin Cunningham turned up for this evening's district development committee meeting of Newry and Mourne District Council, Sinn Fein councillors, led by Pat McGinn, called him a 'tout' and 'informer'. What earned him such abuse was newspaper coverage of his support for the family of Robert McCartney. Copies of the newspaper were strewn throughout the council premises by McGinn in an attempt to demonise Martin Cunningham for his firm stand with the bereaved family.

The family of Robert McCartney has displayed courage and commitment in trying to bring his killers to justice. Many others have a vested interest in seeing the entire matter fade into the background. Neither Sinn Fein nor the IRA should be allowed to feign a humane concerned approach to the family in public while simultaneously undermining its search for justice on the streets.

Murder, cover-up, intimidation—it's time to go.

The Advisocrats: It's All Their Fault

The Blanket, 22 March 2005

For the past week I have viewed with something approaching amusement the rantings by Martin McGuinness that I have been an advisor to the McCartney women as they pursue justice for their murdered brother Robert. A former minister of the British crown throwing criticism at Republicans is hardly a cause of great concern. Needham, Mates, Concannon, McGuinness—what should it matter which former Brit minister has a poke?

Two months ago British diplomat Joe Pilling was the subject of McGuinness' ire when, desperately trying to plug a leaking credibility, he flailed around in search of a convenient scapegoat onto whom he could pin the rapidly depreciating label 'securocrat'. Now to explain away his party's failings in its handling of the McCartney murder, he has cast his line again, this time in the hope of hooking an 'advisocrat'.

There would be absolutely nothing wrong with being an advisor to the McCartney women. In fact, it would be an honour. Just, in my case, I have to forego any misdirected praise because it would be received under false pretences. The allegation by McGuinness is nonsense. On a Radio 4 programme he must have left some listeners underwhelmed when he made the outlandish allegation that I had stated on a radio panel discussion on 13 March that I was an advisor to the McCartney women. There was as much chance of my having declared myself a forward with Manchester United. The only programme I featured on that day was *Seven Days*. Perhaps the securocrats have since wiped the master tape and beamed memory-erasing rays to anyone who listened to the broadcast. The BBC has no record of the said confession, and no one else can recall it. McGuinness made it up. Comical Marty strikes again.

When spinning nonsense it is important to have a kernel of truth even as a fallback position for when the spin boomerangs. McGuinness and truth seem not to be on the terms of even a nodding acquaintance. Frequently having accused himself of not being in the IRA, it is small wonder that few get excitable when the latest accusation shunts off from his lips. As a journalist said last night, things are so bad that when Sinn Fein do eventually tell the truth about something, nobody will be there to believe them.

What does McGuinness hope to achieve by churning out porkies? Seemingly, he reckons that if the McCartney women's campaign can be tainted with the shadow of the 'anti-peace process' lobby, it might bring a few much needed alms of sympathy his way. Unfortunately for Sinn Fein, it has not been too adept in manipulating a wider public into believing that opposition to the peace process and violently dissenting from it are essentially one and the same.

There are lots of good reasons to oppose the peace process, not least of all that the process subverts the peace. In fact, amongst those opposed to the peace process can be found many who genuinely support the peace and cannot therefore endorse the process. Their dissent from the peace process is not violent, unlike Sinn Fein and its militia, who on occasion have sought to violently impose the peace process. Moreover, we would be fools to support a process that effectively provides de facto immunity to those in the Sinn Fein leadership who might seek to order our murder. All should feel free to support Christmas—but not the turkeys.

Perhaps the real irritant prompting McGuinness' advisocrat outburst is his anathema to the concept of autonomous intelligent women operating under their own steam. Women can indeed be seen on the Ard Comhairle of Sinn Fein. Public opinion in modern Ireland would hardly countenance an exclusively male political leadership in any party. But in Comical Marty's secret society, where the real decision-making processes function well beyond the range of any democratic scrutiny, no woman has ever been accused of being on the Army Council. A thirty-six–year life span and not a woman about the place. A Cultra golf club would get past an Equal Opportunities investigator with a cleaner bill of health.

Maybe it is just too much for the great strategist to be turned inside out by such 'lowly mortals' as women whose real place, in his world-view, is at the kitchen sink. He must be acutely aware that he has never once seized the initiative and at times has been reduced to sounding like an incoherent idiot, something borne out by his frequent appearances on *Hearts and Minds*. When Noel Thompson gets him in the hot chair it is like something from Billy Smart's Circus where the call goes up to 'bring on the clowns'. McGuinness never fails to put in a performance that leaves viewers in no doubt that he was born with a 'silver foot in his mouth'. The humiliation is all the greater for the sexist/macho character when women, unheard of in public life eight weeks ago, come across as much more articulate and plausible.

McGuinness' accusatory diatribe has added weight to the charges levelled by the McCartney women that his party has acted in bad faith in its dealings with them. He has demonstrated that the women are not viewed as allies in the search for justice but as hostile forces who must be halted by foul means or fouler. McGuinness, however, labours under a serious handicap in his effort to label the women as pawns in the hands of some external string puller. As his party creaks under the weight of its own dissembling, its organised lying is not as organised as it used to be.

Quis Separabit? The Short Strand/Markets UDA

The Blanket, 29 May 2005

> *Big Sam, Artie, and me were drinking in the Lawnbrook*
> *Social Club. It was discussed that we go out and get a*
> *Taig . . . I remember Artie hitting him with a hatchet and*
> *telling him to keep quiet . . . I reached down and cut his*
> *throat with a butcher's knife.*
>
> — SHANKILL BUTCHER BILLY MOORE

*I*t is not as if Republican society lacked some early warning system. It wasn't—nor did it have to be—state of the art, even mildly sophisticated, but it was there. So dispirited were local Republicans in South and East Belfast that some had taken to terming the local IRA the 'hallion battalion'. Almost a year before sadists and psychopaths converged on Robert McCartney, murder in mind, the *Times* Ireland correspondent David Lister boldly asserted that:

> In the Short Strand and Markets areas, 'justice' is dispensed
> by an IRA unit that counts among its ranks a rapist, a pe-
> dophile, a former joyrider, and a man who once attacked a
> woman by burning her breasts with an iron.

Knowledge about the incorrigible criminal nature of some Republican activists on the other side of town was hardly the sole preserve of the *Times* of London. The Provisional movement knew what it had in its ranks. Beatings, threats, intimidation were a way of life to what one *Irish News* letter writer termed the 'do you know who I am gang'? There was no Republican objective associated with their activity, unless hanging out in bars a la characters out of the movie *Donnie Brasco*, bullying those who crossed their paths at the pool table or who looked the wrong way—resulting in a forced visit to the toilets—had some discrete Republican function that was never explained to the rest of us during political education sessions.

Yet they remained within the ranks of Provisional republicanism, for the most part parasitical on the sacrifices of comrades from a bygone era as they proclaimed themselves the 'RA. On other occasions they would appear as Sinn Fein election workers seeking electoral support for the structure they believed would be most advantageous to allowing them to continue exercising malign power over their neighbours. Some of them avoided Republican activism like the plague when there was a risk to personal safety or freedom, but with the Good Friday Agreement found it easy to puff the chest out and ask menacingly, 'Do you know who I am'? They were the muscle that the Sinn Fein leadership relied upon to fortify its position on the streets. Greenshirt thugs were always at hand to break a leg or kidnap a critic. Now that leadership has joined their lengthy list of victims as they treat with self-serving contempt the calls by Gerry Adams and others for them to do the honourable thing and make themselves amenable.

The latest IMC report has confirmed what was already public knowledge: that the IRA did not authorise the cutthroat killers of Robert McCartney to ply their savage trade. The organisation no more killed him than the RUC killed three men in Sinn Fein's Belfast offices in 1992 when an armed police killer gained access to the building and opened fire on anybody within reach. The killers on each occasion belonged to wider institutions but were on solo runs without the prior approval of those institutions. While it is easy to refute allegations of the IRA being responsible for the McCartney murder, it is more difficult to absolve IRA culture of culpability. This was brought out most vividly in a recent RTE reconstruction of the events surrounding the killing.

There have been few documentaries over the past decade exploring issues associated with the northern conflict that have been put together so methodically as last week's *Prime Time* reconstruction of the events that occurred in Magennis' and beyond on the evening of 30 January.

The public, arguably labouring under the fatigue of persistent media coverage, had their energy reserves topped up with a captivating account that is still being talked about almost a week later. If awards are to go to current affairs programme makers and the people behind this do not achieve one, all faith in the awards system will justifiably evaporate.

The graphic reconstruction of the circumstances pertaining to the death of Robert McCartney constituted a jolting assault on whatever complacency may have lodged itself in our minds in the four months since the murder. As the knife men, organised and purposeful, filed out of the bar some time after the initial clash—belying any notion that it was all a rush of blood to the head—in pursuit of their defenceless victims, the scene could as easily have been a Munich beer hall in the 1930s with a gang of armed Nazis homing in on their defenceless Jewish victims. So immersed were the murderous accomplices in observing the key players it's surprising that they did not address each other as Lenny, Artie, Basher, Big Sam, or Billy—all of Shankill Butcher infamy.

In Chris Petit's book *The Psalm Killer*, there is a horrific scene where a drunken UDA mob toot and hoot while some innocent is carved up while tied to a chair. *Prime Time*, in bringing its viewers inside Magennis' Whiskey Bar in 2005, exposed them to a form of magical realism in which a door opened on a very dark era we thought we had left behind us thirty years ago. Suddenly the primordial savagery that reverses the order of things and leads us to think that apes descended from men was there in full-blown gore.

The sheer arrogance of the Republicans in the bar, unable to brook that some people will not be deferential in their presence, has its roots in a militarist elitism that is as old as the Provisional IRA itself and shows every sign of wanting to outlive the conflict that gave rise to its existence, a most ominous phenomenon. The IRA did not need to be in the bar as an organisation for the killing to have occurred. That its members were present, equipped with the attitude 'we run these areas' was enough. IRA culture was drawn on heavily both to inflict the crime and to cover it up. It is the only barroom brawl in over thirty-five years of conflict that was followed by a methodical forensic sweep on behalf of the brawling party.

Another casualty of the events that took place on 30 January has been the political career of Deirdre Hargey, the young Sinn Fein activist who was present in the bar on the night of the murder. Her reputation has been damaged immensely by the *Prime Time* production. A much respected figure in the Markets where she followed in the footsteps of her late father Jim—who persevered despite long-term health problems in trying to enhance the conditions of life for those within his community—Deirdre Hargey managed to sound like a leadership devotee who was ultimately more concerned with protecting her leaders than addressing the very real issues of justice that the McCartney murder had thrown up. That she was less than forthcoming in an RTE interview about the extent of her own knowledge, no matter how marginal, in relation to the McCartney affair has cast a shadow over a bright political future. A writer watching Deirdre Hargey 'drool' over the leadership later told me that on witnessing such blind adherence she merely sighed, 'Hitler Youth material'.

Although Deirdre Hargey's misfortune was largely self-inflicted, this acerbic observation seemed an inappropriate characterisation of a young woman who allowed herself to succumb to the anonymous pressure of the group. She played no part in the murder of Robert McCartney. While she certainly made a bad judgment call, to drag her down into the gutter alongside the fiends who, John White-like, grew excited at the sensation of human flesh yielding to the force of the knife, is a punishment that grossly outweighs her misdemeanour.

Others, however, deserve no such consideration. Amongst the many things achieved by *Prime Time* was confirmation of the view expressed by former Republican prisoner Rosemary Caskey in the *Irish News* last month that those responsible for the murder were a bunch of lowlife gangsters who should now retreat back into their lairs. It also rubbished the already pathetic perspective of a critic of Caskey, Sean Montgomery, also a former Republican prisoner, who argued that the knife murderers should not be condemned to a lifelong label of being criminals because of a 'drunken row'.

Republican activism is not a license to murder members of the nationalist community in pursuit of self-gratification. Those who engage in it should be given no cover. If they want the cloak of political legitimacy, then, if jailed, they can do their time as political prisoners on the UDA wing in Maghaberry. Jim 'Doris Day' Gray would make ideal company for them.

For now Robert McCartney is a name that hangs over the leadership of Sinn Fein like the sword of Damocles. A party that prided itself on challenging injustice will not be allowed to sleep easily until it delivers it. *Prime Time* was a Sinn Fein nightmare.

CHAPTER 8
Informers

How Stakeknife Paved the Way to Defeat for the IRA

The Blanket, 11 May 2003

For young people growing up in the Markets and adjacent Lower Ormeau area in the early 1970s, Freddie Scappaticci was a household name. A well-known and respected local Republican, he found himself interned twice without trial. Few then could have imagined that three decades later his locally revered name would assume national prominence as a consequence of having become embroiled in one of the major controversies to emerge from the British state's dirty war in Ireland, which has led to fierce media allegations identifying him as the supposed top British agent within the IRA, Stakeknife.

The Republican writer Danny Morrison today urged caution in relation to such reports, flagging up other instances where a frenzy of media activity ultimately proved groundless. It is the type of advice seasoned commentators would disregard at their peril. Morrison, however, does admit that the IRA had on occasion been penetrated by the British state.

While in the H-Blocks of Long Kesh in 1986, I expressed the view to Brendan Hughes that it would make strategic sense for the British to place an agent in the upper echelons of the IRA's internal security department. In doing that they would secure a long-term agent who, unlike those in the operational IRA who habitually risk imprisonment, would serve them as a permanent human listening device.

Whatever the truth of Stakeknife's identity, the allegations that the IRA's internal security had been seriously compromised by the British over such a prolonged period, while unlikely to shatter present Republican strategy, does help explain how such a loser's strategy took hold. Some speculative but dubious journalism that took root after the existence of 'Stakeknife' was made public implied that a sinister hand either in or close to the Sinn Fein leadership was directly working for the British and influencing the peace process. More prudent journalism dismissed such unmediated causality, opting instead to show how a seriously compromised IRA campaign would reinforce a peace lobby within republicanism. Arguably, this is where the role of Stakeknife became crucial.

There is no route more direct through the fog of IRA mystique and secrecy than that of seniority within the internal security department. Those who manage it know most of what is worth knowing. Stakeknife, if one of its senior operatives, may not have been aware in advance of IRA operations, but would most certainly have known the identity of all key operators. His continuing debriefing of volunteers after arrest or as part of the incessant inquiries that characterise the IRA was made workable only by an extensive knowledge of the background. The organisation's weaknesses and strengths, the unquestioning or critical approaches to leadership of its volunteers, the fighters and the shirkers would all have been known to Stakeknife. More importantly, British-placed informers within the IRA could have been protected by Stakeknife, while more committed volunteers may have been set up for arrest or assassination.

Given that his information did not remain the coveted prize of his military handlers and was passed to the desks of various British prime ministers, the British government was optimally positioned to encourage the peace lobby within the Republican camp, punish the enemy of that lobby and reward its friends. It knew the military strength or weakness behind every Republican position and could readjust accordingly. The ultimate aim was to secure Republican acceptance of the British state's alternative to republicanism—ultimately made manifest in the internal solution known as the Good Friday Agreement.

Stakeknife damaged the IRA irreparably and helped pave the way for its defeat. The suggestion that Sinn Fein leaders were conscious British agents as yet remains unfounded. But there is little room for doubt that the hand of the British state was on the tiller of the peace process that the Sinn Fein leadership came to embrace wholeheartedly.

And its grip was made all the firmer by Stakeknife serrating away at IRA capacity.

Stalinville

The Blanket, 19 May 2003

O ut for a walk this evening with a friend, Kevin McQuillan, we
had the misfortune to come across an irate Sinn Fein councillor, Tom Hartley, on the Andersonstown Road. The source of his ire,
strangely, seemed not to be state collusion and the manipulation of
agents for the purposes of murder, or the possibility of water charges
being inflicted upon an impoverished community. Nor was it that the
British had decided to show who was boss and had suspended elections. It was not even caused by a sense of humiliation that party leaders had, in the words of columnist Brian Feeney, grovelled to the Brits
and pleaded for a chance to be allowed to cut back on acute health
services on behalf of Britain once again. No, the ire raging within Tom
Hartley was for me!

Although Hartley these days is as subversive as your average vicar,
myself and him normally exchange pleasantries or platitudes. He mildly
berates me for not thinking the way he thinks I should think, and then
having dutifully gone through the perfunctory motions of inflicting
the party line on me we part ways much the same as we met. Tonight
was different. He was seething. It was as if I had defied a Sinn Fein
banning order prohibiting me from being seen in public. People might
think that I really did exist and was not something that lived in the at-
tic of the BBC, to be wheeled out every now and then—as Big Brother
No. 1 likes to spoof to his RTE audience—to heretically hold forth
against the unassailable wisdom of the peace process. Although we had
bumped into a couple of ex-prisoners along the way and chewed the fat
with them, Tom was the first apparatchik.

The contrast between the activist and bureaucratic levels in republicanism on this occasion could not have been more marked. People,
mere yards apart, inhabited two contrasting intellectual worlds: one
healthy and porous where ideas can breathe, the other pathological,

smothered and stifled where autonomous intellect is only welcome after it has been filtered and stripped of its independence.

Having greeted him, 'Well, Tom' (I didn't even address him as 'Tombstone Tom' to wind him up over his guided tours of the cemeteries), I was immediately subjected to a tirade and told I was 'disgraceful last week'. He did not clarify—clarity not being a concept the peace process rests comfortably with—but merely got very aggressive, finger wagged and pontificated to the effect that there was no room in West Belfast for views that Big Brother No. 1 had not given prior approval to. Seemingly, what I fail to understand is that within West Belfast Big Brother No. 1 just loves his subjects so much that in order to relieve us of our democratic burden he shall do all our thinking so that we are free to concern ourselves with the real things in life like tending the garden, watching football, and all that, a West Belfast version of democratic centralism where Big Brother No. 1 democratically decides for the rest of us. In his infinite kindness Big Brother No. 1 has secured fundamental freedoms—even for malcontents like myself—including the right to be free from making decisions that govern our lives. My view that we should have the right to be free from the decision makers is mere Clever Dick semantics, employed solely to 'confuse the gullible'. An understanding of real freedom is beyond my ken.

In any event, I was left to presume that Councillor Hartley was referring to the views I had expressed through a number of media outlets including *The Blanket* on the Stakeknife affair. In his fulminations he neglected to tell me what it was he was fulminating against. And there was me thinking that Des Wilson was right when he said democracy is always enhanced when people know more rather than less. Not here where it works the other way round. The less we know, the more the leadership will praise us for our intellect and tell us that we are the most politicised people in Western Europe. Ours is a disciplined and collective intellect evidenced by our willingness to tear out of the Ulster Hall and chant in unison 'securocrats'. Anyone suggesting that the controlocrats amongst the liarocracy who devise such intellectually limiting concepts may just have something to explain themselves are dismissed as rejectionists. In our insular little world where we all need each other's falsehoods to reinforce our faith in the incredible, the leadership alone will slay the legions of securocrat and rejectionist dragons—not to mention define who they are. That is of course when they are not secretly meeting securocrats in the form of Michael Oatley or John Deverell to plan the implementation of Britain's alternative to republicanism.

Not being the type to get excited one way or the other about anything Tom Hartley would have to say, and being mildly curious to find out if he would tell me Stakeknife was touting for peace, I asked him, 'Are you defending touts'? His response was to froth even more at the mouth as he stuttered out the words, 'It is you that is a disgrace'. Me—a disgrace. And Stakeknife? Well, he's alright. Bring back Stormont and nobody will mention him. Not vaguely interested in calming the fuming, gesticulating Stalinist that now confronted me I sought to draw him by suggesting that perhaps it was natural for touts to support the peace process. It did not produce any answer other than a snarl, but at least it got rid of him as he took off up the road like a scalded cat, muttering and mumbling, while I stood somewhere between amazement and hilarity wondering at the absurdity of it all. 'Do you think he behaves like that to the Unionists'? I pondered to Kevin. 'What was all that about? He still hasn't told you why you are a disgrace' was his only comment as we walked on down the road, half anticipating to be gripped by one of the many cop patrols doing the rounds, and asked: 'Are you in possession of an alternative idea, sir? Under Section 31 that is an offence in West Belfast. We will need to send for the thought disposal unit to render it harmless'.

What this was all about was a Sinn Fein apparatchik trying to create a poisonous atmosphere that would suffocate any version of events that would call into question the credentials of the bureaucratic structure that endows him with self-importance. The friendly face of moderation when making overtures to the Unionists quickly vanishes to be replaced with a fascistic scowl toward Republicans who will not buy into the bollix. Out goes the tuxedo and the 'I say, old chap' to be replaced with the green shirt and the harsh command of 'verboten'. Make the streets a hostile sea controlled and cruised by goondas whose repressive efficacy is derived from their usefulness to the power structure more than it is on their own talents, and depth charge every alternative idea that happens to traverse along the sub current. Here I was being subjected to an aggressive rant by a city councillor while the party to which he belonged was shouting, 'Get Freddie a solicitor'—Freddie being the man at the centre of the Stakeknife allegations. Seems that both Scappaticci and Hartley thought a good piece of work for the peace process was having a go at me on the same day. Old Freddie, seemingly not the most devout practitioner of omerta, accused me in the *Andytout News* of being embittered and working to an agenda. I read on, hoping he would call me an enemy of the peace process.

Now, I am hardly going to worry in the slightest that Freddie Scappaticci finds me on the opposite side of the fence from him. The peace process deserves his backing. After all, he has been supporting it for years. Perhaps my cardinal sin in the eyes of Hartley has been to ask that awkward question—why?

Spookaticci

Fortnight, April 2004

*T*his book has been long awaited. Since 1999 when allusions to a senior British agent operating in the highest echelons of the IRA began to filter into public discourse, unease mixed with fascination has permeated the psyche of the Republican constituency. Many believed and some hoped that once Stakeknife was unmasked it would reveal a high-profile politician. Uninformed critics of the Sinn Fein leadership harboured hopes that from within its midst a prestigious figure and formidable advocate of the peace process would be dragged shouting, screaming, and lying into the public spotlight. Others more inclined to read Ed Moloney, and therefore more attuned to the background, appreciated that such a 'sensational', if it were to materialise, would be for another day. When the outing came last May, name recognition for Freddie Scappaticci hardly registered amongst the uninitiated.

In the days following the public revelation Scappaticci managed to beguile a sizeable section of Republican opinion. While assisted in this by some weak journalism, a more substantial source of succour came from the Sinn Fein leadership, which, in uncharacteristic fashion, decided that those accused of working for the other side should be provided with a solicitor rather than a unit from the IRA's internal security department. But as the months dragged by, and despite shrill attempts by some subservient local hacks to bounce their readers into believing the story had died within a week of it first appearing, there were few prepared to wager even a small bet that 'Scap' was the innocent victim of a 'securocrat' conspiracy. What residual sympathy remained for him is likely to be torpedoed by the publication of *Stakeknife*.

Jointly written by the *People's Northern* editor Greg Harkin and former British army agent handler Martin Ingram, the book sets out to chart Scappaticci's career as Britain's most important 'civil servant' in the north. It contains little that is new. One of the authors,

Greg Harkin, has extensively covered the detail elsewhere. Ingram's imprimatur is what lends the book its explosive authenticity. Once the darling of elements within the nationalist press for his exposure of British-loyalist collusion, his allegations of similar activity between the British and Republicans cannot be lightly dismissed.

An immediate deficiency in the book is the lack of documented evidence. Nothing that a forensic mind could work with is forthcoming. Yet the authors provide an entirely plausible explanation for this. British security personnel, out of pure self-interest, destroyed anything that could prove detrimental to their man's well-being. And the circumstantial case against Scappaticci is powerful. All the leads point in only one direction. While the existence of taped recordings of the former numero uno headhunter talking to journalists from the Cook report team do not prove Scap is an agent, his denials that he ever met the journalists prove that on the matter of compromising IRA security he is unworthy of belief.

In circumstances where the Republican grassroots were to behave as something other than blind adherents to the leadership line, this book would lead many of them to confront their leaders with difficult questions, not least of all why the leadership strata would seek to cover up for one of its own when it was clear that all was not rosy in the garden husbanded by Scappaticci. The most plausible reason for such a cover-up is the self-serving one of public image. For decades the leadership liked to cultivate the myth that it had directed the most professional and efficient guerrilla army the western world had played host to. And for it to admit that the man it entrusted with the security of its organisation and the lives and freedom of its volunteers was a senior agent of the British state would leave it to carry the mark of Cain. That leadership in suggesting Scap was a victim was not in fact covering for him, but for itself, its incompetence and bungling, which was anything but professional and efficient.

Those put to the sword on Scappaticci's watch—the book claims there were thirty-five—can no longer be regarded as the collaborators the Republican leadership alleged them to be. Undoubtedly some were, but an Army Council that gave the nod for people to be killed on the basis of information provided to it by a British agent itself carries much more culpability than the people it despatched to early graves.

Some still ask if Scap was so dangerous a tout why is he still alive? The answer to that question will be debated and mulled over for some time to come. But what ethical justification would the Republican leadership have for doing to him what it and he colluded in doing to so many others? After all, did he not hanker after the very things the leadership sought? Affluence, a house in another jurisdiction, divesting the IRA of its guns, and the ultimate dissolution of the IRA? No, Freddie Scappaticci should not be killed. He should be on the Sinn Fein negotiating team.

More Spies May Be Lurking in Sinn Fein's Cupboard

Irish Times, 20 December 2005

The year 2005, Sinn Fein's much-vaunted centenary year, has proved to be the party's worst since the beginning of the peace process. Assailed from every conceivable angle for its duplicity and deceit, it took the first steps into the new year to a cacophony of voices chorusing, 'Lies'! at it.

Twelve months later, the phonetics have not changed all that greatly, 'Spies'! now being the new buzz term of opprobrium hurled in the party's direction.

It certainly takes something to give the peace process a touch of élan. The bizarre Kafkaesque act being staged is a good choice for those seeking some form of alternative theatre to the Christmas pantomime circuit regaling yuletide revellers.

Were it not for the periodic scandals that sprinkle the peace process and titillate a long-suffering population, our zest for life would be heavily compromised by those insufferable advocates of the process who, with their fluency in gibberish, have whipped us into a state of narcolepsy.

Last week, which began with the usual Monday nonsense about securocrats, showed all the promise of finishing in similar vein until the Denis Donaldson defibrillator sparked and shocked some serious life into an otherwise tedious seven days.

Donaldson, a senior and crucially positioned Sinn Fein apparatchik, confessed to having been a British spy for twenty years. Give or take a year or two, he is hardly the sole member of this club.

When I first learned of this latest Sinn Fein security debacle, my sole thought was, *And who else?* To think that Donaldson draws the curtain down on Sinn Fein's spy problem, one would need to be as daft as some Short Strand mural artist who, so long as any Provisional leader endorsed it, would readily paint the walls with 'Denis, revolutionary hero of the peace process, was only touting for peace'.

It is the sheer gullibility of large swathes of the Republican rank and file that has allowed the Sinn Fein leadership strategy to last so long, with its persistent affront to Republican sensibilities, without any serious questions being asked of it.

Agents have for long been central to British state attempts to shape the IRA and in particular nudge it toward a peace process.

In 1983 the role of Bobby Lean was crucial. By turning supergrass and securing the temporary imprisonment of key IRA personnel, Lean changed the internal balance of power within the IRA and allowed Gerry Adams to consolidate his grip on the Provisional Republican movement as a whole, opening the way for the current strategy and the abandonment of everything the Provisionals hitherto held dear.

In recent years the role of Freddie Scappaticci, a central player in the IRA's internal security apparatus, came under sustained scrutiny. Scappaticci's purpose as a senior British agent was to help render the IRA's military option redundant, thus allowing the logic of a peace process to take root.

But the peace process had to have some intellectual autonomy rather than exist in a vacuum created by the implausibility of continuing with an armed campaign. This is where agents of influence came into play.

Peter Taylor details in his book, *Provos*, how British military intelligence, working on the premise that 'Gerry Adams would do almost anything to further his political career', sought unsuccessfully to turn Derry Republican Steven Lambert.

His role would be 'to pass on information of the mood within the party, attitudes of particular individuals to particular policies and to implement and push policies' devised by the British. Remarkably, those policies and the core tenets of the peace process are not dissimilar.

It therefore comes as no surprise to find Martin Ingram, a former British army operative, who co-authored a book detailing the nefarious espionage record of Scappaticci, writing on a Web site recently that he had one thing in common with Gerry Adams: Both set out to destroy the IRA and both succeeded.

Consequently, it is even less surprising to trace the lengths gone to by the Sinn Fein leadership to cover for Scappaticci when he was eventually exposed.

For his part, Donaldson also functioned in the agent of influence mode. Even if as a result of Stormontgate his influence had declined, there was no unavoidable reason for the British to out him.

Certainly there were strong suspicions and whispers that the Stormontgate trial was aborted by the British to protect a key informer.

Because Donaldson had been arrested and held on remand for a period as a result of the Stormont spy ring collapsing in October 2002, most people not unreasonably took the view that he was a victim of the informer rather than being the informer himself. However, a search for the informer increased the risk of an agent more important than Donaldson being exposed.

Arguably, Donaldson was outed as a foil against further investigation, the 'tout has now been exposed' dismissal 'so let's get on with the business of the peace process', as Gerry Adams called for last week.

In this perspective, the British give Sinn Fein wriggle room so that it maintains some of its boxing ring craft rather than have it flail on the ropes, as well it might if another informer was to be exposed who, this time, was much more central in the public mind to the peace process than Donaldson ever was.

On last night's *Last Word* programme on Today FM, Martin Ingram confirmed to presenter Matt Cooper that there are senior Sinn Fein household names at present working for the British. Far from the British 'securocrats' moving to undermine Sinn Fein, they are seemingly striving to protect it from serious investigation.

A particular irony in all of this for the voter in the republic is that after decades of being free from British involvement in their part of the island, the dilemma they face is that by voting Sinn Fein they increase the likelihood of returning MI5 to the Dail. Now that truly is an appalling vista.

Poison

The Blanket, 23 December 2005

At the moment Belfast is awash with rumours about the imminent outing of one or more of the many informers currently operating within Sinn Fein or IRA structures. Even some of the drones standing outside PSNI stations demanding an end to political policing have not escaped the finger of suspicion. Nor is the speculation confined to critics of the Provisionals. Party and militia activists alike are giving vent to confusion and concerns. Sinn Fein, unable to fix the party brakes has opted to make the horn louder. 'Securocrat plot' toots out at anybody dumb enough to listen, of which there are many, evenly spread, it would seem, across both Sinn Fein and the media. The party leader is applying Karl Kraus' secret of the demagogue, which is to make himself as stupid as his audience, so they believe they are as clever as he.

That the Provisional movement is extensively penetrated should come as no surprise. Viewed through the Long War prism, it was the logical outcome of a strategy of attrition, in which the attrition was felt more by those waging it than those it was intended to wear down. Activists were reminded that as they grew older with fewer years left to them, the length of time they could expect to serve in prison if captured was increasing by the year. People not on the run and who lived home lives, with partners and children, suddenly exposed to the certainty of losing everything in exchange for a cell found themselves staring at fences they were no longer able to jump. The Long War strategy saw combatants emerge from jail after they had served considerable sentences. If they returned to active service the chill running through their bones reminded them of the price to be paid if captured. The choice was simple: Grow old and grey with imprisoned comrades and wake up alone each morning to the sound of clanging grills; or come to beside a partner and to the laughter of children. Those IRA internal security doyens, not working for the British, with decades of experience observed that the biggest risk factor to the organisation was an ex-prisoner not prepared to return to prison.

For others such as Sinn Fein activists with a public profile, the threat of assassination by loyalists was a constant in their minds. One sure way to retain their profile minus the risk was to work for the British. In turn their handlers would ensure that loyalist death squads were directed elsewhere. It has been argued by Ed Moloney that the primary reason for the security services infiltrating loyalist groups was to ensure that Johnny and his mob did not target British agents within the Provisional movement, Britain's main enemy. When such operations were launched the British would redirect or intervene.

Over the years the role of ideology as a defence mechanism against being turned has been steadily eroded. The abandonment of a Republican ideology by the Sticks was the mainstay of the Provisional critique against them: They were allegedly riddled with informers because they had abandoned the ideological immunisation against touting. Now that Sinn Fein has gone Stick, the same logic must apply. Options previously ruled out now become a pragmatic choice. Martin McGuinness worked as a British minister; Denis Donaldson worked as a British agent. At the risk of oversimplifying, the minister's job is to shaft republicanism; that of the agent is to shaft Republicans. While few outside the ranks of the purists would call McGuinness a rat on this basis, there is no clear blue ideological sea between minister and agent.

While there are patterns, there remains something specific to the life and circumstances of the individual 'turned', which leads to their predicament and which rules out providing an effective firewall in advance, even when they confess there is no way to be sure that they are telling the truth, that they are not merely putting the best possible gloss on their motives. Denis Donaldson is a case in point. Few are willing to accept at face value his explanation that he was compromised at a difficult time in his life. Given that he lived a lie for at least twenty years, why should he be believed in the minute it took him to release his confession? He said exactly what the Sinn Fein leadership instructed him to, even to the extent of lying about the fictional British spy ring at Stormont.

The political implications of touting are one thing but there is an additional factor to be considered. When I look at my own children, I want to see them pass into my postexistence era with something they can carry without it burning their hands. There are things, such as our vocal opposition to power-crazed leaders, that we exercise out of conviction and that many others howl at. The howlers can pass on their own hypocrisies to their children and we can pass on our consistencies. In both cases, whatever divides us, there exists a much wider chasm separating critics and howlers from the tout. How fathers and grandfathers like Denis Donaldson are willing to allow their offspring to go through life unfairly carrying the mark of Cain is hard to fathom. Was he so selfish, cynical, and ruthless that he bequeathed such a legacy to those he brought into the world? His children and grandchildren are not to blame and should be viewed as unique individuals. Donaldson's capable daughter Jane should always be Jane Donaldson or Jane Kearney, and never the daughter of the self-confessed agent Denis Donaldson no matter what ties she may wish to retain with him. He remains her father. And as Camus once observed, when forced to choose between the ideal no matter how beautiful and those we love, we opt for those we love. It is simply untenable to allow a diminution of respect for Donaldson's family to take hold. Those who love him remain as decent as anyone else in these communities.

Provisionalism is now being haunted by a spooky spectre. What blossomed in spring has now become autumn fruit, as poisonous as it is bountiful.

CHAPTER 9
Comrades

A Dark View of the Process

Fourthwrite, March 2000

Interview with Brendan Hughes, *Fourthwrite Magazine,* Journal of the Irish Republican Writers' Group

Q: After such long term involvement in the Republican struggle do you feel a sense of satisfaction at the way things have turned out?

A: No. I do not feel any satisfaction whatsoever. All the questions raised in the course of this struggle have not been answered and the Republican struggle has not been concluded. We were naïve ever to have expected the Brits to get on the boat and go. But the things that we cherished such as a thirty-two county Democratic Socialist Republic are no longer mentioned.

Q: The former Republican prisoner Tommy Gorman in the *Andersonstown News* bewails the absence of radical republicanism and has questioned if it was all worth it. What is your view?

A: Let me answer it this way. When I came out from jail in 1986, having spent more than twelve years there, I found work on a building site on the Falls Road. Some of the people I thought I was fighting for were now seeking to exploit me. I recalled my father telling me stories about earlier campaigns when Republicans such as Billy McKee came out from jail and being employed by Eastwoods for peanuts. And there I was decades later, digging holes for the same peanuts.

Q: But there are many who feel it was worth it.

A: True. But amongst their number are those who have big houses and guaranteed incomes. Of course it was worth it for them. I recall going to the Republican movement and asking that it highlight the exploitative cowboy builders on the Falls Road who were squeezing the Republican poor for profit. The movement censored me and refused to allow me to speak. Once they published a piece that I wrote—or, should I say, did not write, as the thing was so heavily censored as to be totally unrecognisable from the article I actually wrote. Some of the cowboy builders had influence with movement members. Whether true or not, there were many whispers doing the rounds that these members were taking backhanders and so on. In any event this led to a vicious circle in which money created power, which in turn created corruption and then greed for more money. Dozens of ex-prisoners are exploited by these firms. They run the black economy of West Belfast simply to make profit and not out of a sense of helping others.

Q: Is the future bleak?

A: People are demoralised and disillusioned. Many are tired but it would still be possible to pull enough together to first question what has happened and then to try to change things.

Q: But has Sinn Fein not been sucked so far into the system that any salvaging of the Republican project must now look like a very daunting task?

A: While I am not pushing for any military response, our past has shown that all is never lost. In 1972 we had to break the truce in order to avoid being sucked in. In 1975 the British came at us again. And from prison through the Brownie articles written by Gerry Adams we warned the IRA that it was being sucked in. We broke the British on that but it took hard work. And now they are at it again. And it will be even harder this time. Think of all the lives that could have been saved had we accepted the 1975 truce. That alone would have justified acceptance. We fought on and for what?—what we rejected in 1975.

Q: What do you feel when you read that Michael Oatley (formerly of MI6) expresses support for the Sinn Fein leadership, and that David

Goodall, who helped negotiate the Anglo-Irish Agreement in 1985, said recently that it is all going almost exactly according to plan?

A: These are the comments of men supremely confident that they have it all sewn up. What we hammered into each other time after time in jail was that a central part of Brit counterinsurgency strategy was to mould leaderships whom they could deal with. So I get so demoralised when I read about this. I look at South Africa and I look at here and I see that the only change has been in appearances. No real change has occurred. A few Republicans have slotted themselves into comfortable positions and left the rest of us behind.

Q: Has the nationalist middle class been the real beneficiary of the armed struggle?

A: Well, it has not been Republicans—apart from those Republicans eager to join that class.

Q: It seems that the social dimension is your real concern regarding Republican direction?

A: No. There is much more than that. It has been the futility of it all. From a nationalist perspective alone what we have now we could have had at any time in the last twenty-five years. But even nationalist demands don't seem to matter anymore. And in the process we have lost much of our honesty, sincerity, and comradeship.

Q: But could it not be argued that this developed because people are war weary?

A: In 1969 we had a naïve enthusiasm about what we wanted. Now in 1999 we have no enthusiasm. And it is not because people are war weary. They are politics weary, the same old lies regurgitated week in week out. With the war politics had some substance. Now it has none. The political process has created a class of professional liars and unfortunately it contains many Republicans. But I still think that potential exists to bring about something different. And I speak not just about our own community but about the loyalist community also. Ex-prisoners from both and not the politicians can effect some radical change.

Q: Do you sense any radical potential amongst loyalist ex-prisoners?

A: Yes. Very much so. Not only are they much better than the old regime, they have experienced through their own struggle the brutality, hypocrisy, and corruption of the regime against which Republicans fought for so long.

Q: What are your views on the Good Friday Agreement?

A: What is it? Have we agreed to the British staying in the six counties? If we listen to Francie Molloy that is what Republicans have signed up to. The only advantage is that unionism has changed. The landed gentry has been smashed but only because of the war, not the Good Friday Agreement. Overall, the facade has been cleaned up but the bone structure remains the same. The state we set out to smash still exists. Look at the RUC for example.

Q: Do you sense that Sinn Fein is going to settle for something like disband Ronnie Flanagan?

A: Would it really surprise you?

Q: Do you sense that the Republican leadership fears or despises democratic republicanism?

A: The response to democratic republicanism has always been a plea to stay within the army line. Even doing this interview with you generates a reluctance within me. The Republican leadership has always exploited our loyalty.

Q: What do you say to those people who are unhappy but are pulled the other way by feelings of loyalty?

A: Examine their consciences. Take a good look at what is going on. If they agree, okay. If not, then speak out.

Loyalty to the Big Lad

The Blanket, July 2000

*T*here have been many events that have been interpreted as Republicans saying the war is over—to everybody, that is, but the Republican grassroots. All of it is a matter for conjecture. We may never see the definitive statement or realise the defining moment. But there is a strange twist of irony when the first London bomber is trotted out to criticise the last.

Gerry Kelly, armed with courage, commitment, and no votes, bombed London in March 1973. It heralded the opening of a twenty-three-year British bombing campaign that saw many IRA volunteers and others, not all of them innocent, lose their lives. It also gave rise to a litany of false convictions as the British judiciary adhered immutably to the principle of 'innocent until proven Irish'. Gerry Kelly himself suffered greatly due to brutality, hunger strikes, and force-feeding in English jails. He spent a decade and a half in prison as a result of his activities in England.

While right to reject a bombing campaign as a means to secure a British withdrawal, he would have strengthened his position immeasurably had he pitched his case on the grounds of strategic futility. But he did not. In his criticism of those Republicans who filled his shoes he claimed that they were against the peace process. Absent from his comments was any reference to the opposition of those people to British rule being legitimised and administered through the Good Friday Agreement. There was no mention of their opposition to partition, nor of their refusal to endorse a Stormont government far to the right of its 1974 predecessor, which other Republicans, passing through the door opened by Gerry Kelly, sought to wreck. They did so then by blasting a coachload of British soldiers and their families off the M62 near Bradford in February 1974, killing eleven, including two children, in the process.

It is said from within the Provisional Republican movement that loyalty to 'the big lad' has warped Gerry Kelly's political antennae beyond recognition, leaving him void of all sense of political direction and sensitivity. Whatever his motivation, the sum total of his London efforts and subsequent suffering amount to little other than him now being suitably positioned to act as a useful conduit through which others can shout, 'The war really is over if we are prepared to go this far'. The latest London bombers shall not feel failed by Gerry Kelly. Expecting no different from any politician, they will simply ignore him. Gerry Kelly has only failed himself.

A Tale of Two Writers

The Blanket, 11 February 2003

> *Men have been taught that it is a virtue to agree with others.*
> *But the creator is the man who disagrees. Men have been*
> *taught that it is a virtue to swim with the current. But the*
> *creator is the man who goes against the current. Men have*
> *been taught that it is a virtue to stand together. But the creator*
> *is the man who stands alone.*
>
> —AYN RAND

If Sinn Fein and the DUP do team up to administer British rule in the postelection world that awaits us at some point in the future, hopefully the old green shirts do not find some courageous and imaginative reason to buckle and allow big Ian's black shirts to ban TV on the Lord's Day. What could the zealots do, apart from finding somebody who disagrees with them, to hate and smite with the wrath of the Creator as they boom out the words 'have you been saved, sinner'? Armed with the approval of their own God who, just by way of coincidence, as Anne Lamott would point out, happens to hate all the same people they do, they will be hunting victims upon whom they can inflict their truth. What chance does that give people like me and Bap McQuillan, who don't give a toss for the Lord or his day and could happily spend ours in the company of every lecherous sinner who ever smoked dope, exchanged profanities or drank cider while the congregation muttered and mumbled mumbo jumbo in their chapels and churches on a Sunday morning before arriving at their senses courtesy of the plate being shoved under their noses? No doubt, a special hate shall be reserved for those of us who have the audacity—unlike Sheila Cassidy—to disbelieve.

Sunday is bad enough without the Lord's men making it worse by curbing viewing hours. Apart from the papers it is not even a good news day for the north. So last Sunday's *Politics Show* made the afternoon that little bit less tedious. Normally we only get 'the line' from the studios when Sinn Fein representatives are on, valiantly struggling to—what Michel Foucault once said of French Communists—'stand behind a fact that was the total opposite of credible'. For that reason, it was instructive to listen to a brace of Republicans with mutually exclusive views vent irreconcilable opinions on the likely trajectory of republicanism. Danny Morrison these days is a writer and a successful author, and has a weekly column in the *Andersonstown News*. The times in which we live are propitious for a man with his intelligence, ability, and views. Not every door will be opened for him but considerably fewer will be slammed in his face. No longer the pariah of old, the fact that he will state certain views makes him a sought-after speaker or pundit. Tommy Gorman also writes but through inclination is not as industrious as Danny Morrison, for whom writing is a worthy vocation. Most of his writing he submits to *The Blanket*. Because of the views Gorman holds, he doesn't find opportunities knocking on his door. In the Stalinist republic of West Belfast those opposed to the authoritarian culture more often than not are directed to a social Siberia. On one occasion Gorman found that Sinn Fein were applying pressure to his then employer to get rid of him because he was 'writing articles not helpful to the peace process'. His home has been picketed by a Sinn Fein mob and his family have been made to feel the pressure because of his refusal to conform to the great nonsenses of our day. It is part of an old Stalinist tradition practiced elsewhere against the free-flowing pen and brings to mind the experience of the Czech novelist Milan Kundera who, in the words of Olga Carlisle, after the Soviet invasion of his country:

> lost his position as a professor at the Institute for Advanced Cinematographic Studies in Prague, and his books were banned. Little by little, life was made unbearable for him, and he was hounded out of his native country.

While not comparing like with like, the authoritarian similarities are sufficient to permit a comparison to be drawn.

Both Morrison and Gorman are Republicans who have been around quite a long time and know the score. The contrast between the two is best captured in the discursive grids through which they describe the peace process. Morrison, because he was for so long at the top of the Republican movement, tends to give answers, whereas Gorman, seeing matters from the bottom, prefers to ask questions. Morrison expresses it as leaders like it to be said; Gorman poses it in terms not approved by the leaders and for which there is a price to be paid—a swift uprooting from Republican iconography and relocation to the social internal exile reserved for 'enemies of the peace process'. But, as Morrison has contended, 'Better to be honest, even if it means being misrepresented, than to be a hypocrite'.

Gorman dislikes the peace process but not the peace. He views Sinn Fein as having moved completely away from any radical position to one of seeking to become part of the establishment. In a bid to massage this actuality out of all recognition, many Provisional Republicans have resorted to manufacturing fabrication. From the apex to the roots organised lying grinds on remorselessly. For Gorman, the party will do whatever it takes to complete the journey into the heart of the establishment even if it means dissolving the IRA; it will not, however, dissolve its ability to kill or harm those within its own community who threaten the new partitionist basis of power and privilege.

For Danny Morrison, this is all wide off the mark. The struggle had always been about reform in the guise of an equality agenda. To stop well short of the republic is an honourable compromise. What made a united Ireland the goal was only that equality and reform could not be achieved in a six-county framework. The ranks of the IRA were swollen by the introduction of internment for Catholics alone. Republicans have come a long way in terms of advances and this has rendered redundant and unethical other armed Republican groups. He argued that the IRA would not disband; the evidence was that the organisation had said it would not and that to do so would be an act of surrender.

At one level the *Politics Show* permitted some insight into an internal Republican struggle to control the interpretation of events. Logically I could find no fault with the take of Tommy Gorman but I am favourably predisposed toward his position. However, it is difficult to quarrel with success. Gorman's advantage in this regard lies in having predicted from the outset where the peace process was going to take republicanism—to precisely where it is today. On the day of the cease-fire announcement in 1994 when he, accompanied by myself, phoned up Bernadette McAliskey to praise her for her comments on radio that the 'good guys lost', there were howls of opprobrium from those within the ranks who swore he had it wrong and that it was all tactical. The howls turned to scowls when we both refused to go over to the Sinn Fein cavalcade through West Belfast on the grounds that turkeys should not be celebrating Christmas. They have been howling and scowling ever since, dismissing with venom any suggestion that republicanism would end up where it is. When they were not howling, they settled for ostracism, although they always manage to make it look more like ostrichism, their silence caused by mouths full of sand, so deep have their heads been buried in it.

A considerable impediment to finding Danny Morrison's discourse persuasive is that it is almost a 'riddle of the sands'—sand building on sand. It is not as if we have not been here before and could not possibly have any idea of what way things are likely to go. While there is no suggestion that Morrison is engaged in organised lying, it does seem he has succumbed to organised forgetting. For to claim that the IRA will not disband because it would amount to surrender is bizarre, given that by his own criteria the organisation already has surrendered. A while back he wrote, 'There will never, ever, be IRA decommissioning, an IRA surrender . . . There will not be decommissioning. There will not be a surrender . . . even by the year 3000'. And then as if all of that hadn't mattered in the least, he recently informed us in the *Guardian* that the

IRA had in fact decommissioned; and in the *Andersonstown News* told his readership that on two occasions the IRA had put weapons beyond use and were poised on the brink of a third act of decommissioning. Three surrenders and still undefeated? When you build on sandy foundations . . .

Perhaps because he was a leader of the Republican movement he does not want it said that the IRA was defeated. There is then less for leaders to be called to account on. But if the IRA wasn't defeated, why then accept the terms of defeat—the consent principle/veto, decommissioning, no disbanded RUC, no declaration of intent by the British to go, etc., etc.? As journalist Breandan O Muirthile asks so saliently, 'If you bumped into defeat in a dark alley, how would its face differ from what we have now'?

And if we were not led to defeat by our leadership, why do we stand poised to squabble over the renamed RUC? The terms of the debate amount to little more than who will be the prestigious sergeant and who will be the lowly constable? Could we have imagined that being discussed in the prison hospital during the hunger strikes? It took the Armani suit to replace the blanket before that could be contemplated. Seemingly, Joe Slovo of the African National Congress was not wide off the mark when he said if a man wears a suit long enough his politics change. Our leaders, it seems, have wardrobes full of them.

Tommy Gorman, Radical Thought:
The Tom and Vita Cox Memorial Award

The Blanket, 3 August 2004

Wwhen Tommy Gorman first told me about a week ago that he was to receive an award for pushing radical ideas under the auspices of the West Belfast Festival, I thought he was joking. So too did others. One man I spoke to yesterday said, 'Gorman is mixing', when I enquired of him would he be going to today's presentation of the Tom Cox Memorial Award at Conway Mill. West Belfast being the capital of censorship on the island, it is understandable that few believe that there are prizes given out here to those who promote freedom of opinion. It is not that long ago since the stupid white men (and women) swarmed like George Romero's undead outside Tommy Gorman's home in a bid to muzzle him and have him conform to their bizarre beliefs. Yet it was true, he had indeed been selected for an award.

Having it confirmed did little to attenuate my sense of amazement. While books are routinely launched during the festival and their authors are competent, they are not normally what would be viewed as the outflow from independent minds. The individual perspective of their creators rarely appears out of step with the orthodoxy. For all their literary acumen they tend not to raise questions of the established inequitable order that currently prevails in West Belfast. Moreover, many are invited from near and far to speak or sit on discussion panels—including the Unionists. But those real life denizens who actually reside in West Belfast are Republican, who do not support the party of the local MP and seem never to feature on the lists of those asked to contribute. Conformity opens doors in West Belfast. The rewards and sanctions system maintains the hierarchical order of things. Those who think independently must always swim against the tide and risk being marooned by tidal waves of resentment. This makes this year's Tom Cox Memorial Award all the more significant.

The award that Tommy Gorman received has its origins in the human rights advocacy of Tom and Vita Cox. At today's presentation Des Wilson explained something of the background of this U.S. couple. It was their belief that the struggle for human rights in Ireland was a beginning, not an end. They encouraged people to think outside the narrow groove. In keeping faith with their own commitment to the promotion of radicalism they set aside some money to underwrite acknowledgment of the work carried out by radicals. Springhill Community House was nominated to 'talent spot' and arbitrate in the event of a photo finish. On his death bed Tom Cox told Des Wilson, 'Tell the people to keep the faith'. Catholicism wasn't the faith he was referring to either. It was faith in the human intellect to think autonomously, to kick aside the suffocating boundaries of censorship.

Tom Cox was a prolific writer, producing many plays and books throughout his life. He crafted books on Erskine Childers, Michael Collins, and Fenian prisoners in British jails. He also gave of his considerable energy to press for the truth behind the 1984 RUC killing of Sean Downes. In the late 1990s Springhill Community House began its work of presenting the Tom Cox Memorial Award.

Before announcing that this year's choice was Tommy Gorman, Des Wilson gave the audience a glimpse into the life of the Lenadoon Republican who has steadfastly refused to be cowered either by the British or by West Belfast orthodoxy, which seeks to conceal the paucity of its own position by suppressing those who might by their commitment to openness expose it as threadbare. I was honoured to sit in an audience gathered to pay tribute to this Republican activist. I have known him for twenty-six years, first meeting him on the Blanket protest in H4 in 1978. I had known of him for much longer—his 'wanted' boyish face gazing out from our television screens as the British state launched a massive manhunt for him and six of his comrades after they had swam to freedom from the Maidstone in 1972.

Freedom was always central to the being of Tommy Gorman. Not merely freedom from prison walls and the panoptical gaze of British security installations, but freedom from those insidious and invasive techniques of mind control. The standard line on anything was never something to be swallowed by him. When others on protest were saying, 'Political status is just the other side of the hill', because some communication came around from the camp leadership saying so, Tommy never failed to show that the hill was a steep mountain. It could be crossed okay, but not on faith alone.

Des Wilson referred to Tommy's exploits, including his prison escape. He then switched track and spoke of his work in promoting cross community relations at a time when it was not in vogue. For this Tommy was called 'half a Prod' and derided by others. But of real significance were Des Wilson's comments in relation to the unpopular stance taken by the Lenadoon Republican when it came to the politics of the peace process. From the outset Tommy raised the questions that few wanted to hear. On the day that the Provisional IRA cease-fire was announced in August 1994, he rang Bernadette McAliskey to endorse her comments that 'the good guys lost'. An hour later he declined to go to the flag-waving farce through West Belfast. There was nothing to celebrate. It was a mere exercise in fanning away the whiff of defeat through the vigorous waving of tricolours. That is more clear ten years after the event than it was at the time as is evidenced from recent comments by Gerry Adams that 'the British state in the north is a Unionist state. Its symbols and emblems are Unionist. So are its agencies. And its management'. With that as backdrop it comes as no great shock to learn that Tommy Gorman has challenged the logic of a process that has bequeathed this to us.

When it was his own turn to take the podium he, in a voice laden with emotion, expounded on his attitude to the unfettered expression of ideas. Refuting any suggestion that people should prostrate themselves at the altar of Francis Fukuyama who proclaims the end of history and the eternal hegemony of liberal economics, he called for more sustained efforts to widen debate and to respect a multiplicity of voices: 'If you see something that is wrong, speak out and suffer the consequences'. This is asking a lot from those more inclined to believe the exact opposite of what they believed twenty-four hours earlier merely because some leader hit the reverse switch in the back of their necks.

Those who chose to make this award to Tommy Gorman deserve every praise. It takes courage to reach out to the margins and engage with those there rather than seek to draw them into the centre on the terms of the centre. It would have been much easier for Des Wilson and his colleagues to have opted for a safe writer, one who never strays from the comfort zone of the peace process and uses the pen to smudge rather than construct accuracy.

In the audience were members of Tommy's family who shared his burden over the decades. They experienced his prolonged absences while he sat in his second home in Long Kesh. They watched his isolation and ostracism. They heard the whispering campaigns. His wife Anne faced the wrath of the undead gathering outside the family home to protest their opposition to truth. She knows only too well the averted eye contact, the silences, and the myriad expressions of disapproval from those who pronounce, 'There shall be no alternative to us'. Today's award acknowledges their support and loyalty throughout Tommy's challenging political life. His fellow writer Jim McCann was also there today. McCann would hardly agree with Gorman's take on political events but he found it within himself to acknowledge the validity of differing perspectives. By contrast, outside the hall were people who had served time alongside Tommy Gorman in the H-Blocks but who for one reason or another decided not to stray off course by stepping over the threshold into a room where diversity was lauded.

On the drive home I asked Tommy how he felt.

I am overwhelmed. When does anybody ever give people like ourselves prizes for showing that there are opinions other than the official one? I am honoured to have received it from Des. It is all the more special for that.

Tommy Gorman's retention of the rough edges that imbued him with radicalism, and spurred him into opposing censorship and challenging despots are the very qualities that any radical project should extol and value. Who benefits but the powerful when such accoutrements are buffed and polished into mediocre conformity by the peace process? Tommy Gorman's contribution to critical discourse has brought him into conflict with conservative forces whether of the British state, unionism, or the current conservative nationalist status quo. Yet his endeavours in pushing at the boundaries have been a powerful intellectual analeptic, which at all times functioned as the antidote to the mind-numbing sedatives so lavishly applied to the thought processes in West Belfast. In this sense it will never be said that his award was a backhander for silences rendered.

Granny Josie

The Blanket, 28 October 2006

No tyranny is so irksome as petty tyranny.

—EDWARD ABBEY

They carried Granny Josie out of the Ballycolman estate where she had lived up until the time of her death. As in life it was no different in death: Her immediate family were closest to her as she left the estate for the last time. She had eleven children. They in turn provided her with grandchildren. The ripple effect from that was evidenced in the size of the cortege as it crept up the road toward the chapel where the funeral Mass would be heard. Schoolchildren lined part of the route, many of them the friends and classmates of her grandchildren.

Josie Gallagher was a devout Catholic. One of her sons said to me that she possessed a very deep faith. The hardship she encountered during the course of her life was alleviated to some extent by the succour she took from a firm belief in God. In the chapel, one grandchild after another came up to say a few emotionally charged words in her honour. Each spoke of their love for Granny Josie and how her empty chair would be a painful but constant reminder of her presence.

Earlier that morning I had travelled from Belfast to Strabane along with Kevin McQuillan to attend the funeral. Both of us knew the Gallagher family well. Throughout my spells in prison Josie's sons always seemed to be represented in the Republican prisoner population. From what is the norm for families they were overrepresented, three sons in at one stage all serving hefty sentences. Another had served an earlier sentence. In prison I gravitated to them as a duck does to water. They were no respecters of authority, even less so when it was arbitrary and unaccountable.

The Republican prisoner Alex McCrory once observed to me during his second stretch, when the days of seriously battling the prison management were long behind us, that the daily battle for Republicans in jail was to create personal space. There was no shortage of people trying to close it down. The tyranny of the small man is well suited to prison. With literally a captive audience, which as a consequence of enforced proximity is always within fifty yards of some moral guardian, it was easy to see why Alex McCrory thought as he did.

The Gallaghers sought out their own space and helped make it for others. Theirs was an oasis in a desert of boredom and stifling conformity. The Republican leadership in the prison might not have appreciated such a bolthole in the middle of the aridity they so proudly ruled over. But for others who felt Republicans should not try to emulate the lives of frugal monks, the colour lent by the Gallaghers to prison life was welcome. While others were busy ascetically committing to memory the words of some obscure revolutionary, they and the coterie they hung out with were indifferent to what people drank, smoke, read, or expressed. Whether they partook or not, hooch, pot, porn, or free speech were never reasons to be shunned from their company. Small wonder that the friendships forged behind steel doors have lasted long after the final clang of the slammer faded in the distance.

Josie Gallagher shared something of her sons' disdain for authority. She knew that the great and the good rarely practiced what they preached. The forces of good order brought bad disorder to her home. At one point she found herself bound over to keep the peace after hitting a member of the RUC who was violently attacking one of her children. Her home was frequently raided, every year from 1973 to 2002, often several times a year. She saw her sons imprisoned, one of whom went on a lengthy hunger strike after being falsely convicted and who was subsequently brutally beaten on a daily basis by prison staff eager to break his spirit and diminish his resolve. The hunger strike never established his innocence but it kept the NIO paid thugs at bay for its duration and for some time after. His actions had made him into a political hot potato, too hot to be kicked along the cell block. During that fast Josie's husband decided to take on British secretary Roy

Mason in his Barnsley constituency in a bid to draw public attention to their son's plight. An accomplished smuggler of material comforts punitively banned from the prison, Josie defied the prison regime time out of number. In her own words, 'In my own small way I was beating the system and providing my sons with some small luxuries they were being denied'.

With three sons at one point all serving time together for Republican activity, two as INLA prisoners and the third for IRA activities, it would be expected that lots of assistance would be directed Josie's way. She had visited the prisons almost every week from 1974 to 1996. Then in the Teach na Failte booklet *Out of the Shadows* I came across a short contribution by Josie:

> We received no financial assistance for years, maybe a decade. . . . Manys a time I had to thumb it up the road to see them as we had no car and I was not permitted to travel on the Sinn Fein transport as my sons were in on INLA charges. . . . I could never, and still cannot, tell the difference between Stickies, Provos, or INLA as they were all soldiers to me. I remember once thumbing back from Long Kesh and it was snowing and the local Sinn Fein transport passed me. Once I was told I could use the transport to visit my son who was in on Provo charges.

She could not of course use the transport for the purposes of visiting her INLA sons. The power of the small man would prevail; her visiting pass for the day would be checked by the transport police. No mother of imprisoned Republicans would evade their scrutiny. What a crime that would be, letting the mother of the wrong type of Republican political prisoner use the bus to visit her children. 'Papers, please'.

A sceptic might be excused for thinking like John Kenneth Galbraith that under British bosses man oppressed man, but under Republican bosses it was just the opposite. Was our self-righteousness, elitism, and political sectarianism so entrenched that we nurtured an outlook utterly disdainful of an impoverished mother standing at the side of the road in the snow? The bus driver could have thought about a career improvement and applied to become a prison officer. He of course did not devise the policy but was the willing minion at the bottom of the food chain.

Such prejudice against the membership of the Republican Socialist movement and their immediate family was unfortunately not an isolated incident. Those interested in the double discrimination faced by these political prisoners and their kin will find plenty to disturb their sleep at night in *Out of the Shadows*. It is a document that leaves a serious blemish on the standard Provisional Republican accounts of how they managed their own regime within prison. Republican Socialist prisoners endured an experience that was once summed up by an imprisoned son of Josie Gallagher. When on the morning of his release he was asked what he would tell people about the H-Blocks, his response was damning: 'The place is full of bastards and the screws are nearly as bad'.

It is a testimony to the generosity of her character that Granny Josie never held a grudge as a result of this discrimination against her and her family. A mere couple of years after her ban on using the Sinn Fein prison transport she helped three IRA volunteers, two of whom were wounded in a gun battle with British soldiers, escape imprisonment. One of them however, Tommy Brogan, was captured three days later. She hid them, assisted their escape, and destroyed incriminating evidence. On that particular day the whole Ballycolman Estate was cordoned off by the RUC and British army while house-to-house searches were conducted. Josie's home was raided twice that day, the second time after it was noted that smoke was coming from the chimney. It must have been a strange sight, much of the case against IRA volunteers going up in smoke billowing from a chimney on a hot summer day. She knew the volunteers as they had attended the same primary school as her own children. The title of the film *Some Mother's Son* jumps to mind. Josie was proud of the fact that she prevented the mothers of two sons going through what she had—years of trudging to prisons. Prior to that day she had assisted another IRA volunteer destroy evidence that could have led to the imprisonment of a number of his comrades.

Knowing her sons and coming to learn that she was the rock upon which they stood, I regret that I never got to know this tenacious and tender matriarch in life but was honoured to walk in her funeral cortege. While not having a religious thought in my head, I entered the chapel and listened to every word of her funeral Mass. Granny Josie was no Republican ideologue. She cared about her family. There is a side to the Republican struggle that people like Granny Josie and the late Denis Faul graced: a humane side buttressed by remarkable individuals who cared for people, persevered against the odds, and the disapproval of others. Like Denis, Granny Josie was pilloried and ignored and left to stand in the snow because the faces of two of her sons didn't fit the political order.

She got little material reward for her efforts but she never sought it. A number of years ago her sister left her £3000.00 in her will and despite being a pensioner with a weekly income of £60.00 she donated all of it to African children. Recently she was involved in fund raising with her family for the establishment of an orphanage in South Africa that is presently under construction. The group involved in the construction decided to name the orphanage Josie's Place after her untimely death, in recognition of her contribution. For Granny Josie it was about people not property. And in the end, fittingly, it was the people of no property, like herself, who bore her to her grave.

CHAPTER 10
Dissembling

Bertie Talking Bollix

The Blanket, 23 April 2002

At one time on this island there existed a discourse that remained in permanent overdrive as those who shaped it worked with singular determination to ensure the IRA were demonised, banished, banned, and regularly called liars. Those of us in the organisation's ranks were subjected to such pejoratives as terrorists, criminals, and gangsters, the demonology dictionary seemingly required reading for conflict writers and establishment politicians. But now that Peace Process is here to look over us—Big Brother-like in its pervasiveness, monitoring our every word and action lest we say something that 'is not helpful to the peace process' or behave in some manner that is 'opposed to the peace process'—there has been a considerable discursive twist. And it is nowhere more pronounced than in nationalist circles. So fearful have we become of upsetting Peace Process that we tend to appease it, feed it on a diet of its own myths, and tell it nice things about itself, even when it is nonsense. We are all expected to act as a mirror for Peace Process in which it is only ever allowed to see its own deceitful intellectual image tarted up as truth. 'Yes, Peace Process, you are the most exemplary of all peace processes'.

And when the mirror dulls down and its ability to reflect peace as distinct from a mere process is called into question, there is no shortage of word cleaners to come along with new products that explain to us that the dullness is in fact a shine, merely turned inside out, that we need to think strategically and avoid being mesmerised by the tactical manoeuvring of the moment to fully understand it. How else are we supposed to conceptualise the great language of our day such as 'constructive fudge' and 'creative ambiguity'? Without this ability to 'get our heads around it', we could never rest at peace with ourselves having tasted the forbidden fruit, unsuspectingly handed to us by a leading Irish participant at a 1998 Oxford conference on the need for a truth

221

and reconciliation commission: The Good Friday Agreement, all were warned, is 'a delicately balanced compromise that can be destroyed by truth . . . honesty and straightforward talking must be avoided at all costs'.

And nowhere is the evidence of this more substantive than it is within the political leadership of establishment nationalism. Referring to talks between the IRA and the De Chastelain disarmament commission, John Hume once commented, 'The most important thing about the guns factor and those who have used them is when they have said they have stopped that they are telling the truth'.

Gerry Adams—well, he would, wouldn't he—informed his audience in June 2001 that 'the one thing about the IRA, they accept what they have done even when it is unpopular'.

If matters were just restricted to these two minor partners in the nationalist body politic the myth about Peace Process would not be so oppressively encompassing. But when the hegemonic element, represented by the leader of the country, puts his shoulder to the wheel of fiction it then becomes totalising. The regime of truth is established, not constituted by the facts but by all those with the dangerous power to, in the words of Eric Hoffer, 'make their lies come true'.

Speaking after Fianna Fail's annual Easter Rising commemoration at Arbour Hill, Taoiseach Bertie Ahern, echoing Hume and Adams, made the following comment in relation to the Castlereagh theft: 'Down the years when the IRA say they were or were not involved in something, however horrific, it is usually factual. That has been the experience. The Republican movement said from the start that it had no involvement in this particular incident and I've no reason to disbelieve them'.

It is very possible that Mr. Ahern has every reason to believe the IRA when it says it was not involved in the break-in at Castlereagh. After all, the British have neither record of nor reputation for honesty throughout the past thirty-three years. The *Sunday Tribune* (21 April 2002) articles that the British are once again moving to conceal their involvement in the 'dirty war'—this time by blocking a proper investigation into the Dublin-Monaghan bombings—should serve as a reminder that what they say about Castlereagh need not be absorbed like a sponge. And over the years their persistent lying to cover up what took place in Castlereagh interrogation rooms became so ridiculous, it at times sounded like they were being tongue in cheek. In the mid to late 1970s few in the nationalist community would have raised eyebrows if the following statement were to have been released by the British: 'Last night another six prisoners beat themselves up in Castlereagh. One officer who intervened to prevent a suspect attacking himself had his fingernails broken by the suspect's eyes'.

Moreover, even less than the, at best, scant evidence produced in the Colombian case—none, in fact—would suggest Republican involvement in the break-in. The British state has relied on the inevitable innuendo and speculation that would generate as a result of the arrest of a prominent right-wing Republican with media-alleged leadership connections. If the public can be conditioned to presume the guilt of the arrested party, then it is only a small step to make in terms of public perception in order to implicate the Republican leadership. Consequently, a moral panic is created that may have little basis in real terms.

But any historian, rather than a revisionist, of the conflict would instantly recognise Bertie Ahern's comments as nonsense. While his judgment may be right about Castlereagh—the jury is still out on that one—it seemed not to strike the Taoiseach that his sense of timing was going to leave him open to allegations of insensitivity. In the week when the deaths of two gardai brought to public mind the fatalities the force sustained over the past three decades it shall hardly be seen as opportune to forget that the death of Garda Gerry McCabe was a killing carried out by the IRA and immediately denied.

The IRA's history of doing exactly what Mr. Ahern claimed it doesn't is long. Even at the earliest stage of its bombing campaign the organisation remained silent about its involvement until one of its volunteers, Michael Kane, was accidentally killed bombing an electricity transformer at Newforge Lane, Belfast. This practice of remaining mute was resurrected on at least two further occasions: during the sectarian war of 1974 to 1976 when the IRA killed numerous Protestants, and during its campaign in the mid-1990s against drug dealers when the cover name Direct Action Against Drugs was employed.

But remaining silent or using cover names was not the only stratagem employed. In a number of cases the IRA resorted to outright lying. For decades it told the relatives of Jean McConville that the organisation was not responsible for her fate, whatever that may have been. In May 1972, rather than accept responsibility for its involvement in the Anderson Street explosion in East Belfast, which led to eight people dying, including four of its own volunteers, the IRA pointed the finger at loyalists or the SAS. It lied about the Claudy bombing of August the same year in which nine people died, Sean MacStiofain, the then chief of staff, saying an internal IRA inquiry had established that the organisation was not involved. In November 1974 it denied being responsible for the Birmingham bombings. Months later it denied the attack on the Bayardo Bar in 1975 in which five people died. One of those convicted went on to lead IRA prisoners in the H-Blocks during the 1981 hunger strike. In April 1981, the organisation was again lying when it denied killing census collector Joanne Mathers in Derry. This time the finger was pointed at those who were 'frantically attempting to discredit the election campaign of hunger striker Bobby Sands'. In today's language, 'securocrats'.

In November 1987 the IRA blamed British army electronic measures for having detonated the device that killed numerous civilians at the Enniskillen Remembrance Day ceremony. By 1995, according to David McKittrick and Eamon Mallie, IRA sources 'admitted that this "explanation" was just nonsense'. In December 1987 the organisation again lied about having accidentally killed Derry man Gerry Doherty in a bomb blast. In October 2000, the IRA was found to be lying in relation to the Ballymurphy murder of Real IRA member Joe O'Connor, even going as far as to cynically offer condolences to his family.

Eddie Holt, Irish political commentator, surely got it right when he claimed that 'the language of war, like the language of advertising, political ideology and corporations, is a jumble of jargon, euphemisms, and downright lies . . . a sanitising operation, designed to disguise the reality of butchery'.

The litany of lies is far from exhaustive. But that lies are officially manufactured to conceal other lies demonstrates that the peace process is intellectually fraudulent and morally bankrupt. Perhaps if his advisers were to have provided Bertie Ahern with the *Irish Times* more often he may just have noticed that as early as May 2000 the paper was commenting that 'frequent assertions that the IRA are models of truthfulness are not borne out in all circumstances'.

It is perhaps to be expected that the IRA, like all other parties, will peddle its own myths. But for those of us who support the peace but are not beholden to the process because of its counterfeit composition it seems bizarre that others do. From the point of view of Fianna Fail's own self-interest Ahern seems to have lost the plot in ensuring that the sun shone so that others could make hay.

There seemed to be little strategic sense for the party leader to be crediting the Provisional IRA with a general honesty it does not possess at a time when the other side of the house, Sinn Fein, is making a claim to be a party of integrity in a sea of corruption.

The South African writer Nadine Gordimer's observations may yet come to haunt the Fianna Fail leader: 'To serve your society best you have to be honest and frank'. And historians may ultimately ask, was this the turning point at which Bertie Ahern failed to turn?

The Imperfect Peace: Terence O'Neill's Day Has Come

Belfast Telegraph, 18 August 2004

T en years ago as August drew its last breath a buzz of excitement swept through West Belfast. The Provisional IRA had just declared its first major cease-fire in nineteen years. Later in the day Provisional leaders Gerry Adams and Martin McGuinness would be feted with flowers at Connolly House. The Falls was awash with anticipation, the Shankill subdued by suspicion. The mood in both communities would have been vastly different had anyone suggested on that day that a full decade later the British would still be here, having shown not the slightest inclination to leave; that the consent principle, which Republican volunteers had fought, killed, and died to usurp, would reign supreme; that IRA weaponry would be decommissioned; that the Provisional Sinn Fein leadership would be worshiping at Temple Stormont; that it would be openly stating as its objective the reform of the RUC and the disbandment of the IRA. As one time Republican prisoners we had spent decades inside dreading such an outcome, seeing in it only defeat. Yet hardly a word of protest issued from within Provisional ranks. David Aaronovitch of the *Independent* apparently hit the bulls-eye when he later wrote: 'It has taken 3,500 deaths and thirty years for Republicans to understand that John Hume was right all along'.

Sometime in the afternoon of that 'historic' day, I was with one of those former Republican prisoners, Tommy Gorman, when he phoned Bernadette McAliskey to endorse her BBC *Talkback* comments that 'the war is over and the good guys lost'. As we made no attempt to conceal our affirmation of her view the leadership's thought police soon came to learn of it. They were not enamoured toward us. What did they expect? Because they were fluent in gibberish and had the most amazing capacity to absorb nonsense that everyone else should be the same? Days earlier, when a senior IRA member had 'briefed' me that there would be a cease-fire, my first comment was, 'The leadership might have surrendered but we haven't'. The vacant look on his stunned face was so bottomless, revealing a cerebral nothingness, I wonder if the realisation has sunk in even today.

After his call to Bernadette, Tommy Gorman and myself walked down a sun-caressed Whiterock Road. We had not covered any great distance before being approached by an excitable but solid local Sinn Fein member who invited us to join him on the party cavalcade that would shortly wind its way through West Belfast. My response, 'Turkeys celebrating Christmas', seemed to offend him. He genuinely believed that something was coming. We sensed we were about to be shafted. And we were.

At the time, the defeat of the Provisional IRA was hushed up by all sides. It suited. If fudge and ambiguity allowed the leadership to deceive its grassroots about the enormity of the climb-down it was preparing to make, then London, Dublin, and the other main players would provide cover. Only now, when all but the recalcitrant few believe the IRA can't go back to an armed campaign, are observers prepared to acknowledge that the IRA lost the war. Before he died Joe Cahill was openly likened to Comical Ali for being sufficiently immune to public common sense to have been able to say the Provisional IRA had won the war and now it was time to win the peace. Few thought to ask if the war was truly won, why so much difficulty in announcing that it was over?

After our initial forays into that dangerous realm of independent thought, it soon became clear that the bearers of dissent were to be identified as prime candidates for the persona non grata award. Furious party apparatchiks would froth at the mouth at the slightest sign of a hand they did not control going up at a meeting. 'At the end of the day, Gerry is right', the tautological mantra. As the years have passed and everything that was not supposed to happen has happened, it is now clear why the leadership was determined that its strategy would not be questioned. It was based on an utter falsehood. The struggle to achieve 'national liberation' was being abandoned—traded in for an internal solution. In order to protect this falsehood our leaders ruthlessly pursued a policy of organised lying, methodical lying. It took the endeavour of Ed Moloney via his discerning tome *A Secret History of the IRA* to bring it home to greater numbers.

Before the Provisional IRA was founded the Unionist prime minister of Northern Ireland, Terence O'Neill, pompously stated that if the Unionist community would only treat Catholics well and allow them some prosperity, they would stop having seventeen children and come to live like Protestants. His day has come.

Case Unproven

The Blanket, 5 June 2006

peaking five years ago Martin McGuinness made the following prediction:

> There's almost an inevitability that within the next five years Sinn Fein then will be the largest party and the first minister will be a Sinn Fein minister. I could certainly see Gerry Adams as first minister.

Today, the prospects of Adams stepping into the shoes of David Trimble must seem light years away. The downturn in Sinn Fein's fortunes has been so dramatic that the party is reduced to calling for Paisley to be the top dog at Stormont. To make matters worse the man who made the Adams prediction is now embroiled in the type of controversy which in itself, even if the accusations levelled against him turn out to be groundless, may have serious consequences for his long-term political future.

Martin McGuinness has been in the media hot seat so often that he must have worn out more than one of them. No matter what was thrown his way he faced it down secure in the knowledge that he was defending his movement from attack and would have the support of the bulk of those within it. On this occasion the authoritative deportment of old seems absent. Persistent leadership lying has shattered the grassroots confidence on which McGuinness could normally have relied. Dismissing as the 'Sunday Liar' the paper that initially named him as agent J118 rings vacuous against the backcloth of Sinn Fein leadership lies.

Although McGuinness prudently avoided being scooped for a 'world exclusive' interview by the one journalist who 'established' the innocence of Freddie Scappaticci, the language used in his defence is remarkably similar to that brought out to cover for Scappaticci. This has generated uncertainty among the usually certain followers. There is a hesitancy to give full throttle to protestations of innocence on McGuinness' behalf. The delayed intervention of Adams, heard but not seen with McGuinness, has done little to allay unease. The BBC's former security correspondent, Brian Rowan, hardly helped the defence case by calling as witness for the accused every 'securocrat' that Sinn Fein claimed was previously working to wreck the peace process.

McGuinness' attempts to blame former Special Branch Chief Bill Lowry are contestable given Lowry's public admission that Special Branch intervened to shape the outcome of IRA army conventions so that they would produce the result desired by McGuinness and Adams. Against such a backdrop, the goodwill that Martin McGuinness is getting from the Republican constituency boils down to a view that he is unlikely to have been an agent. Prior to Scappaticci, 'unlikely' would have been a term that conveyed so much doubt that those using it would have come under suspicion themselves for displaying something less than absolute faith in the leadership.

Many will find this perplexing considering that the evidence against McGuinness thus far amounts to zilch. Some Republicans outside of Sinn Fein who know him well and abhor him nevertheless conclude that were he an agent, the Provisional IRA would have been brought to its knees long before the 1994 cease-fire. As Eamonn McCann argued on *Radio Free Eireann* Saturday evening, if the accusation against McGuinness is to be taken seriously then it must be Everest-like in stature. At the moment it is nothing more than a pebble. It has legs solely because of past leadership deception and a willingness to cover for informers. Outside of that history, the current story would have died the Sunday it emerged. There seems no reason to be any more suspicious of McGuinness now than there was prior to the appearance of the transcript that it is claimed shows he is a British agent but reveals nothing of the sort.

The transcript at the centre of the McGuinness-as-agent controversy is increasingly viewed with scepticism. This week's *Sunday Times* unpicked its authenticity so thoroughly that to continue believing it is not counterfeit requires a huge dose of intellect suppressants. By linking its emergence to the agent Kevin Fulton/Peter Keeley (who denies any involvement) the *Sunday Times* has obliterated in one surgical strike any potential for the transcript to gather credibility. But like the pacesetter in long-distance running who drops back long before the finish line, the transcript has brought to the fore new competitors.

This is nowhere more evident than in the *Sunday Times*. In a masterly piece of manoeuvring the paper took out the man but kept the ball in play. One article hobbled Martin Ingram who brought the transcript into the public domain in the genuine belief that it was authentic, while another judiciously kept the head of steam growing against Martin McGuinness. This has inevitably given rise to speculation on the part of those who know as little as the rest of us that the *Sunday Times* at some point will disrobe McGuinness. It helps defibrillate a story that would otherwise have reached the flat line.

An inescapable dilemma for McGuinness is that in denying the accusation he adds to its newsworthiness. That alone, without the slightest proof of any wrongdoing on his part, may ultimately make his position as a prospective deputy first minister untenable. In the sectarian jockeying for position against opponents for public office, rather than in anything disreputable on the part of the Derry nationalist, may lie the origins of the current spy story. Allegations of DUP manipulation of public sentiment could turn out to have more substance than at first imagined.

Martin McGuinness is in an unenviable position. While he should be able to win the debate outright, given the weakness of the case thus far against him, he cannot land the knockout punch and instead labours on the ropes because he is an integral part of a Sinn Fein leadership that has long exhibited disdain for the truth. What a complex web this has turned out to be.

The Bogeyman

The Blanket, 19 November 2006

> *The problem with 'terrorists' is that they keep their word;*
> *politicians usually don't.*
>
> —GERRY ADAMS

Taoiseach Bertie Ahern says he believes it. Tanaiste Michael McDowell claims not to. PSNI boss Hugh Orde says it's true, yet his special branch has no knowledge of it. Paul Leighton and Peter Hain haltingly testify to its existence, while Ian Paisley Junior scorns it as some sort of pathetic distraction. The warnings about it came from neither the Garda nor PSNI. The Continuity IRA, Real IRA, and INLA have all denied any association with or knowledge of it.

Whatever about 'it', the truth status of the 'great dissident threat to Sinn Fein leaders' story has kept the media busy in a week that was otherwise much the same as the week before—politicians trying to kick each other off the greasy pole to power. Most people are bored with that, so the 'dissident threat' morsel spices up the news. It is through bemused eyes that the media handling of the story is to be viewed. The invisible threat is reported with great verve but no mention of the fact that those allegedly under threat have spent their entire adult lives threatening others and worse. Nor has the media bothered to ask why, after years of accusing dissidents of being micro groups penetrated by British intelligence and incapable of pulling off any serious operation, should Sinn Fein be concerned about threats emanating from such quarters.

Most people outside Sinn Fein think the leadership lie machine is doing what it does most—spoofing, the purpose being to kill off any debate on policing that is not leadership controlled and as a result rendered anodyne. Widely laughed at when it blames securocrats for its misfortunes or bungling negotiating, the leadership, under new

232

stresses, comes up with new bogeymen—dissentocrats. This mosaic of diverse crats has for years apparently found common cause against Sinn Fein. No skulduggery or mischief is considered beyond the pale of the evil schemers in the crat alliance to stop Gerry Kelly from becoming a peeler.

If, in the interests of best practice, observers bypass the dubious testimony of Sinn Fein politicians, the pseudostrategic discourse of *AP-RN* bamboozlers, or the Dear Leader column in the *Irish News*, what evidence is there of any threat? *The Blanket* sought out the views of a wide but diverse range of opinion within the Republican spectrum that is at odds with Sinn Fein's political project. These days there is no shortage of voices ready to make themselves heard. They all doubted the existence of any threat.

Brendan Hughes, who along with Gerry Adams ran the IRA's Belfast Brigade in 1972 and 1973, dismissed the claim as an election stunt ahead of the March polls:

> There is no threat. They are certainly not under any threat from the Brits! It is all bullshit. The only people likely to be under threat are you, me, Marian Price, Tommy Gorman—anybody who has questioned the hopeless direction this party has travelled in.

Hughes thinks few people will be taken in by it. He said Sinn Fein leaders have been 'lying for so long about everything, nobody is going to fall for this'.

Richard O'Rawe, author of the influential book *Blanketmen*, was equally sceptical of the allegations first made public by Gerry Adams. 'I don't think anybody is threatening this man at all'. O'Rawe believes it is a self-serving two-pronged Sinn Fein construct. On one hand it sends a message to the DUP that Sinn Fein leaders are eager to meet the Unionist demands and are risking their lives to do so. At the same time, it is an attempt to blackmail those within Sinn Fein into staying put. They are being told that if they leave the movement the type of people they will end up with are those who want to kill the leadership. For O'Rawe it is nothing more than a transparent fraud that others should see through readily enough.

Dolours Price, who survived a prolonged hunger strike in British prisons in the 1970s where she was sentenced to life for leading the first IRA Provisional bombing team to target the British capital, and who served under Gerry Adams when he commanded the Belfast IRA, queries the existence of any threat. In her view it is an attempt by Adams to stupefy the Republican base into diving headlong into policing structures. Adams pushes the threat line so that 'he can tell his followers that the best way to have protection is to be part of the state and its armed wing, the police'. She is adamant that there is no threat to Adams or his fellow contras. 'I am absolutely convinced, as a result of my Republican contacts, that there is no threat whatsoever'. She goes on to ask why anybody would bother targeting Sinn Fein leaders:

> The more ridiculous they become, the less anybody would be interested in threatening them. No Republican would want to kill David Ford of the Alliance Party. Gerry Adams is just the same as Ford or any other political leader. Sinn Fein is just another political party. What difference is there between Adams and other political leaders apart from Adams telling more lies?

Price reinforces the view that none of the Republicans critical of Sinn Fein have ever attacked the party physically. 'Sinn Fein has that dubious distinction all to itself. I was visited by the Garda and told that the PSNI had information that I was to be attacked by the Provisionals because I had protested at their meetings'. She is scathing of their motives. 'They want to join the cops. Shame on the first one of them to put on a British uniform'.

Kevin McQuillan, onetime chairperson of the IRSP, feels that the threat claim is a 'cynically contrived no-brainer'. He argues that while there is strong opposition on the ground to the Sinn Fein 'sellout' this does not translate 'in any way, shape, or form into threats against the party'. For McQuillan, Sinn Fein is concerned by what it sees as a realignment of Republicans and the emergence of broad front politics against what Sinn Fein is trying to do. 'The party leadership wants to corral the herd in order to bloc vote through the remaining concessions that the Brits and DUP are demanding it makes to meet the demands of the St. Andrew's Agreement'.

Carrie Twomey, editor of *The Blanket*, derides the Sinn Fein claims:

> As one poster on an Internet site pointed out, at one time if you challenged them they would accuse you of lining up with the Omagh bombers. Now that nobody any longer believes that dissent equates with Omagh, they accuse those who question their strategy of being part of a plot to kill them. Either way, it's a crude attempt at demonising their opposition. Their tactics are transparent, patronizing, as if people are idiots who haven't a brain in their head to see through them. They treat people with contempt when they come out with guff like this and expect it to be believed unquestioningly.

Patricia Campbell, a Tyrone Republican who is a columnist with the radical journal *Fourthwrite*, says she is suspicious about the claims. 'I know that there have been slogans on walls calling Sinn Fein traitors. But the media seem to be blowing this out of all proportion. I have never trusted the media and still don't'.

Tommy Gorman, a former Maidstone escapee and H-Block Blanket protestor, is not surprised at Sinn Fein coming up with the threat idea. 'Not because it exists but because Sinn Fein is in a tight corner and needs to create a bogeyman'. He cites Bernadette McAliskey, who once pointed out that the peace process began like a funnel but over time narrowed to the point where the only option is to be squeezed:

> At the start there is plenty of wriggle room in which to deceive the rank and file. But the further down you go, the tighter it becomes, until there is no room to do anything other than what those who control the funnel want. We always insisted that this was where it would end up. And so it has. The leadership is now willingly pushing through everything it once swore to oppose. Consequently, the scales are finally beginning to drop off the eyes of the grassroots. The leadership is panicking and wants the eyes blinkered up again. They are desperate to stop their own people from experiencing other ideas.

Gorman then draws on an analogy once made by George Galloway when the Respect MP riposted Christopher Hitchens: 'The Sinn Fein leadership has managed to metamorphose from butterfly into slug'. He sums up the party leadership in one word—'pathetic'.

Marian Price, once a former IRA hunger striker and life sentence prisoner, retains the political perspective that motivated her throughout the darkest days of her life. She is scathing of the 'nonsense, absolute nonsense' peddled by Sinn Fein leaders. She is unhesitating in asserting that there is not the remotest possibility of Republicans attacking anybody in Sinn Fein:

> With the Provisionals so far down the road of dishonour, why would people decide to take action of the type alleged by Sinn Fein? Republicans have been pointing out for years that this is where Sinn Fein would end up. There is nothing surprising about it. People who have not targeted Sinn Fein over the past decade or more are most definitely not going to do so now.

Marian Price believes the Provisional movement is boxed in with nowhere left to go but cap in hand into the jaws of the beast. With many of its own members starting to realise that they were sold a pup, its leaders are now desperate to create a smokescreen as cover for the final step in their retreat from republicanism. She argues that the leadership is also determined to ensure its own members do not link up in a common political project with people it calls dissidents:

> They want sympathy. The danger is that instead of coming clean about where they have taken their people they are spreading nonsense that could feed into a feud mentality. Republicans will not fall for it. Republicans will sit back and watch Sinn Fein leaders be exposed for what they are.

John Kelly from South Derry, who was a Sinn Fein MLA before he resigned from the party after being hounded for supporting Republican prisoners in Maghaberry, believes it is a 'smear campaign against those Republicans who do not agree with the leadership. It is Provo black propaganda'. A former founding member of the Provisional IRA, Kelly thinks it highly significant that the only evidence for the supposed threats comes from the Provisionals themselves. 'It is an effort to distract attention away from their stance on policing. It is quite deliberate'. He was scathing of Gerry Adams' cynical attempt to elicit public sympathy on the grounds of his family being alarmed. 'There is absolutely no consideration from Adams for the families of those he falsely alleges are his would-be assassins'. Kelly goes on to say that 'Mr. Adams is being deliberately hurtful to his former comrades in arms. Then again, by his own account, Mr. Adams was a draft dodger so he would not understand the concept of fealty to comrades in arms'!

Seamus Kearney, a former Republican prisoner also from South Derry, regards the threats as nonsense made up by Sinn Fein:

> They can't really complain about being viewed as traitors

after all they have done. They brought Franko Hegarty back and executed him for giving away fewer guns than they did. But that does not mean anybody is planning to kill them. I think Republicans just laugh at them. They could never be regarded as Republicans after getting into bed with the Brits.

Michael Donnelly, a former internee who once had his limbs broken by a Sinn Fein gang, agreed with Seamus Kearney that many people would view the Sinn Fein leadership as traitors and some would probably like to see the back of them:

But this does not mean anybody is serious about threatening them. I suppose people might sound off about them but that hardly amounts to a real threat. They have played the underdog so long that they think by trying it again they will win sympathy. They are on the defensive politically and need a scapegoat.

Donnelly posits an alternative view of the origins of the threat allegations:

They have outlived their usefulness to MI5. They can't deliver because Paisley is not interested in having McGuinness as his deputy. He prefers someone like Michelle Gildernew. So you can't rule out the intelligence services putting the mix in to bring that situation about.

He is certain that there is no basis to the threat allegation. 'It does not exist'. He contends that, in fact, it is the other way round. 'I am threatened by the Provisionals all the time. Recently they threatened to raid a house in search of a computer because they believed it hosted a Web site that challenged their line'. Donnelly argues that many

Republicans in Derry keep talking about the need to look over their shoulder in case Sinn Fein makes a move on them. 'There is a gap in the political process for a while and the Provos might be planning to use it to flex their muscles'.

Tony McPhilips is a Fermanagh-based activist involved in defending the rights of political prisoners. Describing himself as an anti-treaty Republican, he slams the Sinn Fein claims as laughable:

> To suggest that Republicans who have always opposed treaties would suddenly decide to target Adams and McGuinness doesn't add up. The camel's back was not broken by any recent event. The camel collapsed a long time ago. Anybody who wanted to target Adams and McGuinness would probably have done it back then. It is not going to happen. Whose agenda does it suit? Adams and McGuinness and no one else.

Sean McCaughey, until recently a Sinn Fein activist in South Belfast, said he had initially paid no attention to the claims of Sinn Fein, putting it down to yet more drivel. After he did think about it he wondered why he bothered, as the only conclusion he could come up with was it was still more drivel. 'It is a distraction created by Sinn Fein spin doctors to divert attention away from the final dilution of Republican principles as they slaughter the last sacred cow, opposition to a British police force, on the altar of the peace process'.

Ivan Morley from Newry, who in tonight's issue of *The Blanket* writes an article about his late father, Davey, the former OC of Long Kesh, says he is sceptical about the existence of any threat:

> Rather than it being a threat to them it is a threat engineered by them. I think it is to win themselves some kudos. They are brilliant manipulators and like they have done on other occasions they are trying to manipulate the current situation to their own end.

Martin Cunningham, a former Sinn Fein councillor in South Down, is another Republican not persuaded by Sinn Fein's protestations:

> It is attention seeking. They want sympathy as they try to buy time to get into the police. People are asking questions and that is the last thing Sinn Fein want. They need people who will accept being told what to do and question nothing. So they come up with this swindle to keep people obedient. There is no threat.

The former Republican prisoner Brendan Shannon is particularly critical of Hugh Orde's intervention in the matter, arguing that the PSNI boss' concern about Republicans under threat is only newly found:

> He has said nothing over the years when there were very real threats from the Sinn Fein leadership to its Republican critics. What is a serious threat? A member of my family recently received live ammunition through the post. The cops said it was a threat but not a serious one. They have nothing like that to show that Sinn Fein is under threat.

He further argues that Orde's backing of the Sinn Fein position is clear evidence that the party is not even Republican. 'When do the cops ever support anything Republicans say? For years dissidents have been threatened and harmed by the Provisionals and no cop said anything'. He says Sinn Fein is appearing ridiculous in its desperate attempt to cover up for its strategic failings. 'Think about it. If you are a dissident it is much better to sit and watch these people being exposed. Their Republican veneer is being peeled away like the layers of an onion. Much better to see them humiliated than threatened'.

Republicans like Shannon do not rule out Sinn Fein launching a Four Courts–type strike against those who refuse to accept the new political dispensation. He harbours a suspicion that former IRA comrades such as Gerry Adams and Martin McGuinness, on the pretext that it is preemptive, may follow in the footsteps of their forebears, Richard Mulcahy and Kevin O'Higgins, and order a little of Auden's necessary murder. 'It is a Sinn Fein devised tactic aimed at preparing the ground to lash out at its opponents in the full knowledge that the British will turn a blind eye. They are under no threat; it is a load of balls'.

Willie Gallagher of the IRSP repeated to *The Blanket* earlier claims he had made to the *Sunday Times*, *Belfast Telegraph*, *Derry Journal*, and on an IRSP Web site. He said Martin McGuinness, who he described as 'Chief $pin Fein Liar', and Gerry Adams, 'the darling of Bush', have fashioned a strategy to suppress any dissenting voices within republicanism. This had led them to spew:

> bogus rubbish, lies, and spin. I believe that someone in Sinn Fein has concocted this to divert people away from the party's internal problems with the PSNI. It is designed to get the troops to rally round the leadership during this 'great time of danger' and stifle political criticism. These ridiculous claims are a blatant attempt to negate any debate within the anti-PSNI Republican camp by vilifying us as collaborators and assassins so that nobody will have anything to do with us and also to suck up to their masters on Downing Street. 'Look at poor us, Tony, risking our lives in the pursuit of joining your police force'.

Gallagher feels that Adams and McGuinness are themselves targeting for marginalisation those who attended a series of meetings organised by Republicans opposed to the political direction of Sinn Fein. However, he insisted:

> These are ridiculous claims from two proven liars. I am one of the individuals who has attended every one of these

so-called coming together events that Martin McGuinness has referred to and I can assure him that nothing of the sort that he has alluded to was discussed. In fact, to be quite frank, if talk like that came up, we would not be there. There has been absolutely no discussions whatsoever on any type of military action, assassination, or conspiracies, no discussion of any kind of military campaign. We are absolutely opposed to anyone from Sinn Fein being killed. McGuinness and Adams know that quite well as current members of Sinn Fein attended the meetings. What we have discussed is the political capitulation of Sinn Fein. We won't be deflected from our opposition to acceptance of a corrupt British police force nor will we be forced into giving allegiance to a corrupt state or to a corrupt Sinn Fein leadership.

Gallagher, a long-standing Strabane Republican, and former long-term Republican prisoner, shares the concerned view of Brendan Shannon. He believes Hugh Orde's endorsement of Sinn Fein charges that its leaders are under threat is a strategic attempt on the part of the PSNI boss to create the conditions whereby Republican opponents of the PSNI will face repressive measures endorsed by Sinn Fein. 'The very fact that both Peter Hain and Hugh Orde have said that they are also aware of these claims suggests that this is a coordinated spin exercise by both the leadership of Sinn Fein and their British masters'.

Others display a lesser sense of alarm, intuiting that Sinn Fein have become so locked into the peace process that it has become almost impossible for the party to murder its detractors. Tommy McKearney, editor of *Fourthwrite*, doubts that the Provisionals feel threatened to the point where they would want to risk everything by taking military action against their Republican critics. Nor does the former Republican prisoner and H-Block hunger striker think there would be any desire on the part of those critics to literally start taking shots at the Sinn Fein leadership. 'Even if some individual felt so inclined others around them would see the futility of it. I doubt if there is any threat but if it were to exist it would be both deplorable and insane'.

In other times or places, given the scale of their abandonment of Republican politics, Sinn Fein leaders might well have had cause for concern. A bit like the Russian oil oligarchs who stole their country's resources and grew rich on them at the expense of the citizens, these leaders became profiteers by selling off every Republican asset that was acquired through the endurance and sacrifices of Republican volunteers and activists. What belonged collectively to Republicans was privatised in the hands of key leaders who traded off the lot in return for the booty of power and prosperity. They did quite well out of it.

It can hardly come as a surprise, therefore, to these same leaders that their incessant lying, manoeuvring behind the backs of their own activists, acquisition of wealth and property, the power-at-any-price strategy would accumulatively nurture resentment. But even here they try to turn that very legitimate resentment into an asset that can be used to buy more sympathy. Adams and his colleagues, however, may not get the return they anticipated on this. Too long a lie makes a stone of the ear. Few are genuinely listening, although Sinn Fein's establishment friends pretend that they are. There is not the slightest evidence to suggest that Republicans are prepared to follow the most base instincts and pose any physical threat to the lives, families, or considerable property of the leaders of Contra Sinn Fein.

Only a Fool

The Blanket, 19 January 2007

> *There was nothing new in last week's written statement from*
> *Tony Blair on the future role of MI5 in Northern Ireland. It*
> *amounted to no more than a repetition of what is already laid*
> *down in the relevant section (Annex E) of the*
> *St. Andrew's Agreement.*
>
> —DAVID ADAMS

A fool and his money are easily parted. A knave alone would put his earnings on the veracity of the claim that MI5 is not to be involved in civic policing, which will be carried out exclusively, we are told, by the PSNI.

Think about it. The greatest liar in modern British political history tells the greatest liar in modern Irish political history, 'Policing is the responsibility solely of the PSNI. The security service will have no role whatsoever in civic policing'. What seriously are the chances of the Blair-Adams combination producing something totally alien to the two components that make it up? What odds would you get with a bookie for it? The same probably as you would find were you to place your money on the result of two dogs' mating being the birth of a cat.

Yet such a claim is to be peddled to the Sinn Fein grassroots so that those who compose it can get over any reservations they might harbour toward supporting the PSNI. Gerry Kelly tried pulling this one on them: The police will now be protected from the 'malign and corruptive control of MI5 . . . if they act illegally then we have a PSNI that is not signed up to MI5 and that will hold them to account'.

To rub salt in the wounds the guarantor of the Adams-Blair arrangement is an arch opponent of civil liberties, Lord Carlile, who supports both Diplock Courts and ninety-day detention. He, we are asked to believe, shall scrutinise the role of MI5 and hold it to account. James Connolly's appropriate and prophetic words flood the mind: 'Ruling by fooling is a great British art with great Irish fools to practice on'.

Blair and Adams have sought to hoodwink both the Provisional constituency and the wider nationalist community by blurring the issue. It is not MI5's role in civic policing that is the subject of dispute but the PSNI's role in political policing. No one ever seriously thought that MI5 would be sent to Ireland to pursue people who annoy their neighbours, don't pay car tax, or do the double. But the PSNI will most definitely arrest those who extralegally protest against water charges, as well as Republicans who sadly learned from Sinn Fein leaders that violence is a productive form of opposition to the British state.

Moreover, Blair, when pressed, tellingly refused to rule out MI5 involvement in tackling any Provisional movement activity, or that of Sinn Fein's various Republican opponents. Neither did he offer assurances, nor was he asked for any, that both the PSNI and MI5 have pulled all their informers out of Sinn Fein.

In order for Sinn Fein to maintain the sleight of hand it will have to agree with the British that the type of activity Sinn Fein leaders previously ordered young men and women to carry out will now be criminalised so that it may fall under the remit of civic policing.

Activities Sinn Fein previously demanded be rewarded with political status will now have to be termed criminal in order to maintain the fiction of the PSNI as a service engaged exclusively in civic policing. It is happening already as with the Sinn Fein call for the Provisionals involved in the Bobby Tohill incident to hand themselves over to the courts.

Gerry Kelly's wretched handling of the MI5 issue has invited much ridicule from a wide range of people on the streets, journalists and politicians. During the week a friend and shrewd observer of events e-mailed me and commented, 'That fool Kelly said on TV this week that if MI5 did anything wrong the PSNI now will be able to investigate them'. Another veteran Republican said, 'Can you believe the nonsense that spews out of him? The stupidest man in the world is wiser than that fool'.

Gerry Kelly has probably been called many things in his life but a fool was never one of them. A number of years ago it was inconceivable that the word *fool* would have found any space in the lexicon of his critics. Today, however, the frequency of his bizarre public commentary, encapsulated in the exuberant welcome he extended to the Great Liar of London's MI5 statement, has ensured that his intellectual credibility is being called into question on a daily basis: 'We want MI5 out of Ireland; there's no place for it north or south. This gets us a very major step closer to that'. For those who know him it is hard to reconcile the intellectually adept, straight-talking Kelly of the prisons with the inchoate dissembler of today.

Gerry Kelly, throughout the time that I remained friendly with him, was a perceptive and highly intelligent man. Those hoping to win the point against him were wasting their time if they came ill prepared. As well read as he was well versed, Kelly was a formidable adversary in any political or strategic discussion. He can hardly have lost that intellect. He has, however, allowed it to slip into abeyance in deference to the meaningless platitudes of the peace process. This became apparent to me in the spring of 1998 when at a Sinn Fein briefing session he ventured the opinion that the Good Friday Agreement, while not a transition to a united Ireland, was a transition to a transition. It was one of my last Sinn Fein meetings.

It is because Gerry Kelly is judicious rather than foolish that it sticks in the craw of many that Ian Paisley Junior has somehow managed to package himself as a cerebral colossus compared to him. Paisley Junior is much more credible when he asserts that Kelly's party had been 'sold a pup'; that Blair's words amounted to 'a restatement of the fundamentals set out in Annex E of the St. Andrews Agreement'. Mark Durkan of the SDLP complemented this, claiming that British minister Paul Goggins 'confirmed that MI5 are taking over intelligence policing. He confirmed that it will include domestic terrorism. He confirmed that

Nuala O'Loan, [Police Ombudsman for Northern Ireland], will not be able to investigate MI5'. It is embarrassingly all up in the air when the DUP and the SDLP are telling Sinn Fein members the truth and their own leaders are lying to them.

What really decided the issue for Sinn Fein was an agency but not the spook ensemble the party would have us believe. Borrowing from columnist Tom Luby's wonderful analogy, in what would seem to be yet another side deal between Napoleon Adams and Pilkington Blair, agreement was reached to scrap the Assets Recovery Agency. One paper has reported that this was a move to mollify South Armagh Provisionals. Perhaps, but observers don't have to travel to the hills of South Armagh to see Provisional prosperity. The 'greatest negotiators ever' have ceded all the hard-won political ground to MI5 in return for the men of property being allowed to proclaim 'what we have we hold'. In return the men of property will take their place on platforms throughout the north in the coming days to urge support for the leadership's endorsement of the PSNI. Hypocrisy, as the poet John Milton wrote, is 'the only evil that walks invisible'.

CHAPTER 11
Northern Bank Robbery

Bad Santa

The Blanket, 23 December 2004

The intricacy and mastery of detail put into the robbery of the Northern Bank in the heart of Belfast has led to much speculation that the 'perps' responsible for carrying it out belonged to one of the north's local militias. Certainly the most illegally efficient organisational minds on the island were not twiddling their thumbs, or despatching shoals of pickpockets through crowded streets of Christmas shoppers while first-time amateurs tripped over a city centre rainbow and landed perchance on this pot of gold. No—outlaws with a strategic mind were responsible for this.

The reports thus far read like accounts from the 1978 Banstead robbery. A group of London gangsters led by Chopper Knight using a bogus policeman and relying on inside information planned and implemented a sensationalist heist with split-second timing and military precision. The operation in the Blackwell Tunnel went like clockwork and caused untold embarrassment to the British police.

Given that Northern Irish gangs outside the militia world have rarely displayed such cunning and expertise, the bookies' odds on this one narrow considerably the closer the pointer comes to settle on the Provisional IRA. While nobody yet has suggested anything concrete that would lead the finger to definitively point in the direction of Adams' merry men, people's knowledge of the wider world is largely mediated and heavily dependent on inferences. It is the human condition. People watch for patterns, study the form, rule out the ridiculous, consider the plausible, and then make conclusions. It is how we live. Whether the conclusions in this case have caused the film industry to cast around for scriptwriters to pen the potential blockbuster *Jesse Adams Rides Again* remains to be seen. But if the *Daily Telegraph*, based on its briefings from British security sources, is anywhere near the mark, then the film isn't going to be about anybody else.

251

In the media discourse immediately following the robbery there appeared suggestions that one reason for maintaining caution against assumptions of Provisional IRA culpability was that 'despite the signs pointing in their direction, it is very difficult to believe that the leadership of the Provisionals would sanction a spectacular that would inevitably doom the fragile peace talks to failure for another lengthy period'.

To the contrary, such an action dovetails perfectly with current Provisional strategy. If the Adams outfit was responsible, then the final stages of the operation were being put into effect while the negotiations that collapsed earlier this month were taking place. When Gerry Adams stood with Tony Blair and Bertie Ahern, renouncing the IRA devil and all of its works, the one image that flickers to mind is of Michael Corleone renouncing Satan at the baptism of his child in the closing stages of *The Godfather* while his cohorts ruthlessly move through the streets of New York clad with horns, tail and cleft foot.

Provisional involvement in the robbery, if true, adds weight to the view that the Sinn Fein leadership were never serious about reaching the type of deal the DUP thought it was getting. The only way Sinn Fein was signing up for that deal was on the basis that it would sneak the IRA into government. Tom McGurk of the *Sunday Business Post*, thinking the deal had been all but signed, taunted the DUP that after years of trying to obliterate the IRA the only thing the party had achieved was to place the IRA at the heart of government. The DUP was lucky it didn't reach agreement. Once in government with Sinn Fein, and the robbery had occurred, the DUP would have been under serious external pressure not to buckle the new institutions. London and Dublin would have pulled out all the stops in a bid to persuade Paisley's party that it was the work of former paramilitaries beyond mainstream control. Sinn Fein relying on the IRA denial would claim it was an internal bank room brawl prompted by securocrats for the purpose of wrecking the peace process. There would have been no shortage of bungling media hacks blaming the Martians—anybody just as long as they were not peace process linked. From within the DUP and certainly from the ranks of the UUP, Peter Robinson would have been subjected to a barrage of 'Peter Provo' putdowns. And the bookies would take no bets on who would be looking at their own reflection asking, 'Mirror mirror on the wall, who is the smuggest of them all'?

Whether responsible for this week's robbery or not, a functioning IRA is essential to the maintenance of a peace process that from the Sinn Fein point of view has as its objective acquisition of the maximum amount of power north and south. It is a goal aided by the persistent uncertainty that plagues the smooth functioning of the institutional dimension of the Good Friday Agreement, an uncertainty that would most definitely not be as intense in a post-IRA world. Consequently, why not rob and deny it? There will be enough forces in both governments not to mention the police and media that will cover for you, that will insist on such actions as not being deemed a threat to the Good Friday Agreement.

The trick of the peace process is to keep people endlessly participating in a process that somehow never seems to bring peace. And in the meantime the rest of us can just sit around and wait for the next robbery by the Martians. For as certain as the nose on your face it will happen for as long as there is a peace process.

Northern Bank—Open All Day Monday

The Blanket, 6 January 2005

Many like myself do not give a toss for the Northern Bank or its money. Poor bankers are as rare as straight politicians. A common attitude is that the cash stolen from the bank last month came from a broad back. Few in working-class areas care if the fat-cat financiers never see their lolly again. They also know that the poorer sections of northern society will not be the beneficiaries of it either. If, as is being widely alleged, the robbery is the work of the Provisional IRA's Army Council, then it is a matter of the rich robbing the rich. None of the loot will find its way to the victims of the tsunami. The poor and unemployed of Ballymurphy and elsewhere will have to fund that out of their own meagre incomes.

Amongst those convinced that the Provisionals are the guilty party are some who are confidently predicting the construction of luxury villas and holiday homes in the not-too-distant future. A less cynical view, perhaps, would see it as £22 million set aside to bankroll the anticipated bid to take the presidency of the republic in 2011. By that time, the logic goes, the money should have been well laundered, and the Northern Bank as forgettable as any zebra eaten seven years ago on a Kenyan game reserve.

Today it has been widely reported throughout the media that PSNI chief Hugh Orde will name the Provisional IRA as the culprit. If so, he will merely be confirming what most already assume. This is despite Gerry Adams, who denies ever having been a member of the IRA, denying that the IRA was involved in the Northern Bank robbery. The public no doubt will assign equal weight to each Adams claim and reach its own conclusions accordingly. For once, few will be found disagreeing with the DUP's Sammy Wilson when he ridicules Sinn Fein's 'usual tripe about securocrats trying to destroy the peace process'. Like them or loathe them, the Provisionals have become contenders for the bank robbers of the century award by dint of their sheer organisational ability and track record. There is simply no one else within miles of them in possession of the requisite skills. In these matters the 'Green Mafia' is in a league of its own.

When Orde speaks to members of the north's policing board to-morrow, his professional pride will display the bruising sustained as a result of last month's robbery. Toward the end of 2004 the new word swirling around the palates of political pundits was *humiliation*. And just to keep faith with the spirit of the times the firm who fleeced the Northern Bank inflicted the humiliation of the year on Hugh Orde's force. A job that some have speculated involved up to forty thieves with no Ali Baba present to spoil the show found the PSNI flat-footed and cold. One security source was reported as saying, 'With something as big as this you would have expected in the past to have got a sniff that something was going on . . . this was an intelligence failure. There wasn't a single word that this was happening'.

The PSNI have since taken to giving the impression of being deter-mined to look under every stone, if they can find any stones to look un-der. Luckily Al-Qaeda does not treat Northern Ireland with the same inflated regard that its own political class does. Otherwise the PSNI may have learned the population of Belfast had died from botulism poisoning twenty-four hours earlier via Al Jazeera.

To add insult to their injury, when Andy Sproule and Sam Kincaid sent their late risers up into West Belfast's Cavendish Street to hassle a local man, some smart cop decided to decommission his police issue weapon. Despite the absence of any photographic evidence that the said gun had in fact been decommissioned, the DUP were happy to accept the word of the authorities and have been content to slag off Hugh Orde's men ever since.

Whatever the PSNI thinks it attained for its reputation during the year, its competence is now being viewed through the prism of the Christmas heist. In boxing it is said a fighter is only as good as his last bout. The PSNI didn't even manage to get into the ring on this occasion. Outfoxed and outmanoeuvred, it now gives off the appearance of swinging wild punches at an opponent who has long since left the ring literally carrying the victory purse.

Although it is over two weeks since the robbery occurred, Hugh Orde is only now getting around to pointing the finger. This is in spite of the fact that his cops have been targeting the homes of people with long established links to Provisional republicanism. Given his instant response to the Kelly's Cellars incident last February, the tardiness on this occasion can only be explained by considerations other than policing. Orde, the peace process cop, is weighing up the political implications of any public utterance that he might make. He will have come under serious pressure to keep quiet from an array of forces still wedded to the notion that a deal can be done between the DUP and Sinn Fein this side of 2006. If naming the Provisionals as the firm behind the heist were to adversely affect any potential deal, then Hugh Orde would be tempted to sign off tomorrow with a 'to be continued'. If the deal is beyond salvaging at this point, then Orde will place the Adams outfit in the dock.

Truth is indeed the product of multiple constraints. And policing—it is as political as ever.

Changing Fortunes

The Blanket, 10 January 2005

> *When one tears away the veils and shows them naked,*
> *people's souls give off such a pungent smell of decay.*
> —OCTAVE MIRBEAU

I was driving through a rainy Belfast on Friday morning, accompanied by two other journalists, yet there was no heightened sense of anticipation that something new might be learned at the imminent press conference to be given by Hugh Orde. Speculation had been rife throughout the previous twenty-four hours that the finger of blame for the Northern Bank robbery was going to point unambiguously in the direction of the Provisional IRA. From the moment the news first broke at the start of Christmas week, the 'common sense' on the ground, and virtually everywhere else, had eliminated all others as potential contenders.

The venue at the Clarendon Docks headquarters of the Policing Board was packed with journalists. The PSNI press team had laid on tea, coffee, and sandwiches for hungry hacks who might have to wait around a bit. The buzz of conversation that had filled the room tapered off as soon as Hugh Orde, Sam Kincaid, and the PSNI press secretary entered.

Orde seemed the more relaxed of the two cops. He exuded a certain confidence as he eyed his audience, weighing up the challenge. If he spotted any wolves there he showed little sign of alarm. Kincaid appeared subdued. Perhaps that is his usual demeanour but if journalists were scenting a weakness they may have felt it was from the assistant chief constable that they would draw first blood.

When he spoke, Hugh Orde was resolute. He must have sensed instinctively that much of the credibility the British police force in the north had built up with him at its helm was in danger of melting in front of his eyes. The earlier much vaunted professionalism had been hit by a pre-Christmas robbery of tsunami proportion, which capsized it. Twenty minutes after he had delivered his opening lines Orde had steadied his vessel. From the discourse of the journalists present it was clear that Britain's top cop in Ireland had put down an anchor. Suddenly, his force was moored and it was the turn of the opposition, cut adrift from public credibility, to flounder in a choppy sea.

The simple act of unambiguously fingering the Provisional IRA had transformed Orde's fortunes. Had he blamed the UDA, St. Vincent de Paul, or some other group, then his passage would have been much less secure. Whose head would roll for not preempting it would have been the theme from the floor. But the newsworthiness no longer lay in his force's inability to prevent the world's largest cash bank robbery. The charge that the Provisional Republican movement had settled so comfortably in the unfathomable depths of political cynicism had the news field all to itself.

Orde spoke for about ten minutes and took questions from the assembled press for the same amount of time. Only in the closing comments of his monologue did he make the charge that the Provisionals were responsible. There were no exclamations of shock or deep inhalations of breath. He had hardly told us that his force had discovered Ian Paisley was a Catholic. We knew what he would say. On finishing, the press pack turned into a mob shouting over each other. One journalist gave what his colleagues described as a party political broadcast on behalf of Sinn Fein before Orde cut him short. Another berated the PSNI boss for telling journalists anything that might damage the peace process. I kept my hand up throughout but my reward was a sore shoulder. Courtesy gets stampeded at big story press conferences, where 'first shout first served' seems to be the only rule observed by all.

The one weak point of the Orde delivery came when he tried to protect his force from allegations that it was completely blindsided by the robbery. His intimation that this was not true led to a justifiable demand for an explanation as to why such intelligence was not acted on. Orde hesitated and faltered somewhat before recovering. In days to come he may have cause to regret that he did not concede the point on the intelligence debacle, cut his losses, and run. Few would have been interested in pursuing him on that, with another juicier hare firmly in sight. Now he has provided a side dish, which some might turn to when the main course digests itself.

We had hardly left the press conference when reports began to filter through that the Sinn Fein lie machine was taxiing down the runway. When it came to the bit, it never took off. There was no fuel to power it, having been used up telling earlier lies. Few were taking up the party's invitations to come on board. Been there too often in the past seemed to be the prevalent view. These days the lies are not even told in a new manner. Same stale old guff about securocrats trying to wreck the peace process; same as when the Stakeknife informer allegations surfaced; same as every other time. For a party that for long praised itself for being imaginative, it fails hopelessly when it comes to massaging the lie with even a modicum of imagination. Given that it lies as often as others would take a drink of water, perhaps the practice has become ritualised and commonplace. Nobody dresses up just to go to the water tap.

The only thing that resembled the Sinn Fein performance and that of the bank robbers was sheer audacity. But the imagination, ingenuity, organisational skill, and professional brilliance that deprived the Northern Bank of £26.5 million were simply not evident in the endeavours of the lie machine. The image of mismatched twins was hard to escape. One tight, trim, fit, energetic, and direct; the other a fat fumbling liar, too gorged on the good life to even work up the energy to use a tiny fraction of the imagination of the robbers.

The irony is that even if the Provisional IRA has been wrongly accused, the Sinn Fein lie machine has exhausted any residual trust that might have given it the benefit of the doubt. The boy cried 'securocrat' once too often.

Strategically Induced Crises Pay Rich Electoral Dividends for Sinn Fein

Irish Times, 13 January 2005

The Northern Bank raid may have put 'peace' on hold but it will breathe new life into the peace process, and the process is what keeps Sinn Fein growing.

The response of the British and Irish governments to the announcement by the PSNI boss, Mr. Hugh Orde, that the Provisional IRA was behind the robbery of £26.5 million from the Northern Bank was anger tempered by weary resignation.

Anger that they had been misled by the leadership of Sinn Fein pretending that it genuinely wanted a conclusive deal with the Reverend Ian Paisley's DUP; resignation to the fact that in spite of everything the peace process has them transfixed, like the relationship between the moth and the flame.

They know they will go back and as surely will be scorched again. There is no avoiding it. They have succumbed to an iron law of the peace process—that the process must always undermine the peace.

The world's greatest bank robbery came to the accompaniment of the sanguine words of Taoiseach Bertie Ahern that there were only ten hours of work needed in order to secure a deal that would see both an end to IRA activity and the restoration of the north's power-sharing institutions.

'Ten hours from peace' is an accurate characterisation if we are prepared to accept an hour this year followed by another hour the year after, and so on. In between those hours there can only be more of what we have now—strategically induced crises.

Such crises are what maintain the peace in a state of process rather than allowing it to come to fruition as a solution. The Sinn Fein leadership, playing by its own rules, benefits from the permanent state of instability. Its primary strategic goal is not an agreement in the north but expansionism, north and south. The attainment of any deal in the north is evaluated within this overarching strategic framework and never on its own merits.

Sinn Fein's ability to expand in the republic is primarily the result of the statesmanlike profile of its leader, Mr. Gerry Adams. He is its most powerful asset. What puts real wind in the sails of Mr. Adams and makes him different from leaders of other minority parties in the republic is the peace process.

The accruing exposure has made him a celebrity politician with an international reputation. At times opinion polls indicate that he is the most popular political leader on the island.

Central to maintaining that peace process as a 'work in progress', and consequently the profile of Mr. Adams, is the continued existence of the IRA. With the IRA off the scene, the peace process comes to the end of its shelf life and beds down as a solution.

But to be of benefit to Sinn Fein's strategic designs the IRA has to do more than merely exist. It must—employing plausible deniability—continue to disturb the peace, upset the Unionists, and allow Sinn Fein to promote the need for a process through which 'peace' can be pursued against the wishes of agenda-setting 'securocrats and recalcitrant Unionists'.

If, however, Sinn Fein was serious about reaching an accommodation with unionism based solely on conditions in the north, it would not have allowed David Trimble to go into the assembly elections of 2003 without a deal that he could sell to the Unionist electorate.

Sinn Fein fully appreciated that the type of unionism to emerge victorious the other side of that election could only be one that would offer terms to it much less generous than those offered by Mr. Trimble. This signalled the impossibility of Sinn Fein ever reaching an accommodation with the DUP either at the Leeds Castle talks last September or as a result of the subsequent December negotiations.

For the only deal acceptable to the DUP was one that would bring the peace process to a conclusion. And to conclude the peace process before the republic's electorate had been milked for all it was worth never featured in Sinn Fein's intentions.

By continuing to deposit the capital accrued from the peace process in the hearts and minds of the republic's electorate the party's Dail representation may well double at the next election. The election after that, possibly in 2010, may be an optimum moment for Sinn Fein to trade in the IRA in return for handsome electoral dividends. From such a strong springboard base Mr. Adams will be poised to make a bid for the republic's presidency in 2011.

Senior Sinn Fein member Jim Gibney has argued that the peace process has stood the IRA on its head, evidence that the Sinn Fein leadership is in total control. There was little in the way of internal opposition. The organisation could quite easily be put out to graze, but the time is not yet right. Too large a hiatus between concluding the peace and the 2011 presidential bid could seriously arrest the forward momentum of the party.

When commentators wail that the peace process has been destroyed by the robbery, they miss the point. On the contrary, it has been given even more life. It will smoulder but will never be extinguished. After the British general election, almost certain to occur this year, the embers will be fanned, the governments will proceed tentatively at first as they try to bridge the gaps. Then they will move to announce yet more ultimate deadlines, which will be put back endlessly.

At that point the peace process will be back to where it was before the December heist. And banks will continue to be robbed until Sinn Fein's ability to expand is thwarted by such activity.

Why give up a winning formula?

When a Leader Deserts His Men

Fortnight, February 2005

Andy Sproule, the senior PSNI member running the investigation into the robbery at the Northern Bank, has reported that on the evening of the theft, a couple with a child approached a traffic warden and made it known that two men wearing wigs and carrying baseball bats were in the immediate vicinity of the bank. The information that the traffic warden in turn passed on to the police was of the type that would lead only Inspector Clouseau to think Halloween revellers were having a lark. This is all the more so since the revelation by Suzanne Breen on RTE's *Prime Time* that the PSNI were in possession of information that a robbery of a Belfast bank by the Provisional IRA was imminent. By the time the cops arrived, however, the robbers had gone—along with their substantial haul of notes.

As if things were not bad enough for the PSNI, a diffident Sproule went on to assert that his boss Hugh Orde had made no claim to be in possession of actual evidence but was nevertheless in a position to identify the group behind the heist. Setting aside the debate about where the boundary between intelligence and evidence sits, the PSNI performance both before and after the robbery has left many of the force's advocates jittery. A cloud of suspicion still hangs over the PSNI that its professional and technical prowess was far outmatched by that of the robbers.

Using the type of language that has come to characterise most PSNI pronouncements thus far, even the evidence for the existence of evidence, was evidently not evident when, on the same news report Ulster Unionist MP David Burnside could be seen angrily gesticulating as he took advantage of parliamentary privilege to name a former Republican prisoner as being responsible for the bank heist. Given that the same man was named by the Hennessey Report as being behind the massive 1983 escape from the H-Blocks and has featured in public discourse in relation to a series of alleged IRA activities, it is all too easy to create the dots and then join them any way you want. Shouting a well-known name is evidence of an ability only to shout a well-known name. It can as easily be the result of guesswork as it is the product of reliable intelligence. The upshot of the blame game is that neither Sproule nor Burnside has firmed up public assumptions about culpability, managing only to reinforce a view already out there of investigators peering into a black hole.

But as ridiculous as the meanderings of those determined to pin the rap on the Provisionals at times seem, they pale in comparison to the absurdity displayed by those seeking to deflect barrages of fingerpointing away from Sinn Fein's alter ego. There is more heavy lifting to be done in defending than accusing on this one. Finding anyone who thinks the job was not the work of the Provisionals is as challenging a task for journalists as locating those responsible for pulling it off is for detectives.

In their denials of Provisional IRA involvement Sinn Fein have exuded the demeanour of men with forked tongues managing to protrude through every cheek. Martin McGuinness at one point took to calling the robbers criminals. No doubt he would insist on this to the family of Bobby Sands if they were to ask him if the IRA were involved.

Perhaps more than anything else this displays the cynical opportunism of Sinn Fein. In 1976 Republican prisoners began a protest within the H-Blocks of Long Kesh to refute a British government lie—that IRA activities were criminal. Five years later ten Republican volunteers died defying the lie. A major consideration in those young volunteers readily giving up their lives was to create space for people like Martin McGuinness, understood by those hunger strikers to be their chief of staff at the time, to publicly proclaim in defiance of the British state that IRA (and INLA) actions were political in motivation.

The hunger strike was the most intense moment in the history of the Provisional IRA. It has assumed the status of sacred. Those of us involved in the blanket protest still shake with emotion when the memory of ten men dead visits our consciousness. When we approach their graves we do so with the respect reserved for hallowed ground. To see Martin McGuinness, who went on to gain so much from their deaths, virtually spit on their sacrifices and demean their agony by employing the term *criminal* to describe what few could possibly deny is an IRA operation is more galling than having to listen to Margaret Thatcher, in the days before Bobby Sands died, pontificate 'a crime is a crime is a crime'.

Thatcher and the Tory government could not make criminals of the IRA. McGuinness and the Sinn Fein leadership most certainly did.

CHAPTER 12
Policing

A Wasted Journey

Irish Republican Writers Group, 23 September 2000

The turnout was poor. Not just among the audience either. Even some of the panellists failed to show up. Poor advertising was one excuse. But this hardly affected those billed to appear on the panel. It is unlikely that they needed to read the *Andersonstown News* to find out that their presence was expected. West Belfast's debate on policing promised an inauspicious start—and not to any new force.

Brendan Behan once opined that the first item on the agenda of any Republican meeting was a split. Not this one, though. The split occurred before it even began. Only the Republicans on the panel turned up. That did not stop curious agendas emerging. In fact it may even have caused them. The first motion for debate was that there should in fact be no debate. The audience agreed virtually unanimously, forcing some to wonder why they bothered to come along to begin with. It was all Alex Atwood's fault, we were assured. He did not treat his audience with respect.

All that may well have been so, but having bothered to turn up some of us felt that the remaining panellists could treat us with respect by allowing us to hear what they had to say. Most of us were not primarily interested in what Alex Atwood of the SDLP had to say. He would say the same as his party had been saying on policing for the past twenty-seven years. On the policing question at least the SDLP have been remarkable for their consistency for the best part of three decades. Sinn Fein's views on the matter were potentially more interesting. They had demanded the total abolition of the RUC and with Patten had achieved anything but.

Alex Maskey—admittedly weary looking and probably longing to get home—told us that the Sinn Fein view was widely known given the coverage the party's position had been afforded in the media. A strange response for a party used to complaining that Republican 'dissidents' are the media darlings. But it did bring to mind the observation of the Ireland correspondent for one of the British broadsheets that to find what passed for the Sinn Fein view on anything you should go to their Web site. Anything else was like talking to an answering machine.

But our efforts at persuasion in favour of a debate were in vain. We just had to settle for the reality that the great and the good came, saw, and—feeling that they could not conquer us with their logic—ignored us. I left with a friend who felt that without the SDLP presence Sinn Fein's position would fall under intense scrutiny and they, not being able to conduct any charged flak into the person of Alex Atwood, would be struck by the lightning of alternative ideas themselves. And the major alternative idea to be shunned was that Patten should be rejected outright. Anything less leaves Sinn Fein debating what type of RUC they want implemented—Patten's version or that of Mandleson.

Yes, Yes, RUC—It's the Force to Set Us Free

The Blanket, 14 September 2002

> *Since when is a Minister of State not part*
> *of the Establishment?*
>
> —FINTAN O'TOOLE

South Down was always viewed by Republicans as a strange place. In prison, Pat Livingstone was fond of saying that the bulk of Catholics in the RUC hailed from that neck of the woods. 'Big Liv' would also point to Eddie McGrady, the area's SDLP representative, by way of illustrating his point. In his view, McGrady was the epitome of the most conservative elements within a not very radical party—the type of nationalist Catholic cops would vote for.

Sinn Fein MLA Mick Murphy, aware that his tenure in Stormont is now on a very short lease given that he has been deselected by his colleagues in Sinn Fein, may now be calculating that if he is to remain a denizen of the one parliament in Ireland administering British rule, he too may need the support of Catholic RUC men. How otherwise are we to explain his recent comments, reported by the *Sunday Business Post*, that the RUC (or PSNI as Mick Murphy prefers to call them) is failing to clamp down on the Real IRA and is giving them a free run in order to split the Republican movement? 'You would nearly think they were working to bring down the Good Friday Agreement along with the likes of the DUP. There is a lot of dissident activity in the area, but the PSNI has done nothing about it'. Murphy's party colleague, Councillor Francis McDowell, in language strikingly similar to that used by the DUP in relation to the Provisional IRA over the decades, complained that the PSNI know who the Real IRA are 'but continue to work to their own agenda. This has been going on steadily for three or four years'.

None of this is really surprising. The only people likely to be shocked by it will be the type that couldn't even see decommissioning coming; those who, by their own admission, find somebody like George Orwell too 'intellectual', and thus deprived of his incredibly simple but piercing insights about the twists and turns of the power crazed indulge in 'cultic idiocy', believing any old nonsense they happen to be told by whatever leader is about on the day. But as Gerry Adams admitted in the televised debate, in which he trounced the inept Labour Party leader Ruairi Quinn, Sinn Fein is an establishment party. And what else does an establishment party do but support the forces that safeguard the establishment, even if they do display a bit of tardiness in getting there?

In the autumn of 1983, Cathal Goulding, a former chief of staff of the IRA and first chief of staff of the Official IRA, could be found supporting the British state's use of supergrass evidence in the north. In an ironic twist Mick Murphy was to come into prison shortly after Goulding's comments on the evidence of a supergrass. While there he found the decision by Sinn Fein to enter Leinster House so unpalatable that he resigned from the Republican movement and, if my memory is right, aligned himself with Republican Sinn Fein. How the worm has since turned.

Gerry Adams on yesterday's BBC Radio Ulster said that a friend observed of the PSNI that if they look like the RUC and behaved like the RUC, then they were the RUC. What may we say, therefore, about those who sound like Cathal Goulding and behave like Cathal Goulding? Perhaps as one of Mick Murphy's Sinn Fein MLA colleagues told Kevin Bean in England, 'We are all Sticks now'.

The PSNI Threat

The Blanket, 16 December 2003

> *Opportunity can often sway even an honest man.*
>
> —LATIN PROVERB

Acouple of years ago Martin Salter, a British Labour MP, posed the question, 'What on earth has happened to the early 1970 radicals like myself who have found themselves in parliament twenty-five years later. Have we sold out or simply grown up'? An interesting question, and one that should be considered by any 1970s radical considering embracing all the things their radicalism once pitted them against. But the force of the question was blunted by the answer it only half sought to disguise. Suggesting a maturation attained by 'simply growing up' is yet another self-justificatory discourse aimed at alienating alternative voices by ascribing to them the characteristics of infantilism. Obliterate one's own egregious metamorphosis, not by explanation, but by silencing those who would flag it up. And when backs are against the wall, what more useful a weapon to impose silence than the police?

The problem of policing in any society has not yet been solved by those eager to add their number to the 'thin blue line'. Even at its most adventurous, it is not easy to conceive of an entryism that manages to maintain at the centre of its vision a problematisation of the police as distinct from the problem of policing. There is more to suggest that regardless of the initial motives of the radicals determined to hold the police to account, little time passes before the power of the policing institution comes to inscribe itself in the being of those inside it. The individual exchanges his or her own identity for an institutional one. They may start out sporting their new institutional dimension only as a mask, but invariably the mask absorbs and constitutes the face. Their discourse becomes little other than a mere word in a wider sentence. It

273

is only defensible to themselves and intelligible to others when situated within a longer chain. The institutional sentence, not the individual word, is the foundation upon which meaning is based. Despite the optimism of the Pollyannas that any chain is only as strong as its weakest link, the chain can easily dispense with the link if it doesn't fit—the link is nothing without the chain, hooked on it as it is. Eventually, the poachers become gamekeepers, their energy expended in protecting the police against the policed.

But no amount of ducking and diving evades that thorny old question as old as society itself—who guards the guards; who shall police the police? If those most opposed to the police join them, then in a bid to minimise criticism of their decision they shall seek to minimise criticism of the police: 'They are alright now because we are part of it'. So when Martin McGuinness says that Sinn Fein is 'very determined to bring about the kind of change that would encourage young nationalists to step out of their front doors with their uniforms on, with their chests out and their heads held high', the doubt that gnaws at the mind is who then is going to hold these people to account? There are Republicans who have stated that although they served jail time alongside Gerry Kelly, they fear that if he were to become minister for justice he would revoke their licenses and return them to prison. That he may never is hardly the point. People believe it and envisage no safeguards against it. They see no sign of autonomous Republican grassroots activism that would stand up to leadership rightism. Past practice does not augur well for future behaviour. The former Sinn Fein health minister closed down hospitals and cut back on acute health services not because she was a Thatcherite ideologue but because she opted to take up a position, which once occupied allowed for no other option. Yet there was no public Sinn Fein criticism of her. Is it to be the same with policing?

The British state is at ease with its position in Ireland. There is no serious threat to it. It no longer requires the type of police force once deemed essential to meet the challenge of subversion. The only issue confronting it in relation to policing is the potential fallout from inquiries that don't do what they are supposed to do and end up highlighting past policing malpractice. At most this embarrasses the government of the day but will hardly cause it to short-circuit. The faulty wiring was installed on another's watch.

Yet, it is clear that the British state in spite of Patten has done little to tackle the fact that the police remain a problem. On three separate occasions the PSNI have been found making concerted attempts to subvert forensic science practices for the purpose of framing people in the courts. A leading forensic scientist, Ann Irwin, has complained that police officers had for many years attempted to coerce forensic scientists into tampering with forensic evidence. How many people are now serving sentences as a result of PSNI-contaminated forensic evidence? Furthermore, former CID (Crime Investigation Department) sergeant Johnston Brown has claimed that the police have used 'serial killers' as informants and have ensured that no prosecutions were brought against them. Many of these people populate loyalist organisations and will not be brought to book for the crimes they perpetrate on those they regard as nationalists or unfortunate members of their 'own' community.

Last month a member of Ogra Shinn Fein was arrested by the PSNI and charged with taking a photograph of a protest by his colleagues at Omagh barracks. Pat Doherty claimed that it was an act of political policing carried out by 'heavily armed PSNI thugs'. It seems to be an attempt by the force to do as they attempted with *The Blanket* in July of this year—suppress and obstruct news coverage of events that is not in tandem with their own account. Doherty unfortunately learned nothing from Pastor Martin Niemoller, otherwise he would have spoken out earlier before they came for him or his party. A sign of things to come even with a nationalist justice minister. On message nationalists will be protected; the cops can take the hindmost.

The PSNI pose a serious threat to civil liberties. Because the conflict is no longer as intense, the imperative to behave as it did before its name change is not as striking. But it retains from the days of old what functions, illegal and otherwise, it needs to repress. The forces needed to hold policing to account are diminishing by the day. Society without an opposition is a totalitarian nightmare.

From Up the 'RA to Up the Rozzers

The Blanket, 22 October 2006

> *Policemen so cherish their status as keepers of the peace and*
> *protectors of the public that they have occasionally been known*
> *to beat to death those citizens or groups who question*
> *that status.*
>
> —DAVID MAMET

In Ballymurphy the other evening the PSNI made an arrest of a man in the immediate wake of an incident that resembled a punishment attack. The now rare hum of the once ubiquitous helicopter droned its way into our homes. Police land rovers roamed the area. PSNI members, batons pounding their shields and sides of their vehicles, stood menacingly, poised to aggressively confront anyone who might interfere with their business of the day.

I was not there so did not see it. But witnesses to this display of PSNI zero tolerance toward some forms of violent activity in West Belfast complained that those who once postured as defenders of the community against a British police force raiding nationalist homes 'skulked' away rather than give some leadership. There was no sign of the promised policing of the police. But what leadership could they have provided apart from leading the police into the homes to be searched? Things have been inverted so much that those who once called Pearse Jordan *comrade* have no destination but that certain day when they shall address those who killed him barely half a mile away as *colleague*.

Since February, there have been close to 700 related incidents of violence or intimidation in Ballymurphy, many of them life-threatening. Apart from the catalyst for this violence, the murder of Gerard Devlin, there have been few arrests and no record of anyone being apprehended in circumstances similar to the Ballymurphy arrest the other evening. A family who claim their home was targeted by a thirty-strong gang yesterday evening allege that the PSNI told them not to ring for assistance if it happens again as the force was fed up responding to emergency calls from the estate. Not half as fed up as the people making them.

The Ballymurphy arrest demonstrates that the police acted because they considered the supposed punishment beating a subversive act that had to be politically policed. The quality of life of people in Ballymurphy has not improved one iota due to that arrest. The arrests that would make a difference have not been carried out because the police show little interest in tackling antisocial crime. Actions that threaten to destabilise the political equilibrium, no matter how marginally, will be robustly dealt with, whereas more serious actions that damage the well-being of a working-class community will accumulate by the hundred with minimal police intrusion.

There is little doubt that antisocial activity and violence against the vulnerable has become a scourge in working-class nationalist communities. People who once had the power to stand up to the armed repression of the British state now feel impotent in the face of hoods. Without the ultimate power to coerce their tormentors, they face a further depreciation in the quality of their lives. Those who claim to have a legitimate monopoly on the exercise of such coercion, the British state and its armed police, the PSNI, show little sign of using it unless it is to apprehend someone they might believe is engaged in violent Republican activity.

Peter Hain has argued that by reversing its long-standing policy on the RUC, Sinn Fein would allow some badly needed succour to arrive in the communities they represent; crime and antisocial behaviour could be tackled. This underlines how policing remains a politically loaded issue. Why individual citizens, including Republicans who may wish to avail themselves of it, should have their right to be defended from violent gangs contingent on Sinn Fein supporting the police is not explained. Surely the democratic right of the weak to be defended against the strong is a stand-alone justice issue not to be bartered over on grounds of political expediency.

Sinn Fein support for the police will increase the number of people willing to report their neighbour over minor disputes or tout on others doing the double. It will do nothing to end antisocial behaviour. The type of crime that stalks working-class communities will not be affected by Sinn Fein supporting the police. The most salient effect of that support will be to legitimise British force in Ireland. That is why there is such an emphasis on securing it. It has nothing to do with Peter Hain wanting to curb the hoods of Belfast any more than he wants to put manners on the gangs of Cardiff. Why would the British police be successful in curbing antisocial behaviour in Belfast but not in Liverpool, Glasgow, or Birmingham? The failure of British policing in this respect is evidenced only today in a report from the Institute for Public Policy Research in Britain, which showed that more than any other European society the British are afraid of teenage gangs.

The type of crime that plagues working-class communities from Limerick to Liverpool, from Cork to Cardiff, from Belfast to Bolton, fuelling a generalised fear and immiserising numerous lives is largely impervious to modern policing. Working-class communities need a multi-agency approach that is supported by more resources rather than more rozzers.

In Britain such communities pragmatically acquiesce in policing. They do not normatively endorse the police. The police are those who arrest you and lie on oath in court to send you down. What a turn-around it would be for Britain's fortunes in Ireland if there are to be more people applauding a British police force in Ballymurphy than in Brixton.

Meeting Hugh Orde

The Blanket, 7 November 2004

When it was announced that *The Blanket* had conducted an interview with PSNI boss Hugh Orde, many people from a range of backgrounds were interested to know had I not found it a strange piece of business to pursue. Since I travelled to Knock PSNI headquarters a fortnight ago along with *Blanket* editor Carrie Twomey, the most frequent question to come my way has been, 'What was he like'? They knew already what Hugh Orde had to say, as a transcript of the full interview appeared online.

The Knock interview was the fourth and not the first occasion on which I had met and spoken with the leader of the British state's police force in the north. It was also the most sustained and intense exchange. The previous encounters were fleeting affairs: once at a conference, another in the rest room of a downtown restaurant, and on the third occasion at a commemorative appreciation for the late Jack Holland. It was at the latter that *The Blanket* editor approached him and asked for an interview. That's how it works—the eye for opportunity bags the prize.

I knew he hadn't horns and consequently felt little anticipation as we crossed the city. Previous journeys to police stations were much more contentious affairs. On one occasion, my return ticket could not be used before seventeen years had expired. This time it was different, mainly for two reasons: I knew I would be out within the hour and I could do something other than either lie my way through the session or remain silent. Our demeanour was relaxed. Our driver, up until a few months ago a Sinn Fein member, bantered with us about history in the making. He brought a camera so that he could snap us on the way out.

The groundwork had been done. We had earlier taken soundings from a variety of people, those who never have the chance to address people in positions of authority. We sought out the most marginalised. Their concerns were reflected in the questions asked. In as far as was possible we strived to make our questions reflect a constituency much wider than our own intellectual curiosity. In a sense we were democratic to a fault—some of those who engaged with the PSNI chief through the medium of *The Blanket* have themselves scant regard for democratic sentiment. Nevertheless, they represent the gaps, the hidden voices, the silences that never fail to tell us something the powerful want smoothed over and pressed out of the narrative. While conscious of those who would see in us a means to prise open the clamp that the state imposes on the free flow of information, there was no intention on our part to play to the gallery and behave in a hostile manner to Hugh Orde. But we were determined not to give him the type of interview that in the business is called a robin. Our questions would be probing, direct, and engaging.

The interview was straightforward. We had our questions typed out in front of us, copies of which we handed to Hugh Orde and his press secretary on arrival in his office. It would speed up the process by rendering unnecessary any need on our part to repeat sometimes lengthy questions. The PSNI press office had not asked for a copy of them in advance, although it had suggested that a general indication of the areas we intended to cover would permit more rounded answers. Reasonable enough. When we arrived, there were only a few minutes waiting around until we were ushered into the office of the chief constable. Coffee was served and the interview was under way.

Over the years I have had call to deal with many of Hugh Orde's subordinates and have been in quite a few rooms with them, usually very spartan places—three chairs and a table, myself on one side and two interrogators on the other. Only weeks ago I accompanied a local kid to the station as a 'competent adult'. He was asked to attend to be questioned about some minor fracas. The 'interview suite' may have a nice ring to it but it looked much the same as they always did. They are not exactly constructed with a welcome in mind. Now and then, during my own interrogations, my chair went unused as I was forced to stand. On the very infrequent occasions when they would try to spread-eagle me against the wall I merely sat on the floor ignoring them. The cops, unlike the military, usually provided me with a chair.

This time it was different. For once a friend accompanied me in a police station, and the cop I was facing had a smile rather than a scowl. His companion was not some burly rugby type brought in specifically for the hard cop/soft cop routine. It was a press aide. The seating was brown leather, which I sank into upon sitting down. Most striking of all in terms of contrast, however, was that on this occasion I asked the questions. It was the most I had ever talked in a police station and later it brought a wry smile to my face when I read in the *Village* magazine that an 'ex-IRA prisoner interrogates Hugh Orde'.

Some people are of the view that it is a sign of how things have changed that someone from my stable was actually able to gain access to the chief constable. To an extent there is truth in this but the nature of that change is instructive. Few now believe that Hugh Orde heads a police force that sees its primary objective as the repression of nationalists. But the force is what the RUC always was—despite Republican assertions that the RUC was primarily the armed wing of unionism—the police force of the British state and no other. I knew I was going in to meet a new police chief but not, crucially, the chief of a new police force. When the Patten report was published, Danny Morrison writing in the *Sunday Tribune* commented that it did not constitute the long sought Republican objective of RUC disbandment. Maurice Hayes later waxed ironical on the notion of Republicans elevating Patten into some form of Holy Grail when in fact it was proof of the failure of republicanism to secure anything remotely like the disbandment of the RUC. The real change, which formed the backdrop to my Knock exchange with the police leader, was that on all my earlier involuntary visits to police stations I was a member of an army that was fighting a war. I was there because those holding me sought to inflict a defeat on the army of which I was a part. This time my visit was voluntary. I was going in as a former member of a defeated army to meet the head of a victorious British police force who would answer what concerns I might have about British policing. The very fact of its Britishness requires little else to be said.

Hugh Orde was sharp, relaxed, genial, witty, robust. He was not afraid to engage. In fact, by agreeing to the interview, he was making it clear that he was prepared to face questions from an element generally regarded to be more hostile to the force he commands than most other sections of society. If he could field the questions from that quarter, then he would close down the space for those who continue to argue against the new policing arrangements. Intuitively, we were aware of this but felt it would be cowardly not to press him for fear that his answers would trump our questions. Should we only play games we know we are going to win?

Did we win? I don't think so. On the day, Hugh Orde acquitted himself very well. While there was nothing to suggest dishonesty on his part many of his answers were political. But then he is a political cop, as the head of any British police force in Ireland must always be. We left Knock feeling we asked the questions that were relevant. If the answers were not what we would have wanted, the importance of raising the questions as a matter of public record should not be understated. Our task was to demonstrate that there are still serious questions to be asked of the police.

The morning after the interview was published in full a friend sent an e-mail praising *The Blanket* for having the courage to take it on but suggesting we stand by for flak from the Left, Sinn Fein, and traditionalist Republicans. We were unconcerned. As they say, those who matter won't mind and those who mind won't matter. In any event we met no hostility. Most people seemed interested in the dialogue that had taken place. One said he had never seen a senior cop asked such a wide range of questions. Other *Blanket* readers were interested in the questions posed about racism, investigative journalism, and street traders. An American friend felt Orde was a good cop but the British state's cop nonetheless. Many, whom I anticipated being more blinkered and antagonistic, surprised me firstly by saying that *The Blanket* was right to do the interview but secondly by conceding that Hugh Orde put in a solid performance. One word featured in all the commentary on the PSNI boss—'astute'.

As a result, speaking after the interview, strangely enough to a former prisoner who is still wedded to the perspective of physical force republicanism, I expressed the reservation that because Hugh Orde had responded so firmly to our probing that in a sense we, as Republicans opposed to the police, may have helped his case look more plausible. His response—'You are only responsible for your questions, not his answers'.

We can live with that.

Toome Debate

The Blanket, 21 December 2006

Aweek ago today I went along to the Toome debate on policing organised by Concerned Republicans. Whether officially concerned or not, those concerned appear to be growing in number. Nevertheless, it would be an untrained eye that would read too much into that. If only I had a pound for every time over the past ten years it had been pointed out to me that the Sinn Fein vote will go down next time around. Still, there is a rustling and an oppositional energy like never before in the history of the Provisional abandonment of republicanism.

On this occasion the size of the panel had gotten larger, four rather than three. The SDLP, still holding its nose at sharing platforms with the 'wild men' of republicanism, failed for the second time to turn up at a policing debate promoted by Concerned Republicans. Sinn Fein probably gained more from that. The SDLP rather than Concerned Republicans would be better placed to measure the accuracy of claims made on its own behalf by Sinn Fein vis à vis the negotiations with the British on the policing issue. The story has it that Sinn Fein offered not one word of opposition to the St. Andrews document on the question of MI5. Late in the final day at St. Andrews when the document was being churned out for the parties to read, a halt was brought to proceedings because Sinn Fein had raised three objections—not one of which dealt with MI5. Now the party is in brouhaha mode over the spook agency. That type of detail would be the SDLP forte at public debates on policing.

The debate in the Elk Hotel was well attended. Sinn Fein had a bigger presence amongst the Toome audience than in the earlier event in Conway Mill. Many party members appeared to have been bussed in for the event. It is as legitimate as anybody else being bussed in. Sinn Fein appears to control who in its ranks attend. For Concerned

Republicans it is a free-for-all. While a high-powered team of Sinn Fein activists turn up, away from the venue and out of sight of television cameras other party members and supporters report the visit to the house or the quiet word on the street or in the pub. The message is the same—your presence is not required.

A lot has been written on Web sites about the Sinn Fein contingent trying to intimidate the rest of the audience. It was not the impression I got. It was good to meet up with old friends from the South Derry region who remain in Sinn Fein. Apart from banter about the size of each other's belly and the ageing process, there was nothing that could be remotely described as a clash. One member of the audience said the tension in the room could be cut with a knife. I didn't feel it.

If anything, the Sinn Fein members in the audience treated the panellists with respect. The only heckling of any speaker came from the anti-Sinn Fein lobby. Many of their colleagues later expressed dismay at the heckling, feeling it is thwarting genuine discussion. Heckling is tantamount to censorship. It is not just an assault on the panellist's right to speak but on the audience's right to hear.

There was a sense that Sinn Fein put in a weary performance. Its speaker Declan Kearney was not as polished as on his earlier outing at Conway Mill. He complained at having to sound like a stuck record, facing the same questions. It seemed not to have occurred to him that the audience might be fed up with the same answers.

Declan Kearney's case is argument by assertion. From a Republican perspective it is logic-deficient. Not without merit he accused the 32 County Sovereignty Movement of engaging in theology, but overlooked that his own contribution amounted to codology. He hammered on about the need to end political policing but completely evaded the question of how this is to come about. The paradox at the heart of the Sinn Fein position, it was put to him, was one of being prepared to support political policing that will put Republicans in jails for armed resistance to the British state. If the party is not prepared to perform such functions at the behest of the British state and the DUP, then it will never attain the justice ministry. The leaderships who send young men out to fill Maghaberry Prison, he argued, should face that question.

I thought it was a question they were facing. One need only look at the letters pages of the *Irish News* to see as much, where disquiet pertaining to the events surrounding the kidnapping and torture of Bobby Tohill has been vented. One former IRA prisoner asked:

> Did anybody even think that there would be a time when the IRA would send four volunteers on a sanctioned operation and when it all went wrong Martin McGuinness would without embarrassment tell those volunteers to hand themselves over to British justice?

All in the service of helping to fill Maghaberry.

Nevertheless, Kearney does articulate a strategy, which an 'off night' does not invalidate. It is a reformist strategy but a strategy nonetheless. His opponents between them have revolutionary positions but no strategy for making those positions attractive to the support base, without whose endorsement such positions remain intangible.

If an overall assessment were to be made of the debate, for three of the parties it could be measured against their performance at Conway Mill. Sinn Fein's was poorer. The 32 County Sovereignty Movement stayed the same, largely due to the use of what John Hume once termed the Single Transferable Speech. Only the IRSP seemed to advance, although only incrementally. Paul Little was very relaxed as some of the audience tried to pose awkward questions. A wealthy Belfast Provisional quoting from a tabloid, which he acknowledged is never that reliable, asked the IRSP man if the party intended challenging Sinn Fein in elections. Little's put-down, while not providing the clarity that the Sinn Fein man wanted, won much applause from the audience.

The Sinn Fein strategy on the night against the 32CSM and IRSP speakers was to persist with the hardly unreasonable question of what alternative is postulated to Sinn Fein policy. Little, wary of prescribing a blueprint from on high, argued that the communities must be given the latitude to both debate the matter and decide on how they wish to be policed. A logical enough response if viewed as a holding position but not one that can be expected to flourish in the political marketplace where over-the-counter gratification is preferable to a deferred result.

Francie Mackey persisted in Jesuitical style to focus the debate on the question of national sovereignty. There is little in what Mackey said that a Republican traditionalist could find fault with. But it was like listening to the Mass in Latin, fine for the small number of traditionalists but little that would be understood by those large swathes not imbibed on traditionalist assumptions.

The three panellists were overshadowed by the presence of a fourth, Larry O'Neill, who recently resigned from Sinn Fein. It was the first time I had seen him since we shared a cage in Magilligan Prison back in the 1970s. Then he was unassuming. It was a characteristic he seemed not to have lost, preferring to avoid the limelight. On this occasion he felt things had gotten so bad under the autocratic Adams leadership, the defining feature of which is control freakery, that he had no choice but to step in front of the spotlight.

O'Neill told his audience that he was a lifelong Republican who had finished his education at primary school. His comment that he had not swallowed a dictionary like others on the panel and would not therefore fill his listeners' heads with mad dogs' shit was met with rapturous applause.

It was a timely appearance by the North Antrim activist. With Sinn Fein trying to persuade the wider public that there is a threat posed to it by Republicans, O'Neill alleged that the one Republican whose safety he is genuinely alarmed about is Dominic McGlinchey, one of the organisers of Concerned Republicans. The son of murdered parents, McGlinchey is said to have been warned on a number of occasions that his life is in danger.

O'Neill addressed the issue of the threats, in spite of his desire to keep the debate within the confines of the policing question, only because IRSP representatives in the audience were adamant that Sinn Fein was being disingenuous in its allegations that some of its leading members' lives were in danger. The IRSP pointed out that it had a meeting with Sinn Fein leaders after the threats were supposedly made aware to the Sinn Fein leadership but not the public. This meeting took place on 3 November. At it Sinn Fein raised the debates being organised by Concerned Republicans but made no reference to the supposed threat. The IRSP at Toome asked why the threats were not raised then given that, according to Gerry Adams, speaking on 13 or 14 November, he knew of the 3 November meeting that INLA members were amongst those posing the threat.

The lack of any persuasive response caused my mind to wander back earlier in the evening to when Paul Little had parried a question from a Sinn Fein member in relation to possible electoral intervention by critics of the party. Such was the Sinn Fein member's anxiety that it struck me that what Sinn Fein really fears is not a physical assault on their lives but an electoral assault on their constituencies.

Concerned Republicans seem to be on a roll at the minute. Sinn Fein replacing some of its elected representatives with even more malleable candidates has added to the party's woes and the confidence of its critics. Leaving the Elk in Toome, I felt that for the first time in the peace process, the Sinn Fein leadership had to explain itself. The authoritarian levee has long held out against the encroachment of democratic grassroots sentiment. The levee is far from collapsing but only the party's grovelling grunts can claim to believe it has not been breached.

CHAPTER 13
Strategic Failure

All the Crown's Ministers and All the Crown's Men Will Put Humpty Dumpty Together Again

Irish Republican Writers Group, 5 February 2000

Sinn Fein's isolation on the question of decommissioning is grow-ing more pronounced by the day. And it is difficult to imagine that the party leadership were unaware that this would be so when they cautioned the Republican base not to be mesmerised by the tactical manoeuvrings of the moment and have not prepared for it with a view to moving on to the next boring round of supposed negotiations. All of which will result in the type of nontransitional settlement outlined in the Good Friday Agreement including decommissioning in some form or another. Although things may seem in a state of disarray, it is hard to see Humpty Dumpty not being put together again. Such reconstruction goes against the way of things but no more so than a situation in which Republicans call for the retention of Stormont and Unionists seek its abolition.

In general, London, Dublin, and 'nationalist Ireland', together with most political parties, the nationalist press, and its British counterpart have blamed Sinn Fein. The *Chicago Tribune, New York Post, Washington Post*, and *New York Times*, to name but a few of the North American dailies, were no less hostile. Republican sensitivity to this outside senior leadership level accentuated rather than challenged this isolation. A small number of Sinn Fein members gathered outside the Unionist Party headquarters in Belfast's Glengall Street to chant, 'Make poli-tics work—don't suspend the institutions'. On Red Nose Day people making clowns out of themselves as a means of raising money for char-ity is the generous thing to do, but in the eye of what is claimed to be a political crisis—which if it is to be resolved through continuing engagement shall leave republicanism facing humiliation—it was quite absurd, pathetic even.

This totally irrelevant gimmick underlined how the whole process has dissuaded Republicans outside leadership from thinking strategically, for which leaders shall no doubt be grateful. Why should people think when there are politicians to do that for them? In a sense a situation prevails similar to that within the British Labour Party of whose leadership it has been said, 'Hate people who are popular and have an independent base in the party'.

Such determined characters would not be found in a Red Nose protest chanting nonsense. They would demand as a right to be fully informed of all that was happening. They would not oppose Gerry Adams and David Trimble meeting again but would demand that it take place on a public platform in West Belfast's Conway Mill where everyone could see what plans were being worked out for our future. They would no longer have to sit and guess about the accuracy of reports alleging that the Sinn Fein leadership either promised decommissioning by January or not. And no more could Deaglan de Breadun of the *Irish Times* report that 'the reason the media were given the cold shoulder during the Mitchell review was that too often in the past politicians went into talks and made compromises that they immediately had to disown under media interrogation . . . [and] . . . Word has it that the meeting was unsatisfactory from Dublin's viewpoint because of the size of the Sinn Fein delegation. Taoisigh and prime ministers like to deal with Gerry and Martin alone, it appears'.

Why? That one resoundingly democratic word at least echoes further than any amount of Glengall Street chants.

Republicanism's Surrender by Instalment

Guardian Web site, 26 June 2000

*T*he report to the International Independent Decommissioning Body from Cyril Ramaphosa and Martti Ahtisaari, which states that IRA 'weapons are secure and cannot be used without their becoming aware that this has happened', was significant but not surprising. In a sense it marks a further down payment in the process of 'surrender by instalment', which the leadership of the Republican movement have been pursuing for a number of years now.

The major question that historians will ask is not why the Republicans surrendered but why they fought such a futile Long War only to get brought back to accepting less than what was on offer in 1974 and which they rejected outright.

It has not been unconditional surrender. And it has been infinitely better than continuing to fight a futile war for the sake of honouring Ireland's dead yet producing only more of them. But let us not labour under any illusions that the conditions were good. The strategic logic of engaging with Republicans from the British point of view was to establish a process that would be inclusive of Republicans but would exclude republicanism. The extent of British success can be gauged by the ground conceded by republicanism. The consent principle and by logical extension, partition, has been accepted; the RUC has been modernised; the northern parliament has been re-established. Sinn Fein stands poised to prove republicanism wrong—and demonstrate that the northern state can be reformed.

In this sense republicanism is effectively decommissioned. Discursively it lives on but this is little more than lip service. In substantive terms republicanism has been reduced to vampirising the ideas of the SDLP and the latest move on decomissioning now opens the way to colonise the SDLP constituency. Some might yet conclude that John

Hume was prepared to sacrifice the SDLP as a party to ensure the triumph of SDLP ideology.

What does the future hold? Sinn Fein as the expression of state republicanism and a party of votes as distinct from a party of ideas will move to straddle the middle ground. Those marginalised that sustained it during the hard times will not experience the good times. That is the trophy of the nationalist middle class. The marginalised will remain and will be either serviced or exploited in some form or other by nonstate republicanism. If republicanism re-emerges, let it be democratic rather than elitist. Army Councils only ever lead us to despair or disaster.

Right Honourable Rotters

The Politician, July 2000

*R*ecent events, which occasioned both the inspection and securing of IRA arms dumps, have led to much speculation about the future of republicanism. Too many commentators have hung their colours on the mast of technicalities and as such have denied their readership access to more analytical considerations. The decommissioning of IRA weaponry was never the Republican baby but merely the bathwater—to be cast off long after the baby had deserted the bath. Republicanism may have conditionally surrendered but that was not as a result of arms inspections. Rather it was enshrined in the Good Friday Agreement of 1998. That agreement specified the conditions of the Republican surrender; after that it was a case of those conditions being met.

There are of course those who have told us that a former Republican prisoner plus a colleague in government cannot be construed as surrender. It is all too easily forgotten that placing former Republican prisoners in government was an objective secured by the SDLP, when the late Paddy Devlin, a onetime IRA member, served in the Stormont government of 1974. Republicans termed him a member of the British war machine for having done so, yet he managed to remain far to the left of anyone in the present Stormont regime.

What republicanism accepted with the Good Friday Agreement was, as Tony Blair stated, an outcome that gives:

> Unionists every key demand they have made since partition eighty years ago. . . . The principle of consent, no change to the constitutional status of Northern Ireland without the consent of the majority of people, is enshrined. The Irish constitution has been changed. . . . A devolved assembly and government for Northern Ireland is now there for the taking.

All of these were the terms of 'the enemy'. British Home Secretary Reginald Maudling as far back as 1972 was suggesting such. This, coupled to a weak Irish dimension grafted on, has formed the core of British state intentions since.

The Sinn Fein leadership is attempting to render republicanism obsolete while holding on to the vocabulary as it ditches the policies. In a recent RTE interview Danny Morrison's one revealing note of concern pertaining to those he described as Republican dissidents was that they could be proved right in their assertion that the northern state was beyond reform. But that was always at the core of the Republican belief system. One hardly qualified as a Republican dissident by holding that position. Republicanism is by its essence irrevocably opposed to the existence of the Northern Ireland state regime. State republicanism is merely a different and slightly more radical-sounding name for constitutional nationalism, the philosophy of the SDLP. Nonstate republicanism will continue to survive in one form or another. It will do so because parties such as Sinn Fein that seek party growth through electoralism rather than ideas invariably move to straddle the middle ground. Sinn Fein will strive to usurp the SDLP in the north not by establishing the hegemony of ideas that are traditionally associated with what the loyalist Billy Mitchell describes as 'the working class, the workless class, and the underclass' but by becoming the hegemonic site of middle-class ideas. In the south, Sinn Fein will enter a right-wing coalition with Fianna Fail. This leaves those who are marginalised remaining on the margins. Nonstate republicanism will emerge to articulate their discontent.

The question being pondered in many minds is in what way shall republicanism seek to achieve this. Up until now the signs are not good. Much of the intellectual opposition to the NI state is being articulated by individuals like Tommy McKearney, Tommy Gorman, and Carrie Twomey of the Irish Republican Writers Group. None of these people advocate a return to armed struggle. Indeed, a recent *Sunday Times* piece stated that the group generally regarded armed struggle 'even if they don't say it straight out, as a waste of time and of life'. But the group is small in number and despite extensive media coverage does not seem to be expanding in the manner that groups associated with the physical force tradition are.

The stark reality facing Tommy McKearney and his colleagues is that politics per se now looks anathema to a gradually increasing body of grassroots Republican opinion. The abandonment of resistance politics and its replacement with administration politics means that those who feel republicanism should have a future are now reduced to watching 'right honourable friends' in suits calling each other 'rotter'. In such a sickly environment the lesson is easily forgotten that it was the sterility of military politics that produced such a scenario. We can only hope that some do not insist on reinforcing failure.

Never, Never, Never

The Blanket, 26 January 2002

> *Arise ye dead of Skibereen and watch Sinn Fein take
> an oath to the queen.*

*D*uring the week there was an amusing sports report referring to the luck of two punters at the horses. During the race one of the jockeys came off his mount. The two racegoers immediately ran to the racecourse bookie and bet two pounds each that the rider would remount and go on to win the race. Their entrepreneurial instinct was rewarded with a payout of £2000. Their gamble had paid off. But would any bookie give you 1000/1 odds against Sinn Fein eventually taking their seats in Westminster?

For the party to be where it is today amounts to an amazing turn-around. Franz Kafka would have had difficulties conjuring up that labyrinthine plot for any of his novels. Gerry Adams once told us that Guy Fawkes had the right attitude to the Houses of Parliament: a point heavily underlined when the IRA bombed those who led the House as they met, slept, partied, or planned repression in Brighton's Grand Hotel eighteen years ago and that prompted the remark from the Sinn Fein president that the attack was a blow for democracy.

Of course to lessen our sense of bafflement at the latest shift we shall for the moment be assured that it is a beachhead on the road to a united Ireland, a new phase of struggle, a courageous and imaginative initiative made possible by the undefeated IRA, a momentary tactical manoeuvre, even a patriotic act that helped save the peace process—again. George Orwell would have marvelled at the doublespeak employed. It is so self-evidently embarrassing that even David Trimble can confidently joke about it.

By now we should be well accustomed to this being the type of fig leaf given to every defeat or broken promise. Watching the Sinn Fein

MPs sitting beneath the large Irish tricolour flag in their new London office the acerbic comment of a journalist friend crossed my mind—the bigger the flag the greater the sellout. But it passed as quickly as it had arrived. Terms like *sellout* always conjure up images of a fundamentalist stridency on the part of the user rather than provide insight into the motivations and behaviour of those against whom the allegation is levelled. In its place, however, I was reminded of the old joke about the idiot who lost his key in the dark but began to search for it beneath the light. In response to suggestions that the search was futile as the key had not been lost at the spot where the idiot was searching, he replied, 'I know I lost it in the dark but it is easier to look for it in the light'. Sinn Fein is off in London searching for a republicanism long since lost! What are the chances of it being found again in a British parliament where the antithesis of any republicanism—the monarchy—is sovereign?

While the Sinn Fein leadership are by no means idiots, our friend the bookie would have a field day if enough people proved sufficiently idiotic to queue up to bet that bums on seats shall not be the end result of the Westminster foray even if the oath is allowed to be taken in Irish. He may even offer a double—George Bush will declare America Islamic before his term of office expires.

Apart, perhaps, from those who tell us we shall have a united Ireland in 2016 few are brave enough to claim they can predict the future. So it is not an iron law that Sinn Fein will take their seats in Westminster. Yet plausible projections can be made from consistent trends. Brian Feeney in one of his columns remarked that Sinn Fein had 'unsaid everything they said in the seventies and eighties and ultimately settled for less than the SDLP got in 1973, which Republicans regarded then as a sellout'. So when Gerry Adams stated that his MPs will never take their seats in Westminster as the centre of political gravity lay elsewhere for the party, it was almost as if a game of intellectual Russian roulette was being played to see how far the rank and file could be pushed and treated like mushrooms before a voice would say 'enough'.

Yet in terms of dissent the trigger only ever hits an empty chamber. It is so humiliating to think that Republicans on the ground are treated, and in many cases behave, as victims of what Jenny McCartney once called goldfish syndrome, perpetually condemned to forget that they swallowed the same old nonsense time out of number. Nonsense such as 'I can give you a commitment on behalf of the leadership that we have absolutely no intention of going to Westminster or Stormont. . . . Our position is clear and it will never, never, never change. The war against British rule must continue until freedom is achieved . . . there will never, ever, be IRA decommissioning, an IRA surrender'.

But once this latest beachhead in the struggle for a united Ireland is secured there will appear a new strategic height to win and a new radical arena of struggle to be created. And who then would bet against the emergence of Lord Gortahork privatising his way to a socialist republic from the revolutionary upper house?

A Secret History Gets Told in Galway

The Blanket, 29 June 2003

> *With one continuous breath*
> *I absorb the pungent night air,*
> *never dreaming*
> *that from all our years together*
> *this moment only will sting.*
>
> —ANNE KENNEDY

*I*n April, the Cuirt International Festival of Literature took place courtesy of the Galway Arts Centre. It was in its eighteenth year. The Town Hall Theatre played host to most of the main events and as a sign of the high literary stature of the occasion names such as the Chilean writer Ariel Dorfman had been billed to attend. I had always liked Dorfman who, from the point of view of the powerful, has the irritating habit of deflating their sense of self-importance. Once commenting on the ill health of democracy in his own country, he astutely observed:

> What politicians have done in Chile is that they've made democracy fragile by saying it's so fragile we can't touch it. Well, no. You've got to bring people into the process of defining democracy, testing it and pushing it. If you don't, it's not true democracy.

A situation not unlike what we have inflicted upon us here, where people get told they are 'mischievous' and 'enemies of the peace process' if they ask a difficult question. On another occasion Dorfman wrote:

303

Dictators aspire to total power in order to seek refuge from the demons they have unchained. As a way of silencing their ghosts, they demand to be surrounded by a rampart of flattering mirrors and genuflecting counsellors that assure the tyrant that yes, you are the most beautiful of them all, the one who knows more.

These words have powerful resonance for anyone familiar with the authoritarian culture that has gripped Provisional republicanism under the leadership of seeming Sinn Fein president for life, Gerry Adams, who views an idea not his own as if it were a SARS-like contagious disease his functionaries must prevent other people from catching. Although eighteen months ago Adams sought to demonstrate his revolutionary credentials—in defiance of those to his right within the party—by visiting Castro's Cuba, it struck me after reading Ed Moloney's *A Secret History of the IRA* that many readers may conclude that he shares more in common with the former ruler of Dorfman's country, Augusto Pinochet, than with the leader of the Cuban left.

Ultimately, it was in anticipation of Moloney—rather than Dorfman—delivering the Anne Kennedy Memorial Lecture that attracted me to Galway. Anne Kennedy was a poet, writer, photographer, and broadcaster who hailed from Orcas Island, off the coast of Washington State. She came to live in Galway in 1977. And it in turn has established a tradition of honouring her literary acumen. It was my first time in the city and its cosmopolitan mix made the visit all the more appealing as well as demonstrating the broad social appeal of the festival. Fourteen hours on a bus there and back—my sole companion a biography—was a lot to endure but the lecture was worthwhile and meeting up again with Ciaran Irvine, who sometimes features in *The Blanket*, made the night's postlecture drinking all the more entertaining. Little chance of hearing self-serving peace process elasticity in that company. And it was a fulfilling experience to talk with Maura Kennedy, the daughter of Anne, in whose memory the lecture was being delivered. This was the fifth annual Anne Kennedy lecture. Before dying in 1998 she had published two books of poems, *Buck Mountain Poems* and *The Dog Kubla Dreams My Life*. Maura is central to the Cuirt project and when I asked her how she felt to see her mother honoured in such a fashion she simply said it was a 'great honour' to carry on with her mother's tradition.

And what a vibrant tradition it seemed to be. I could not imagine Ed Moloney being invited to give his lecture during the West Belfast Festival. And if he were it is not too difficult to envisage some Sinn Fein members handing out SARS-type masks accompanied by instructions on how to fit them over the ears. Author Robert Fisk is welcome to our festival because he is expected to tell the truth about forces we do not like. And when he leaves we loudly praise him for extolling the value of truth and silently breathe a sigh of relief that he ignored our addiction to equivalence. The problem with Moloney is that he would not be coming to tell us what murderous horror the Israelis inflicted on Palestinian civilians or how many civilians the Argentinian military disappeared. No, his narrative in large part interrogates the character we, as a community, elect to represent us as MP in the British Parliament. Consequently, it makes us uncomfortable to feel the moral high ground shift beneath our feet and take on the appearance of someone else's neck, while our shouts of 'human rights abuser' are turned back on us. But if we want genuine rather than political truth then this is the price we have to pay for it, otherwise it is merely about poking the other side in the eye. Because, unless we subscribe to some intellectually limiting metanarrative, there is no one great system of pure evil that works 24/7 to oppress one great system of wholesome good. Uncomfortable as it may be to digest, Napoleon's comment that 'among those who dislike oppression are many who like to oppress' leaps out to tear away our eye patch—that intellectual attire we like to sport when looking inward—compelling us to view what we can otherwise pretend exists only in 'the other'.

The purpose of Moloney's lecture was to demonstrate how:

The future of the Good Friday Agreement now rests with a party that began its existence dedicated to the destruction of the government of Northern Ireland and the partition settlement that underlay it, but the same party has ended up utterly and absolutely dependent on them.

So sure were the British establishment that republicanism was firmly trapped in the snare that the only way out was for it to shed its teeth—the purpose of ensnaring it to begin with—that the media no longer treated alarmist calls of crisis in the peace process with even a modicum of seriousness. At an early point in the lecture the audience was treated to a witty account of how fifteen dead sheep in Tyrone was considered a more newsworthy item than our terminally boring political saga. Moloney argued that such an attitude was predicated upon an awareness that the peace process had brought the IRA campaign to a definitive and irreversible conclusion.

The packed town hall was told that Gerry Adams' alternative to the armed struggle had been in place for years, even when others were racking their brains trying to escalate the war. That it was a strategy of deception aimed at conning not only the Republican rank and file but also other members of the leadership came in a very illuminating comment:

> There was never a chance that Adams could have gone to an Army Council in which figures like Slab Murphy, Kevin McKenna, or Michael McKevitt sat and said, 'Listen, lads, I have an idea: How about we recognize Northern Ireland and agree that we won't get Irish unity until the Prods say so, we'll cut a deal with the Unionists to share power, Martin here can become a minister—and Barbara—meanwhile you guys will call a permanent cease-fire, give up all those Libyan guns, recognise a new renamed police force, and eventually we'll wind down the IRA and disband it. If we do that, then

Sinn Fein, under my leadership of course, will become the new SDLP and Fianna Fails of Ireland'. Does anyone here seriously think Adams could have gone to the Army Council with such a message and survive the experience?

At a time when so much fudge and ambiguity has been given free reign Moloney certainly did not pull his punches. While Adams is about to launch a second book about not being in the IRA, Moloney told a very different story:

> By the time he led the IRA in Belfast, Adams' list of military achievements was already a lengthy and impressive one: He had made his home Ballymurphy the strongest IRA area in the city; as commander of the second battalion in Belfast, his IRA units had pioneered the use of the car bomb and had forced the British to introduce internment before their intelligence on the IRA was complete, with the result that internment was a military and political disaster. He had ordered the importation of the ArmaLite rifles from America, which for a while made the IRA in Belfast better armed than the British army. With the destruction of an undercover British spy ring in West Belfast, he made a name for himself as a counterintelligence genius on a par with Collins and he had also made a reputation for ruthlessness, as the disappearance of Jean McConville and others would also bear grim witness.

Ultimately, Moloney asserted, Adams succeeded because of the existence of two dual peace processes—the sham one he sold to the IRA's Army Council that helped disguise the real one to the point where its success—and the defeat of the Provisional IRA—became a foregone conclusion.

Yet we are forced to ask how the sham one ever took hold. Surely it must have been obvious to the dimmest bulb in the tree that something untoward was afoot. Otherwise we can only conclude that, as Jenny McCartney once wrote in another context, virtually the entire leadership along with the rank and file functioned as 'goldfish perpetually fated to forget that they swallowed the same thing six seconds earlier'.

The question and answer session that followed indicated that few in the audience had been rerouted away from the real lesson of the peace process. In some ways it could all be summed up by George Orwell, who claimed that nine times out of ten revolutionaries are social climbers with bombs. And despite all the buildings destroyed by IRA bombs throughout this war, quite a bit of building work has been carried out since constructing new second homes for members of the Republican leadership. Some animals are more equal than others.

A sure sign that Moloney's outstanding work on how the IRA was effectively defeated through the peace process has made its mark is the launch of the paperback version of his widely acclaimed book, *A Secret History of the IRA*. For those of us who sought a different and better outcome—more just, more egalitarian, more democratic, more honest—read it and weep.

Bad Tactics

The Blanket, 11 February 2007

*T*hat Sinn Fein has an authoritarian leadership is self-evident. As the *Irish Examiner* stated the day after the party's policing Ard Fheis, 'It's symptomatic of the complete command and hold that Adams has on republicanism that yesterday's vote was portrayed as a victory, as a breakthrough. . . '. But it does not follow that authoritarianism necessarily leads to silly decisions as it did on this occasion.

It was a shortsighted but grave strategic error for the former Republican Party to approve the policy shift on the British PSNI by such a huge majority at the end of a conference likened more to a procession than a debate. Delegate after delegate telling the leadership just how great it is hardly qualifies as a debate. Moreover, the absence of proper discussion manifested in the almost unanimous support for an endorsement of the PSNI, rather than the decision to support the PSNI per se, has handed the DUP a significant tactical advantage.

The displacement of a debating chamber by a sycophant convention was an ill-judged move that will ultimately undermine Sinn Fein's negotiating strength. The party decision to support the British PSNI may well mean that the ball has been tossed into the DUP court but the margin of victory will deprive Sinn Fein of any strategic advantage over the DUP that it would otherwise have secured. Paisley's party will be able to claim that the ball kicked by Sinn Fein has landed in a small court and the space in which to manoeuvre unlike Sinn Fein's is heavily constricted. Dissent, it will be said, is more widespread and exists at higher levels within the party than in Sinn Fein. The situational logic is such that, as a consequence, Adams' movement will be asked by the big government players to pony up again. It is the price a caudillo can expect to pay when he prioritises showing the world just how loved a leader he is over any concerns he may have about ceding ground to an opponent.

Sinn Fein seems not to have learned from the Trimble experience. The then UUP leader used his internal weakness as a negotiating strength until such times as the Blair government heeded its NIO mandarins and decided that a deal was more doable if the DUP were to lead unionism. Because there were always critics biting at the heels of the UUP leader, the imperative to 'save Dave' concentrated the minds and consumed the time of the British government in particular. David Trimble could always point to a seemingly innocuous leadership contender such as Martin Smith making an effective challenge to his leadership. Trimble won the day, 57 to 43. Adams as a party leader never faced a challenge like that.

An insight into the way in which the British reckoned they could always calculate on the Sinn Fein leadership to deliver British state objectives at the end of the day came when a British ambassador said to a prominent Irish journalist at a function in Dublin that Adams and McGuinness could always push through what was necessary; they were Stalinists after all. Dean Godson's Trimble tome *Himself Alone* illustrates all very well how Sinn Fein could not comprehend the concept of internal resistance to the leadership within unionism. The Adams team forever badgered why Trimble couldn't just manage his base.

Sinn Fein has managed its base and managed it well, but only in so far as it has served internal management purposes. In the wider strategic arena the suffocation of grassroots autonomy may have freed the leadership from the constraints of its own base but it has left it a hostage to fortune. Unable in future negotiations to cite the circumscribing power of a critical base, Sinn Fein has room only to cede even more ground to a DUP able to channel the pressure generated from within its own ranks into a negotiating pincer designed to hold what it has and take what it has not. Whether it continues to insist on sackcloth and ashes or not, theocratic unionism stands poised, Bible in hand, to smite those deemed to have sinned against its state.

GLOSSARY

32 County Sovereignty Movement	Political adjunct to the Real IRA.
Alan McQuillan	Assistant chief constable of the RUC in 1992.
Albert Reynolds	Irish prime minister from 1992 to 1994.
Alex Atwood	SDLP politician.
Alex Maskey	First Sinn Fein lord mayor of Belfast.
Alliance Party (AP)	Centre ground political party.
Anderson Street explosion	Accidental explosion of an IRA device in 1972 that resulted in eight fatalities, including four of the IRA's own members.
Andy Sproule	Senior PSNI officer at the time of the Northern Bank robbery.
An Phoblacht/Republican News	*AP/RN*. The weekly newspaper of the Provisional Republican movement.
Ard Comhairle	Ruling body of Sinn Fein.
Ard Fheis, ard fheisanna	Sinn Fein annual conference, conferences.
Ballot box and ArmaLite strategy	Term given to the 1981 Republican tactic of combining military and political activity into one single strategy.
Barney McDonald	Tyrone man murdered in 2002 by suspected IRA members.
beak	Slang for judge.
Bernadette (Devlin) McAliskey	Republican political activist. Served as MP at Westminster from 1969 to 1974.
Bertie Ahern	Irish prime minister from 1994 to 1998.

Bill Lowry	Former head of Belfast Special Branch, the RUC's intelligence arm.
Birmingham bombings	IRA attacks on an English city in 1974 that resulted in twenty-one fatalities.
Blanketmen	Republican protestors in the Maze Prison from 1976 to 1981.
Bloody Sunday	Refers to 30 January 1972 when British paratroopers murdered fourteen unarmed civilians during civil rights march in Derry.
Bobby Lean	IRA volunteer who fingered his colleagues on behalf of the RUC in a celebrated case in 1983.
Bobby Sands	Leader of the IRA and INLA hunger strike of 1981 and the first of ten hunger striking prisoners to die in an effort to be recognized as political prisoners.
Bobby Tohill	Former Republican prisoner who was tortured and abducted by the Provisional IRA in 2004.
Brendan Behan	Former 1940s IRA prisoner and renowned author.
Brendan Hughes	Charismatic IRA and Blanket protest leader. Also known as 'the Dark'.
Brendan 'Bik' McFarlane	Charismatic leader of IRA prisoners during the 1981 hunger strike.
Brendan O'Brien	Irish political journalist and author of books on the IRA and Sinn Fein.
Brendan Shannon	Former IRA prisoner.
Brian Cowen	Taoiseach of Ireland.
Castlereagh	Notorious police interrogation centre in Belfast.
Charles Bennett	Civilian killed by the IRA in 1999.

GLOSSARY

Charlie Haughey	Irish prime minister from 1979 to 1992. Widely regarded as being corrupt.
Chris Patten	Author of a major report on policing, which became known as the Patten Report.
code of omerta	Code of silence.
Connolly House	Sinn Fein's Belfast Headquarters.
consent principle	A stipulation in the GFA assuring that the status of Northern Ireland as a British statelet cannot change without the consent of the majority. As the statelet was created to have a Unionist majority, critics see 'consent' as a safeguard precluding a unified Ireland.
Continuity IRA	Group that split from the Provisional IRA in 1986. The critical point of contention was its opposition to abandoning abstentionism, the Republican tradition of never taking a seat in the Dail Eireann.
cumann	Irish for committee.
Dail	Parliament of the Irish Republic.
Danny McBrearty	Derry civilian shot and wounded by the Provisional IRA in 2002 for challenging its authority.
Danny Morrison	Sinn Fein publicity director for much of the conflict. Imprisoned in 1991 for his part in a kidnapping.
David McKittrick, Eamon Mallie	Northern Irish journalists and joint authors of books on the peace process.
David Trimble	Former leader of the UUP and Northern Ireland's first Good Friday Agreement first minister from 1998 to 2001.

Declan Kearney	One of the most astute Sinn Fein strategists.
Des Wilson	Radical Belfast priest, activist, and writer.
Diplock courts	Nonjury courts used in trials of people accused of 'terrorism'.
Downing Street Declaration	An agreement struck between the British and Irish governments in December 1993 in a bid to entice the IRA to end its campaign.
Dublin-Monaghan bombings	Loyalist bomb attacks in 1974 that resulted in the largest fatalities sustained during the Northern Irish conflict.
DUP	Democratic Unionist Party. A Protestant party that advocates British dominion over Northern Ireland.
Easter Sunday	The anniversary of the 1916 Easter Rising, the most senior event in the Republican calendar.
estates	Public housing developments in Northern Ireland.
Falls Road	The main nationalist thoroughfare in Belfast and the site of the August 1969 fires that gave rise to the Provisional IRA.
FARC	*Fuerzas Armadas Revolucionarias de Colombia*, Colombian Marxist guerrilla group.
Felons Club	Belfast social club for 'felons', former Republican prisoners.
Fenians	Refers to members of fraternal organization established in the nineteenth century dedicated to the establishment of an independent Irish republic.

Fianna Fail	Largest political party in the Republic of Ireland.
Fine Gael	Leading political party in the Republic of Ireland.
Four Courts	Site in Dublin where the Irish Civil War began in 1922.
Framework Document	Document produced by both British and Irish governments in 1995 that charted a course for the political future of Northern Ireland.
garda	Irish for police. Used in the Republic of Ireland.
Gareth O'Connor	Dissident Republican and suspected police informer who disappeared for two years before his body was recovered from the Newry Canal in 2005.
General John de Chastelain	Head of the international body for de-commissioning of weapons in Northern Ireland.
George Galloway	Leader of the British party, Respect.
Gerry Adams	Sinn Fein president since 1983. Chief of staff of the IRA from 1977 to 1978.
GHQ	General Headquarters. The department chiefs who plan the IRA's military campaigns.
Glenbryn loyalists	Belfast group that sought to violently prevent four-year-old Catholic school-children from walking to school in 2002.
Good Friday Agreement (GFA)	The power sharing arrangement in Northern Ireland agreed to by Britain and Ireland in 1998.
GPO	General Post Office. Site in Dublin of the Easter Rising in 1916.

Green Shirt	Reference to Social Credit Party in Britain.
Housing Executive	The regional housing authority of Northern Ireland.
Hume-Adams Document	The 1993 agreement between John Hume and Gerry Adams. Considered one of the significant moments in the peace process.
Ian Paisley	Leader of the DUP for almost forty years. Became first minister of Northern Ireland in May 2007.
IMC	International Monitoring Commission. Body appointed by the British government to monitor violence.
INLA	Irish National Liberation Army.
Irish Republican Writers Group	Group of writers formed after the Good Friday Agreement to resist censorship within republicanism and to promote free inquiry.
IRSP	Irish Republican Socialist Party, political wing of the Irish National Liberation Army.
James Connolly	Irish Socialist leader executed by the British following his involvement in the Easter Rising of 1916.
Jeffrey Donaldson	Senior Unionist politician.
Jim 'Doris Day' Gray	UDA leader murdered by the organisation in 2005.
Jim Gibney	Senior Sinn Fein figure and political columnist.
Jim Monaghan	Irish Republican activist arrested in Colombia in 2001.
Joe Cahill	IRA chief of staff from 1972 to 1973.
John Deverell	Senior British intelligence officer.

GLOSSARY

John Hume	Former leader of the SDLP and frequently mistaken as the architect of the peace process.
John Kelly	Founding member of the Provisional IRA.
John Joe McGirl	Republican veteran who abandoned his beliefs to back the Adams strategy.
John White	UDA leader notorious for knifing his victims to death.
Kelly's Cellars	Belfast bar from which a Provisional IRA unit kidnapped Bobby Tohill.
Kevin Bean	Liverpool academic specialising in Irish republicanism.
Kevin O'Higgins	Irish government minister killed by Republicans in 1927.
Leinster House	Preferred Republican term for Dail Eireann, the seat of government in the Republic of Ireland.
Lenny Murphy	Loyalist psychopath who led the UVF Shankill Butcher gang.
Liam McMillan	Leading member of Official IRA. Killed by INLA in 1975.
Long Kesh	The preferred Republican term for the Maze Prison.
Long War	Term given to the IRA's military strategy from 1977.
Lord Gortahork	Spoof name for Gerry Adams.
Loyalist Commission	Body representing the views of loyalist paramilitaries.
MacSwiney	Terence MacSwiney was an IRA hunger striker who died in 1920.
Martin Ingram	Former British army agent handler.
Martin Mansergh	Senior Irish diplomat.

GOOD FRIDAY

Martin McGuinness	Current deputy first minister in the Northern Ireland executive. IRA chief of staff from 1978 to 1982.
MI5	British intelligence agency.
Michael Howard	Former leader of the British Conservative Party.
Michelle Gildernew	Sinn Fein Westminster MP.
Mick Collins	Legendary IRA leader from the early twentieth century.
Micky Donnelly	Former Republican prisoner whose leg was broken by the IRA after he had questioned Sinn Fein strategy.
Mitchell Principles	Set of principles agreed to by Sinn Fein, which included a commitment to non-violence. Named after their sponsor, George Mitchell.
Mitchell Reiss	U.S. diplomat and envoy to Ireland.
MLA	Member of the Legislative Assembly in Northern Ireland.
Mo (Marjorie) Mowlam	British secretary of state for Northern Ireland from 1997 to 1999.
Mountain Climber	Code name for a British representative who secretly negotiated with the IRA.
NIO (Northern Ireland Office)	A British agency created in 1972 to support the Secretary of State for Northern Ireland.
O'Bradaigh/O'Conaill	Media shorthand referring to the former leadership of the Provisional Republican movement, ousted by Gerry Adams.
OC	Commanding officer of an IRA unit.
Ogra Shinn Fein	Sinn Fein youth wing.

Orange Order parades	Exclusively Protestant and loyalist marches primarily celebrating the Protestant faith and loyalty to Britain. They have led to confrontations, riots and violence.
Owen Carron	Election director for Bobby Sands during the 1981 hunger strike.
P. O'Neill	Nom de plume of IRA public relations officer.
Padraig Pearse	Executed by the British for his role as leader of the 1916 Easter Rising.
Padraig Wilson	Former Blanket prisoner and leader of IRA prisoners in the Maze at the time of writing.
partition	Term given to the division of Ireland into twenty-six counties in the south known as the Free State or Republic of Ireland, and six counties in the north occupied by Britain and called Northern Ireland.
Pat Finucane	Belfast solicitor murdered by loyalists.
Paul Leighton	Senior PSNI officer.
Paul Murphy	British Secretary of State for Northern Ireland from 2002 to 2005.
peeler	Term for police in Northern Ireland.
Peter Hain	British secretary of state for Northern Ireland from 2005 to 2007.
Peter Mandelson	British secretary of state for Northern Ireland from 1999 to 2001.
Prod	Protestant.
Provisional IRA/Provos	Provisional Irish Republican Army. The main armed Republican guerrilla body waging an armed campaign against the British state. Frequently referred to as the IRA.

Provisional Republican	Term for the IRA body that sprang up in 1969, breaking away from the Official Republican movement.
PSNI	Police Service of Northern Ireland formerly known as the RUC.
'RA	Provisional IRA.
Real IRA	Group formed from a split within the Provisional IRA in 1997.
Republican movement	Name used to denote Sinn Fein and the IRA.
Republican Sinn Fein	Body that broke from the main body of Sinn Fein in 1986. The party rejects the Good Friday Agreement and is headed by Ruairi O Bradaigh.
Ronnie Flanagan	Last chief constable of the RUC prior to it being renamed the PSNI.
RTE	Radio Telefis Eireann, the main broadcasting authority in the Republic of Ireland.
Ruairi O Bradaigh	President of Sinn Fein prior to Gerry Adams.
RUC	Royal Ulster Constabulary. Former name of the Police Service of Northern Ireland (PSNI).
SAS	Special Air Service. British Special Air Force that inflicted heavy casualties on the IRA.
screws	Prison guards.
SDLP	Social Democratic and Labour Party, Northern Ireland's main constitutional nationalist party and rival to Sinn Fein for the nationalist vote.
Sean O Faolain	Renowned Irish writer.

GLOSSARY

Section 31	Broadcasting Authority Act. Legal tool used in the Republic of Ireland that effectively censored Republicans.
securocrats	Largely imaginary beings invented by Sinn Fein as scapegoats for the party's failings and duplicity throughout the peace process.
Sinn Fein	Political wing of the IRA.
Sinn Fein on Sunday	Spoof title for one of Ireland's Sunday newspapers with a reputation for unquestioningly swallowing the Sinn Fein line.
St. Andrews	Site in Scotland where the deal for the power-sharing executive was clinched in 2006.
Stick	Republican term for a member of the Official Republican Army, a splinter group that developed a Marxist approach in 1969.
Stormont	The Northern Ireland parliament.
Stormontgate	Name given to allegations in 2002 that Sinn Fein was running a spy ring within the Northern Ireland parliament.
Sunningdale	Site in Berkshire where historic talks in 1973 resulted in the Sunningdale Agreement, a power-sharing arrangement in 1974.
supergrass	An informer who testifies against his accomplices.
taig	Protestant epithet for Roman Catholic.
tanaiste	Irish for deputy prime minister.
taoiseach, taoisigh	Irish for prime minister, prime ministers.
Tariq Ali	London based political writer and analyst born in Pakistan.

Teach na Failte	Support group for INLA prisoners, former prisoners, and their families.
Tirghra	Republican body that organises commemorative events.
Tories	British Conservative Party.
UDA	Ulster Defence Association. Loyalist death squad.
Unionism	The belief that six counties to the North of Ireland should remain under British rule.
Unionist veto	The term given by Republicans to the consent principle.
Unity by consent	The terms set by the British state as the only acceptable means for Republicans to achieve a united Ireland.
UUP	Ulster Unionist Party. Northern Ireland's leading party.
UVF	Ulster Volunteer Force. An armed pro-British group responsible for killing many Catholics.
War of Independence	IRA war against the British from 1919 to 1921.
West Belfast	The main nationalist area in Belfast.
Wolfe Tone	Died in prison in 1798. Regarded as the father of Irish republicanism.
Workers Party	Political wing of the Official IRA.